Death of a Hornet

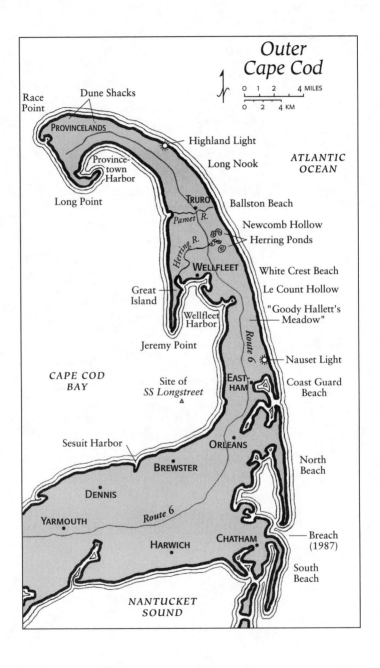

Death of a Hornet

AND OTHER CAPE COD ESSAYS

Robert Finch

COUNTERPOINT

WASHINGTON, D.C.

LIBRARY OF CONGRESS CATALOG CARD NUMBER: 00-022659

ISBN 1-58243-049-7

First Printing
Book design by Amy Evans McClure
Printed in the United States of American on acid-free paper that meets the American National Standards Institute Z39–48 Standard.

COUNTERPOINT
P.O. Box 65793
Washington, D.C. 20035–5793
Counterpoint is a member of the Perseus Books Group

10 9 8 7 6 5 4 3 2 1

This book is for Beth, who made half of it;
for my family;
for the townspeople of Brewster;
for Harriet White, who gave me my first volume of Robert Frost;
for June Lay, who fed my early hunger for books;
for KS, First Reader;
and for Ollie, bounding into spring.

Contents

Preface

Things change, Grendel's dragon said. I would add, especially on Cape Cod. My last collection of essays was published fourteen years ago. Some of the essays in this volume go back at least eighteen years in their composition, and some even farther in the experiences on which they are based. Some of the places, and even landforms, described in this book no longer exist, or have altered beyond recognition. Where a particular event or date is pertinent to understanding the essay, or where long-term change is itself the subject (as in "The Once and Future Cape"), I have tried to include enough information to keep the reader from being confused—about the facts, at least.

When the first group of these pieces were written, I lived in the town of Brewster with my family. Most of the second group were written after my wife and I divorced in 1994 and I moved to Wellfleet, a distance of some twenty-six miles. Marathon runners are not the only ones who understand that twenty-six miles can be the longest distance in the world.

Thus the names of the two halves of this book. The order of essays, too, is approximately chronological, though a

reader who attempts to find strict setting or sequence will be
unnecessarily frustrated. Rather, it reflects what Robert Frost,
the hovering spirit of this book, called "roughly zones."

It is my belief that a personal essay is not the same thing
as a memoir or an autobiography; it is not even primarily personal, and certainly not confessional. An essayist's life may
be the source, the quarry, the raw material, or the spring-
board for a story, but it is not the story itself. I have tried to
balance the minimum amount of personal information necessary for the orientation of the reader with the minimum
amount of intrusion into the privacy of others. Wherever the
two seemed to conflict, I hope I have erred on the side of
privacy.

Robert Finch
Wellfleet, Cape Cod
January, 2000

Death of a Hornet

I

BREWSTER

Death of a Hornet

For the past half hour I have been watching a remarkable encounter between a spider and a yellow hornet, for which I was the unwitting catalyst. I have found several of these hornets in my study recently, buzzing and beating themselves against the glass doors and windows, having crawled out, I presume, from the cracks between the still-unplastered sheets of rock lath on the ceiling. Usually I have managed to coax them out the door with a piece of paper or a book, but this morning my mind was abstracted with innumerable small tasks, so that when another of these large insects appeared buzzing violently, like a yellow-and-black column of electricity slowly sizzling up the window pane above my desk, I rather absentmindedly whacked it with a rolled-up bus schedule until it fell, maimed but still alive, onto the window sill.

My sill is cluttered with natural objects and apparatus used for studying and keeping insects and other forms of local wildlife—various small jars, a microscope box, a dissecting kit, an ancient phoebe's nest that was once built on our front door light, an aquarium pump, pieces of coral and seaweed, etc.—none of which has been used for several months. They now serve largely as an eclectic substrate for several large messy spider webs.

In one corner is a rather large, irregular, three-dimensional web occupying a good quarter-cubic-foot of space. It was into this web that the stricken hornet fell, catching about halfway down into the loose mesh and drawing out from her reclusiveness in the corner a nondescript brownish house spider with a body about three-eighths of an inch long. The hornet hung tail-down, twirling tenuously from a single web-thread, while its barred yellow abdomen throbbed and jabbed repeatedly in instinctive attack. The motion could not really be called defensive, as the hornet was surely too far gone to recover, but it was as if it were determined to inflict whatever injury it could on whatever might approach it in its dying. Defense in insects, as with us, seems to be founded not on the ability to survive but on the resolution to keep from forgiving as long as possible.

The spider rushed out along her strands to investigate the commotion and stopped about an inch short of this enormous creature, three or four times her own size, with what seemed an "Oh, Lord, why me?" attitude, the stance of a fisherman who suddenly realizes he has hooked a wounded shark on his flounder line.

Whether or not her momentary hesitation reflected any such human emotion, the spider immediately set out to secure her oversized prey. After making a few tentative jabs toward the hornet, and apparently seeing that it could do no more than ineffectually thrust its stinger back and forth, she approached more deliberately, made a complete circuit around the hanging beast, and suddenly latched onto it at its "neck."

At this point I went and got the magnifying glass from my compact edition of the *Oxford English Dictionary* and stationed myself near the window corner to observe more closely. The spider did indeed seem to be fastening repeatedly onto the thin connection between the hornet's head and thorax—a spot, I theorized, that might be more easily injected with the spider's paralyzing venom.

While she remained attached to the hornet's neck, all motion in the spider's legs and body ceased, adding to the impression that some intense, concealed activity was taking place at the juncture. If so, it proved effective, for within a very few minutes almost all throbbing in the hornet's abdomen had stopped, and only the flickering of its rear legs indicated that any life remained.

During this process, the spider's movements were still cautious, but also somehow gentle, never violent or awkward as my whacking had been. She was almost solicitous, as if ministering to the stricken hornet, as carefully and as kindly as possible ending its struggles and its agony. Her graceful arched legs looked, through the glass, like miniature, transparent, bent soda straws, with dark spots of pigment at the joints, like bits of sediment clogging the leg segments.

Now the spider seemed to have made the hornet *hers*—her object, her possession—and her movements became more confident, proprietary, almost perfunctory in contrast. She no longer seemed aware of the hornet as something apart from her, foreign to the web, but rather as a part of her now, ready to be assimilated. She appeared to begin dancing around the paralyzed insect, her rear legs moving rapidly and rhythmically in a throwing motion toward the object in the center. I did not actually see any silk coming out of her abdomen, nor did her legs actually appear to touch the spinnerets there, but gradually a light film of webbing, a thin, foggy sheen, became visible around the hornet's midsection.

She would spin for several seconds, then climb an inch or two and attach a strand to a piece of webbing overhead. I thought at first that she was merely securing the hornet from its rather unstable attachment, but after she had done this a few times, I saw that, with each climb upwards, the hornet itself also moved a small fraction of an inch up and to the side. It was soon clear that the spider was *maneuvering* this enormous insect, in a very definite and deliberate manner, using her spun cables like a system of block and tackle, hoisting and moving her prey among and through the seemingly random network of spun silk.

In between these bouts of spinning and hoisting, the spider occasionally stopped and approached the hornet, now totally motionless and with one of its darkly veined wings bound to its barred side. She would place herself head down (the usual position for a spider in a web when not spinning) just above the hornet's head and, again becoming totally motionless as if in some paralysis of ecstasy, seemed to attach her mouth parts to those of her prey, as though engaged in some long, drawn-out death kiss. The two, insect and arachnid, remained attached so for ten to fifteen seconds at a time, after which the spider again resumed her hoisting and fastening. Was this some further injection of venom taking place, or was she beginning to suck the juices from the wasp's still-living body even as she was moving it somewhere? I was struck, mesmerized by this alternation of intimate, motionless contact of prey and predator, and the businesslike, bustling manipulation of an inert object by its possessor.

All in all the spider has moved the hornet about two inches to the side and one inch upward from the point where it landed, out of the center portion of the web and nearer the window frame, where now she crouches motionless behind it, perhaps using it to conceal herself while waiting for another prey. I pull myself away from the corner and put down the magnifying glass, feeling strangely drained from having been drawn in so strongly to watch such concentrated activity and dispassionate energy. There is something about spiders that no insect possesses, that makes it seem right that they are not true insects, but belong to a more ancient order of being. I like them in my home, but they will not bear too close watching.

I look back at the window corner and see that the characters of the drama are still there, once more in miniature tableau. All is quiet again; the spider remains crouched motionless behind its mummified prey, in that waiting game that spiders have perfected, where memory and hope play no part. There is only the stillness of an eternal present and the silent architecture of perfectly strung possibilities.

A Winter Burial

In mid-March, about a week before the vernal equinox, there was a burial in the small church graveyard nearby. The deceased was a woman in her eighties, a native of the town and a neighbor of mine for several years. She had "not been well" this winter and had moved from the small old Cape where she had lived all her married and widowed life into her daughter's home down the street.

Two days earlier a pile of tarps and inverted rugs of AstroTurf had been deposited just inside the cemetery's wooden fence, in front of her husband's stone, which had been erected thirty years earlier. The following day I walked over and found that the grave had been dug and the concrete vault placed within it. Tarps covered the hole, the mound of dirt beside it, and the vault lid lying on the ground.

I stood there, on that bare, cedar-studded knoll, beneath the damp wind and grey skies of March, while wet flakes of snow fell on my head and shoulders and on nearly two hundred years of local graves surrounding me. I felt a strong sense of loss, though it was not personal in nature. True, I had known the deceased for nearly a decade, but it was only as a neighbor whom I had visited infrequently. She had shared many local stories and much neighborhood history with me, yet I had found her formal and reserved, difficult to warm to.

No, her death was, for me, more representative than individual. What I felt was a sense of fundamental change rather than personal loss—a deep change in the life and makeup of the neighborhood that had nothing to do with personal character. Until a few years ago, for instance, she had played a direct role in most of the infrequent burials that took place here. As one of the oldest residents in the area, she had been escorted to the cemetery each time by the funeral director to look over the proposed gravesite and pronounce it "clean," since, in her words, there were many "bones without stones and stones without bones." A strongly-rooted knowledge of place, I realized, was passing with her.

A night of wind and heavy rain left only a tattered and sodden blanket of the weekend's snow on the ground. The early redwings, singing in the nearby marsh, had been right after all. The burial service was scheduled for two o'clock that afternoon. During the morning, a truck from the funeral home roared unceremoniously up the road. Two young rough-shaven men got out and erected over the grave site a large green canopy, with canvas walls on the east and south sides as a protection against the expected prevailing winds.

At 1:30 I shaved, put on an overcoat, and walked over to the cemetery. The weather was still raw, grey, and wet. Several cars had already arrived, and soon the little triangle at the intersection of the two country roads was ringed with vehicles. The people, mostly older friends and neighbors, walked up the short cemetery road and, with canes and help-

ing hands, negotiated the tall stone step at the opening in the
fence and walked over to the canopied grave site. Some forty
people in all came, including grandchildren from Florida, a
town selectmen, a farmer, the town archivist and the president of the local historical society, a landscaper, the rural mail
carrier, and a retired lobsterman and his wife. Except for the
grandchildren and the undertaker, few people there were
under sixty.

The family and the most elderly of the mourners sat on
folding chairs inside the canopy, while the rest of us stood,
mostly bareheaded and silent, in the cold March wind for
some twenty minutes, waiting for the last of the visitors to
arrive. I was impressed by the number of mourners and by
the cumulative years of friendship they represented, but even
more by the organic fabric of personal ties visible in the
assembly. Many of those here had played and gone to school
as children with the deceased, and their families had inter-
twined over the years like the roots of catbriar growing down
the bank. I realized that this was not just a gathering of
friends, relatives, and acquaintances come to pay respects,
but also a true community ritual, a witnessing of another of
its own passing.

The canopy, from outside, appeared like a green prosce-
nium, giving those seated within the air of participating in a
curiously domestic scene, as if they were all visiting her in her
sitting room, or at her bedside. The coffin—made of dark,
massive, polished walnut—was raised on a bier and mounded
with flowers (one basket had "GRAM" embroidered on a ribbon), so that it seemed larger than life, hiding, rather than
emphasizing, the presence of an actual body within, as
though she were already down in the earth with her husband.
(I found myself musing, Would he be pleased to have company again after such long solitude? Or disturbed? Or perhaps, as Thornton Wilder suggests of the long dead in *Our
Town,* merely temporarily inconvenienced and unremem-
bering?)

The minister, indistinguishable from the other people in his heavy overcoat, read a few predictable verses from the New Testament, including that curious pronouncement of Christ's from the gospel of John: "In my Father's house are many mansions: if it were not so, I would have told you." Then why, I always think, why raise the doubt?

And that was all. The assembly quickly dispersed, many of them heading back to the daughter's house for some food and talk. As a casual acquaintance, I would not be going, but I went up to the daughter, a handsome, grey-haired woman in her late fifties with a gentle, sweet face. I said that I was glad to have known her mother and that I would miss her, which was true. She thanked me and said how much her mother had enjoyed some of my books.

There followed a long, awkward moment of silence as we stood facing one another. I knew I should have simply returned the thanks and withdrawn, but I felt the need to say something more, to connect a little more closely with the occasion. I clasped her hands and blurted out, "I'm glad to have known *you*, too!"

"Oh," she smiled sweetly, "we plan to be around for a while, I guess."

I started to stammer something about not meaning that, of course, but, instead, I gave an awkward chuckle and sidled away, having learned once again that you can't force belonging. As I did, an elderly woman with a cane came up to her, touched her arm, and said, "She didn't quite wait for spring, did she, dear?"

Words and Music

Earlier this month I went down to the local herring run to see if the fish had come in yet. I did not really expect to find any, though it was mid-March and a sunny, seasonally warm afternoon. The rule of thumb regarding the arrival of alewives (as these migratory herring are locally called) is that they will begin to enter the estuaries from Cape Cod Bay and migrate upstream into their breeding ponds when the temperature of the outflowing water exceeds that of the estuary into which it empties. The mill ponds above this stream had only broken up from their long winter freeze the week before. Thin crescents of ice were still retreating into their western coves and some remaining fragments of old snow crumbled among the ruins of last year's marsh reeds.

And so, although some of the red maple buds had already cracked their thin shells, extending pale, filamentous pistils, and the long yellow branches of the willows swayed enticingly over the brimming, crashing torrent in the stepped pools of the fish ladder, the waters themselves remained empty, as empty as baseball fields, tennis courts, and other sites of spring rituals yet to come.

So I settled instead for birds. Seated on a large glacial rock that juts out into a narrow channel of water just above the mill race, I watched and listened to a pair of male red-winged blackbirds engaged in a song battle on the other side. These birds, whose response to a warming trend is quicker and sometimes more foolhardy than the fishes', had arrived in the neighborhood a couple of weeks earlier, on March 3 to be exact. When they arrived, they had a bedraggled, drab look, but now they appeared newly minted, their black bodies shiny and sleek, their shoulder epaulets glowing with deep, brilliant scarlet underscored with bands of bright yellow.

These shoulder patches, so conspicuously displayed during the breeding season, present something of a mystery. When a male red-wing sings, the wings are slightly lifted and puffed out, making the patches seem even larger, so that, seen head-on, the entire sides of the bird sometimes appear red. Yet recently the role of these prominent markings in establishing territory and attracting mates has been called into question. Experiments by researchers at the Cornell Ornithological Laboratory have demonstrated that males whose epaulets were painted black still competed successfully with unpainted males. Yet when a bird was deprived of his voice, even the most garish displays of color did not intimidate his rivals, and he soon slunk away.

Voice, it seems, remains primary in birds in defending territory, at least in blackbirds. It also remains a perennial attraction and a puzzle for us, in its teasing and deceptive resemblance to human song and human words. For over a quarter of an hour I sat on the rock, listening to the two red-wings hurling their raucous challenge back and forth at one another at an average rate of about one every twenty seconds. And as I did, I found myself unconsciously trying to vocalize their song.

The generally accepted representation of a blackbird's song in most field guides is *kong-la-ree*, or *konk-ler-ree*, which does successfully suggest its distinctive mixture of harsh liquescence. But it can hardly be called an accurate translation. It is more of an auditory metaphor, or mnemonic device, than a mimicry.

A better rendition, it seems to me, would be something like *wh-DIDdle-EEE(t)*, with the primary accent on the second syllable. Yet even this is a poor approximation, less useful than the first, and already straining language and punctuation. Even if I were to use the entire arsenal of musical notation and diacritical markings to refine such representations, they would still, I know, fall far short of the mark.

Birdsong, like most poetry, does not lend itself to literal translation, and our attempts to do so usually succeed more in conveying the limitations of our language than the true nature of the song. The best we can do, it seems to me, is to find, as the most successful poetry translators do, some "equivalent translation," such as *kong-la-ree* for redwings, or *Drink-Your-TEEE!* for the rufous-sided towhee, or *Old-Sam-Peabody-Peabody-Peabody* for the white-throated sparrow. Such representations are not very useful to anyone not already familiar with the songs in question, but they can give a sense of them to the ear remembering how they sounded.

Today, of course, we have such aids as bird recordings and audiospectrograms, or "Sonograms," which electronically graph the "shape" of a bird's song. The former is a convenient substitute for going out and hearing the song itself, while Sonograms provide impeccably accurate and objective representations. Yet few birders I know actually use recordings to learn birds' songs, and even fewer, except professional ornithologists, use Sonograms to confirm them.

The urge itself, to verbalize birdsong, may seem trivial, even ludicrous, yet it is something we have always done and still catch ourselves doing, in spite of its lack of much practical value and scientific accuracy, much as painting has continued to thrive long after the invention of the camera. It seems part of a deeper, more persistent urge in our natures, one that goes beyond mere imitation and is deeply rooted in specific cultures. (My friend Richard Nelson, who lived and studied with the Koyukon Athapaskan Indians of Alaska, once told me that their transliteration for the song of the American Robin, which in our culture is commonly rendered as *Cheer-up, cheerily, cheer-up, cheerily*, was *My-brother-in-law-is-down-in-the-creek-bed-vomiting-slimy-worms*.)

The aim, after all, is not so much scientific representation as it is to mix ourselves in nature's voice, to put the human in the natural sound. It is, in fact, hard, if not impossible, to hear any natural sound purely: it is always altered, changed somewhat from what it is by what we have brought to it, what we have been taught to hear by previous listeners, by the stories, poems, songs, and sayings we have weaved around it, so that, as Frost put it, "Never again would birds' song be the same."

I don't think this is to be regretted any more than it can be avoided. For it seems to me to be as much our destiny to assimilate nature, mentally and imaginatively, as to manipulate it with our technology and our machines. Just as birds use song to define territory, so language remains our primary tool for humanizing this strange universe in which we find ourselves. Once we have verbally insinuated ourselves into something—a bird's song, the sound of the surf, another culture—once we have storied and versed it, it then becomes a part of ourselves and we bleed when it is hurt. Exterminate wolves and whales, poison robins, cut down old-growth trees, bulldoze a meadow, and our human life is diminished. And yet a distant galaxy, still unnamed, though it be thousands of light-years across, may perish without a ripple, without the whisper of a sound reaching our ears.

Shadow on the Pond

I went down to Berry's Hole this morning, taking along a notebook and binoculars, thinking I might write and record what I saw there for an hour or two. The weather was beautiful after heavy, dark rains the week before. Now it was in the mid-sixties with only a slight breeze, yet just enough to make things in the yard—leaves, birds, limbs—seem almost weightless, as objects rest lightly on the bottom of the ocean, making me aware of a physical connectedness between things through a common medium.

Chickadees, titmice, jays, and woodpeckers all sang loudly in the yard. The phoebe pair, back for several weeks now, are still flitting around the rear side of the house, making indecisive feints toward the corner under the eaves where I have built a nesting shelf for them. The grass in the yard is beginning to green, and a clump of clover has poked its way up between two of the back steps.

I walked down the toboggan run into the kettle hole, noticing how the beech buds were beginning to swell, and lifting up the small, leathery green leaves of the mayflower plants along the leaf-littered slopes to see if the first of their diminutive blossoms had opened yet.

From below I could hear the scattered, intermittent calls of the woodfrogs—wooden, explosive, arrhythmic sounds, like strings of miniature fireworks going off. As I approached the bog at the bottom of the hollow, I caught a glimpse of a black, shiny plated shell in the water—a turtle! This was the first time I had ever seen one in this small wetland, whose shallow, fluctuating waters are too inconstant to support permanent fish or other vertebrate populations. What kind of a turtle was it, and where could it have come from?

But before I could fumble my binoculars out of their case, the turtle spotted me and scuttled down out of sight into the mud. Nature watching, it seems, is largely a losing game of trying to see things before they see you.

The bog is technically a swampy marsh, or a marshy swamp, I suppose, ringed with shrubs and with a center island of small trees and more shrubs, but with good-sized patches of open water when the rains have been generous. When I reached the edge, I could see a mixed clump of a dozen or so egg masses near the shore: the smaller, clear globes of the woodfrogs and the larger, cloudier masses of the yellow-spotted salamanders. The light breezes sent the water shimmering and skittering to the far side, while water skaters and whirligigs hopped and slid across the surface. Light played with sound, as the dead oak leaves, hanging intact in dry clumps on the white branches, rustled on the hillsides.

I worked my way around to the far side of the bog where some large swamp maples loomed out over the water. I was planning to circle the entire perimeter before settling down, but, following a sudden urge, I laid my glasses case and notebook at the base of the largest maple and climbed up its trunk out onto one of the more substantial limbs that overhung the bog. I stayed up there for almost an hour.

Reaching the highest and farthest-extending branch that I thought would support my weight safely, I looked down and saw the bog in a way I never had before, from a bird's eye (or at least a squirrel's eye) view, seeing straight into its muddy mind, its murky workings. As I looked, other masses of amphibian eggs began to appear here and there in the bog; light-colored, translucent globes and opalescent strings, emerging like daytime stars against the reflected sky.

The largest clump, nearly two feet across, was directly beneath me and attached to a half-sunken limb. Others were attached to twigs near the surface, or stuck to rocks deeply embedded in the muck. Some of the clumps were already partly exposed to the air, and I knew that if in the weeks to come the level of the bog dropped further, many of the eggs would be doomed to desiccation. On the other hand, the rains could fall in abundance, inundating the blueberry roots along the shore and flooding out some of the small pine saplings that have begun to take hold in places during the drought of the past two years. But that is nature's way. One gets nothing for effort or endurance. It is all accident, help or hurt.

Then I saw the turtle again, almost directly beneath me. This time I didn't need binoculars to see that it was a painted turtle, a large one nearly six inches long, lying just at the surface, its hind half submerged, the white scute lines and red rim around the shell showing plainly. It was drifting freely, and as the light wind blew some floating surface leaves around it, it kept its place by alternately stroking its front left foot and rear right one.

The breeze also moved the limb on which I lay, stretched out along its rough length. Slowly, almost imperceptibly, it lifted and lowered me with great restrained force and rhythm, distilling and resolving the thin dispersed wind into a more confined but authoritative movement. It was a kind of flying.

Then a second turtle appeared, a few feet away from the first, a smaller one perhaps four inches long, surfacing next to a half-submerged branch. Very gradually, like the hands of a clock, it moved out of the water and up onto the branch:

first the notched blunted snout, then the slitted eyes, then a wrinkled neck veined with yellow, and red, long-nailed fore-claws—so slowly that its dark shell dried as it emerged. I lay very quiet and still in the tree above it, while the woodpeck-ers rattled and the chickadees threw their contrapuntal songs back and forth across the hole.

It did not seem that either of the turtles was aware of me, great red-shirted thing in the trees overhead. Perhaps they do not recognize humans in strange or unexpected locations. I have noticed, for instance, that I can sometimes swim within a few yards of shorebirds resting on the bank of a tidal creek—birds which, were I on land, would not let me approach within a hundred feet of them.

After a while the larger turtle swam off toward the center island, giving me an unusual opportunity to observe clearly the sequence of its swimming motion. It seemed basically to be one of alternate coordination: right-front and left-rear together, followed by left-front and right-rear, with the rear swipe or thrust lagging slightly behind the front each time, resulting in that characteristic side-to-side "waddle" motion of turtles. It struck me that this was exactly the movement of my daughter's plastic mechanical bathtub turtle, an unex-pected bit of commercial biological accuracy.

When do these turtles *do* something? I wondered—some-thing besides hibernate, sunbathe, or practice their side-to-side strokes? So often the animals we observe—herring gulls, frogs, seals, squirrels, snakes—do not seem to be doing much of anything at all, as though they wished to pretend in front of us that their existence is merely a matter of assent, and only we were thrown out of the Garden. In a sense this *is* what they are pretending in our presence, keeping their more vital activities hidden from view.

But I was not really impatient. In fact, I found myself strangely serene and unruffled, unaware of time or place. I seemed to have adapted myself to the turtles' tempo, lifted and lowered gently there in the soft April breezes above the dark bog. Not only did the turtles appear not to notice me, but shortly thereafter I also saw a cat before it saw me—an extremely rare occurrence. This was a large grey and white feral that had paraded by my house many times. Now I saw it padding down into the hole and noiselessly circling the bog, though there was no potential prey in sight. It stopped, lounging and licking itself for several minutes before it finally seemed to sense something above it. It looked up, but even then, from the strangeness of my location or my stillness, it chose to ignore me, and continued on its rounds without haste.

I had, it seemed, by assent to a series of unforeseen opportunities, inclined and climbed my way into a position of utter centrality and perspective, heretofore unattained in scores of previous trips made to this bog. I looked down again, and this time I saw reflected on the surface neither dark water and turtles and buried leaves, nor the darkened image of the overhead sky and clouds, but a pattern of shadows stretching out across the entire bog—the meshed, depthless maze of branch and limb. And there, in the center of the pattern, was my own foreshortened silhouette—hulking, looming like some huge gall-like growth out of the tree, moving only as the tree shadows themselves moved, slowly, smoothly, resolved in the wind.

For once, then, momentarily suspended ten feet above the bog, I found myself a part of this maze of intersecting patterns, accepted by it, carried along with it. Turtles, waterbugs, and unseen tadpoles swam through my image. I harbored within myself the clouded and seed-sprinkled globes of egg masses. And then, from out of my floating shadow, as though out of a cocoon, the lovely form of a mourning cloak butterfly emerged into daylight.

Phoebe Journal

March 28

All morning a phoebe has been flitting around the yard and house, giving his spunky, raspy call and flipping his tail up and down. One of the first of our northeastern songbirds to return in spring, he owns the bare oak woods these days and tonelessly proclaims his territory with his name. Likely he is the same bird that showed up this time last spring, one day earlier (March 27) to be exact. I built a little shelf for him then under the bathroom eaves, hoping he would find a mate and nest, but nothing came of it.

The Eastern Phoebe, so familiar around old New England farmhouses, has always been much less common here on Cape Cod than on the mainland. Hill's *Birds of Cape Cod, Massachusetts* (1965) estimated only six or eight breeding pairs on the entire peninsula, and Bailey's *Birds of the Cape Cod National Seashore* (1968) allows "1 or 2 pairs... in each town where there are suitable nesting sites—an undisturbed shed, porch, or barn providing a shelf on which the mud nest can be built." The latest Cape Cod Bird Club checklist still considers the phoebe a "rare but regular" nester, yet my neighbor had a successful nest only a few years ago, and now this bird has shown up for the second year in a row. Let us see if Finch (1981) can coax him to stay this time.

April 3

Heavy, dark rain all day. Phoebe still about, flitting and calling in the downpour, but no sign of a mate yet.

April 15

Back after having been away ten days on a family vacation. While we were gone a female joined our male phoebe, and the pair of them, I find, have been building a nest under the roof overhang on top of the light fixture next to the front door. It is nearly finished and seems to be constructed mainly of wet leaves and moss packed together. In shape it is a thick, shallow bowl, about four inches across, and for the last two days the phoebes have added long tresses of moss to the outside, which hang down several inches on both sides of the light.

It has not rained for two weeks, and I thought at first they had been wetting the nest material from the half-full rain barrel nearby. But after watching them, I find they are bringing bits of material in their beaks up from the small bog down in the kettle hole behind our house. Some of the oak leaves are black and look as if they were pulled from the edge of the water.

I have read that phoebes like to nest near water, which they use for bathing, drinking, and as a source of insects and nest material, but phoebes will also travel to water from a considerable distance for the sake of a suitable nesting site. In this case they seem to have struck a satisfactory compromise. Our front door is about a hundred yards from the bog and some sixty feet above it. In one hour I counted twenty-seven separate flights by both birds. I am sure it was only our chance absence at the right time that allowed them to build in such a heavily trafficked spot, so I have locked the front door and posted a sign on it—"PHOEBES NESTING—USE OTHER DOOR"—to give them a chance. A neighbor boy read it and asked, "What's a fobee?"

April 27

This morning, alone in the house, I watched from the hall window as one of the phoebes worked on the nest. It approaches cautiously and circuitously, perching on a tupelo branch about ten feet off the ground and fifteen from the nest, then dropping down in a series of consecutive loops to successively lower and nearer branches, at last alighting on the rain barrel under the overhang, or on the bare ground underneath, holding some insignificant fragment of twig or grass or moss in its dark, pointed, little bill.

From there it looks around and up, and then, as though discovering the nest for the first time and by pure chance, flutters up to the light fixture. There it places its cargo and proceeds to shape the nest by wiggling its body down into the cavity, while its dimpled tail is pushed straight up, wrenlike, against the wall behind it. After less than a minute on the nest the phoebe flutters down again to a spot on or near the ground before taking off again for the bog. This groundward approach characterizes all its forays to and from the nest.

Once, landing on the ground from the nest, it began rummaging around in the leaves under the stoop. Then, curiously, it leaped up and fluttered several times at the lowest cedar clapboard just above the foundation, as though attacking it. I thought it had spotted some bugs along the wall, but soon I could see that it was attempting to shred off some cedar fibers from the clapboard for nesting material. This it managed to do and carried them back up to the light fixture to set in place.

Thus, by such incredibly small accretions, the phoebe builds its nest, with an implicit patience or reliance upon the

expanse and allowance of time; or rather, with the acquies-
cence of time itself in the face of such a pure, unhurried,
undesperate, and measured industry. I thought of Thoreau's
mythical artist of Kouroo, near the end of *Walden*, who
determined to make the perfect staff. The artist, wrote
Thoreau, considering that "in an imperfect work time is an
ingredient, but into a perfect work time does not enter . . .
said to himself, It shall be perfect in all respects, though I
should do nothing else in my life."

So it seems the phoebe approaches its work, unhurried by
time, unanxious to make mortgage payments or to meet construction schedules, wholly absorbed in a process and a form
that it carries inside itself and gives shape to with its own
body. As Thoreau said of his artist, "The material was pure,
and his art was pure; how could the result be other than
wonderful?"

The bird even waited patiently on a nearby branch, showing no visible anxiety, while our cat sauntered by, fat gut
swaying beneath him, and rolled languidly in the dust
beneath the nest, then stalked on. The phoebe watched with
no more apprehension than one waiting for traffic to go by
before crossing the street, though the chances are not small
that the cat will get it some day.

Meanwhile the phoebe exhibits, in a world of chance and
threat, that commitment, completely independent from consequence or result, that is the hallmark of all wild animals, a
pervasive lack of desperation and uncertainty that is perhaps
nature's greatest value to our age. It is more than a sense of
belonging; it is a manner of living that includes all other lives
around it, that feeds into and from all it touches—what natu-
ralist John Hay has called "a depth of devising."

Yet there is also in these little birds (as there was not in
Thoreau's obsessed Hindu) that element of play in the very
midst of vital endeavor which seems common among many
of the higher animals and is perhaps a means of releasing

inner stress. A little later both phoebes showed up, and one remained perched on a nearby branch, as though to watch, while the other worked for several minutes about the nest. Then, with no warning, the one at work suddenly flew at the onlooker, and both took off through the trees in wild arcs, chirping at one another in playful chase. At least it *seemed* playful, though I suppose it could have been a reproach by the one bird to its lazy mate, urging it to get off its butt and work.

April 30

The phoebes have apparently finished their nest building. Now it remains to be seen if they will stay; for often, if something is not to their liking, these birds will desert a nest immediately after finishing it.

It is, however, a fine, round, full, bushy nest, shaggy with moss, mud, and matted leaves on the outside, the inner bowl lined with dry grasses and stems, and the whole as craftily shaped and rounded by their bodies as any potter's bowl. Around the rim is a delicate trim of what I first thought was down, but which on closer inspection looks more like grey fur (perhaps the shed hair of the cat that lolled in the dust beneath the nest) or a similar synthetic fabric found somewhere, so airy and light that it looks like the condensation of the phoebes' breath around the edge, or a bit of fog or smoke settled about the nest. This delicate trim is their extravagance, their manifest decorative finishing touch—or it would be if the nest itself, fashioned out of so many uncounted trips down into the mud and muck of the bog, was not already such an unlikely, imponderable extravagance.

May 3

The phoebes have not been heard or seen since finishing the nest. Perhaps they have deserted after all, or perhaps they want to take another year to think about things. Some birds,

I have read, are capable of reabsorbing fertilized eggs if conditions are unpropitious for family raising. How many women would welcome that option?

At any rate, we sense after a while that nature's dramas are by and large ambiguous, inconclusive, and finally undeterminable, so that we tend to rush in and supply them with plots, motives, and endings uncalled-for by the facts. The difficult thing is to give shape to our accounts without shaping the events accounted for.

What, for example, if the birds have left and do not come back? What shall I make of this abandoned nest? Shall I say it had no purpose, was a waste of time and effort in the all-too-serious game of survival and perpetuation in the wild, a bad joke on the birds' dedicated labor—just another example of nature's indifference, incompleteness, and inefficiency? But efficiency is a human invention, a product of limited time and resources, with which nature has nothing to do.

Did the birds take any satisfaction in building the nest? How can we know? Did the cave artists at Lascaux 15,000 years ago take satisfaction in their primitive and consummate renderings of bison and antelope and plunging horses? Or does the labor of the phoebes go beyond such detached responses, toward some deep and total participation in life, unconscious perhaps, but bespeaking other ways of being and knowing, of being *unconditionally* in nature?

May 9

After a week's absence following the completion of their nest, the phoebes appear to have returned in earnest. My wife, Beth, suggested they were just off on a little vacation and rest. All day the female remained on the nest, keeping a low profile, but alert.

Despite a conscious effort to avoid it, I cannot help thinking of her situation in human terms. Is she being "deprived of stimulation," like a worker on an assembly line? Yet she has the male, who all day sang loudly from a nearby branch, determinedly, as though to keep her on the nest.

At noon I happened to look out the window and found her gone. Carefully unlocking and opening the front door, I stepped up on a chair and, leaning out, peered into the nest above the light fixture. Five perfect white eggs, each about the size of my thumbnail, were nestled in the bottom of the bowl. I felt as though some bit of deep domesticity had attached itself to our house, more significant, more sanctioning to our presence here than any occupancy permit could be.

Shortly she returned and sat on the nest throughout the rest of the afternoon. The cat climbed up and sat on the rain barrel under the eaves, not more than five feet from the nest, casually ignoring it and licking his paws. The nesting phoebe gave no sign of alarm, but I shooed the cat and moved the barrel anyway.

Thinking about the nest, its sturdy delicacy and rough perfection, I realize I might conceivably explain all of its components as functional or adaptive, even the decorative trim. But if I do, doesn't that only show that our shapes of human beauty are deeply rooted in the necessities of nature?

May 11

Rain—rich, soft, and binding—fell yesterday and through this morning, finally bursting spring's bubble. After an unusual delay everything seems to have come out with a rush and a tumble in the last ten days, so that even some late bloomers seem to have been sucked out prematurely. Locusts in the cemetery next door are well along, ahead of our tardy yard maple. The beeches have all gushed spiraling green fountains of limp spearmint leaves fringed with fine caterpillar hair. Beach plum blossoms are everywhere, the shadbush suddenly gone by, while the oaks with their long-bearded catkins and scalloped pink leaves are taking their own sweet time.

But the auditory assault is even more pronounced.

Catbirds, thrushes, orioles, ovenbirds, and several waves of warblers have all arrived in the last few days and have been drowning out the phoebe's solo in their chorus. A mourning dove's nest, incredibly crude and fragile-looking, built in one of our pines, was ruined in the rain and has apparently been abandoned; but "Mrs. Phoebe," as my young daughter, Katy, calls her, sat faithfully all weekend on her nest.

Which brings up a point: Is it only the female that broods? It seems obvious it is she when the male is nearby singing, but he is not always there. I have never seen him bringing her food on the nest, but I have never seen them switching places either. Sources are divided on this subject. One I consulted says the female alone incubates, but another gives both sexes credit. I have observed too little and too irregularly to testify in the matter, but it seems odd that such a simple question about such a common and sociable bird should have remained unresolved for so long. It undercuts the scope of human knowledge not to know the phoebe's domestic arrangements.

May 14

Checked the phoebe nest today and found, in addition to the five phoebe eggs, one cowbird egg, slightly larger and speckled. I remember having seen a pair of these birds around on the lawn this weekend. The phoebe is never off the nest for more than a few minutes at a time these days. Cowbirds work fast.

I plucked it out and held it in my palm. It was light, translucent, and warm with the warmth of the phoebe's body. How is it that, seeking only to be hosts or witnesses, we end up meddlers before we know it? The old, unrealized prejudices rise, turning us into judges, arbiters, and finally advocates, in spites of ourselves and our own boasted knowledge of nature's disinterestedness.

Haven't I defended cowbirds in the past against narrow

judgments of human morality? Don't I know that phoebes are among the most common hosts of cowbird eggs, that over seventy-five percent of their nests are parasitized, and still they flourish? I cannot say why I removed the egg, except that I had accepted phoebes to the house, not cowbirds. Within five minutes she was back on the nest, unaware she had been saved from an involuntary adoption.

May 20

As the phoebe broods on the nest, I brood on why the pair did not choose the little wooden nesting ledge I had so thoughtfully provided for them on the back side of the house. So much more sensible, and less trouble for us. Now we have to keep the front door locked and the light off at night, lest we cook the eggs; and she is much more exposed there, more apt to be disturbed by unknowing guests who might come to call.

I am tempted to view it as another example of the "illogical" behavior of nonhumans. But is the behavior any more illogical than that of children who stubbornly refuse to choose the type of life their parents so unselfishly place before them? And how do I know what her needs are, what she sees, senses, follows, in the choice of one place over another? Won't I do better to wait and see if the site she chose works, give her the benefit of her race's success over what I think is good for her, and see if I can discover what led her to where she is? And even if such an attitude does the phoebe no good, won't it serve me better in my dealings with other creatures, cultures, and generations? Kindnesses without expectation of acceptance are the hardest sort to offer.

May 29

Have been away for a week. This morning, after everyone left the house by way of the back door and the phoebe left her nest, I open the front door, set a wobbly stool on the doorsill, and teeter out over the nest. In its shallow bowl I find a small pool of grey fuzz with four pale yellow beaks sticking out of it, four dim pairs of unopened but huge eyes (as though birds are born wide-eyed to the world even before they begin seeing it), four inseparable, nestled bodies with pink points and naked bumps of assorted wing tips, elbows, and knees protruding here and there, all breathing in unison, all beating together under the dark overhang, like some single unformed dream of a bird.

May 30

Whatever the brooding arrangement is, I saw both phoebes actively feeding the chicks for the first time today, often with large white grubs. Instead of any relief ceremony, the adult who was feeding would often chase the other away from the "approach twig." They use the same hesitant, indirect manner they employed in building the nest, approaching it in a series of short flights, feeding one chick, flying back to a branch, then back to the nest to feed another. Both look wet and bedraggled after last night's heavy rain, crewcuts awry and tailwagging dampened. The male has not been singing lately, probably too busy.

June 4

The chicks are visible now above the rim of the nest, and the adults seem to have stopped sitting on them. Today when I looked in (only when the adults are out of sight), the chicks filled their cuplike nest almost to overflowing. They sport pinfeathers now, and their eyes are open when feeding. I blew gently on them, but they pretended not to notice and only sunk down into a deeper semblance of sleep as their remaining natal down shook lightly under my breath.

June 6

Last night the rain returned. When I went out the front door to open the rain barrel cock, I shone my flashlight up at the nest. The mother was there, covering the chicks as best she could, staring at me sideways out of her black, worried eyes, but not flying off. These birds become tenacious about staying on the nest once the chicks hatch.

The young birds grow visibly larger every day now and can be seen over the nest's rim even when not being fed, stretching and preening (their flight feathers are over an inch long). The male has once more taken up singing loudly around the nest.

June 13

Sunday morning, June 10th, the phoebes left suddenly, swiftly, and successfully. I remember looking out the window about 9:30 A.M. and seeing only two chicks, but assuming the rest were hunched down. A little after ten Beth came over to me, looking worried: "Something's happened to the phoebes." We looked, and the nest was empty.

I had seen no indication of the chicks' trying out their wings during the past few days. Unlike most other songbirds, young phoebes don't usually have the chance to sidle off the nest and out onto some branch to practice flapping. Like murres and auks on the cliffs of Labrador, they must leap, unknowing, out of the nest into space, plummeting downward, flailing untried wings. All must have made it, though in doing so they apparently knocked out (or the parents deliberately pushed out) the one unhatched egg, which lay broken open in the dirt below the nest, revealing a partially formed embryo inside.

They gave no warning of their departure and left without ceremony. I think we felt a little deserted. They had made themselves a part of our house and its life for more than seven weeks, and it has taken us several days to get used to using the front door again.

One curious footnote: the day after the phoebes left I took down the empty nest and brought it inside. There, in the exact center of the bowl, was a small, perfect, yellow and brown spiral seashell. Only a quarter-inch long (an estuarine dove snail, I think), it seemed as if it had been left for us on purpose, perhaps as a souvenir of their enterprise, at once fitting and improbable.

The Kindest Cut

Early last summer, in a mood of expansiveness, I cleared some land by the garden to construct a carriage shed. This required the cutting of a large pitch pine, one of only a dozen or so left on the property. It was more than forty feet tall and nearly a foot thick, and when it came cracking and crashing to the ground, it enveloped my son, Christopher, who was holding the end of the guide rope, in a great cloud of yellow-green pollen. As the dust began to settle and he stepped out of the sulphurous bloom coughing and wiping his streaming eyes, I thought of the various trees I have cut here over the years and the relationships I have had with them.

The first were a phalanx of oaks I felled over ten years ago on the rise where the house now stands. Their long, thin, crooked trunks lay about me on the ground like fallen soldiers, and I felt toward them that same assumption of power and responsibility others have felt toward animals of the hunt. My house, my life here, I thought, must be as strong and rooted as the lives I am usurping.

A year later more trees were cut and uprooted to make the garden. Among the maze of pines, viburnum, and catbriar, I found a spindly young apple tree, grotesquely elongated by a wild attempt to reach sunlight. It seemed to possess grit, so I directed the bulldozer operator to perform a crude transplant by digging a hole just behind the garden and dropping the tree into it. I gave it a severe pruning and lots of water, and it not only survived, but has thrived, producing a modest crop of fruit most years.

A few years later, when we placed solar collectors on the roof, I had to cut some trees on the south slope behind the house to let in the autumn sun. I took only those I needed to, though, following the sun's decline week by week with my chain saw until the leaves finally dropped and I could spare the rest.

There have been a few others. A young and handsome scarlet oak stood farther back from the garden. Every autumn it blazed forth in glorious hues, but it was also beginning to shade out the only large red cedar on the lot. I agonized for several seasons over that one, as each October the oak argued its case brilliantly. But at last, one bleak February day, I took it down. Despite repeated mowings, however, the roots send up a little fountain of green shoots each spring, as though to give me a chance to reconsider.

When I look back on it now, mine seems mostly to have been a history of decisions *not* to cut trees. I chose for a driveway an old wood road running through the property, primarily so that I would not have to cut down any large trees in order to get into the house site. In an excess of conservation, I cut only those trees necessary for the house foundation and for a small yard. Since then, during every northeaster or the rare hurricane, I wish I had been more liberal in my cutting.

During one early burst of arboreal enthusiasm I even imported some trees from Maine: a white pine, two balsam firs, and a larch. The pine thrives in the middle of the drive's open turnaround, but the larch languishes in the shade of overhanging oaks. The firs, never native here, simply stand, refusing to grow, with the sullen resignation of involuntary immigrants.

So much is involved in the space taken up by a tree—and so much lost in its removal—that I find myself considering at length the character of any tree I plan to cut. I will climb its branches, sit beneath it, surmise its history, and then, after felling it, measure its girth and length and count its growth rings. Sometimes I even recognize individual trees when I feed pieces of them into the stove box.

When I came to cut that pollen-laden pitch pine last June, I climbed some twenty-five feet up its trunk, first by way of an aluminum ladder and then up the trunk, using as hand- and foot-holds a series of dead, rotten branches, in order to loop the guide rope at the highest possible point (risking my life somewhat in order to take the tree's). Then I paused and looked back over the garden, the house, and the woods beyond—a familiar scene, yet novel. This tree afforded a unique perspective, one I had never enjoyed before and never would again. In order to gain more space on the ground, I was losing a certain vantage point on my own history.

Our history in any place is a history of choices, intentional or unconscious, and the more intimately we come to know a landscape, the more complex those choices become. We can ignore the complexity and enjoy the clear resolve and vigorous purpose that comes from seeing the world in simplistic dualities, of human will against passive nature, of progress without loss. Or we can embrace the world for what it is, a place where action is possible, but never without cost—where what we alter also alters us in unpredictable and unknowable ways.

Bird's Eye View

For the past week or so I have been laid up with a pulled calf muscle I received while fantasizing I was Larry Bird in a basketball game with my teenaged son, Christopher. I would like to say that this condition has given me new insights into the world of the handicapped, but it hasn't, really. I have merely gotten the chance to see that it is, in fact, pretty much as it has been depicted, and that there is nothing intrinsically interesting about being incapacitated.

The biggest difference it has made has been my inability to take daily walks. I do not usually just sit still and watch things. Oh, I am as likely as anyone to stop if something catches my eye, sit down upon a rock or a dune or a chair and watch it, for hours if necessary, until it reveals whatever it has to reveal. I have watched a starfish open a clam, cicadas hatch out of their larval shells, snowflakes build up in the crook of a tree branch, and so on—but these are things that usually catch me as I am walking, that interrupt my natural tendency to keep moving, however willing I am to be waylaid. It is, I suppose, a typically Western approach to nature—action succeeded by contemplation—as opposed to the

Oriental attitude, first espoused here by Thoreau, of sitting still and letting the life of the woods appear before you.

Lately, however, I have been something of an enforced Buddha, an involuntary pivot around which I have had to let the rest of the world revolve. My farthest independent excursions outdoors have been limited to going out on the deck that goes off my study, which is about nine feet off the ground. Yet even this modest elevation, I have found, puts me up in the world, among the maple and oak branches. Flickers shoot by like fat patterned darts a yard or two above my head, and from time to time a cardinal or woodpecker or some other bird lands on the railing a few feet away, gives me quick, curious stares as though surprised to see me in its stratum, then flits off again. It is a curious reversal of roles, like being on a thrust stage where the actors are in the audience. But it puts me in their sphere, so that their presence is not only more vivid but also undeniable, less like visual adornments or accessories for the mind, and more like life with a will of its own.

This morning I noticed two new bird nests from my vantage point on the deck. I do not know whether birds deliberately place their nests so as to be less visible from the ground than from above, but I am sure I would have missed both of these if I had simply walked past their respective trees.

One is already finished: a blue jay's nest, made of stout twigs and stems, in the crook of a fairly large white oak, perhaps fourteen feet off the ground. The eggs are apparently already laid, for the pair take turns sitting on the nest. Jays are supposed to be rather secretive birds during the nesting season, preferring secluded woods. Maybe they still regard my house lot as "secluded"; that would be nice. They certainly know I am here looking at them, but they also seem to sense my immobility and fly up to the edge of the deck wall every so often to peer down at me.

Next to the jay's nest, but twice as high, in the top-most

branches of a tall, slender, black oak, an oriole nest is being built. It is still in its first stages, and so far I have only seen the female working on it. It hangs there, glistening in the sun, a gauzy, airy shell spun of yarn and dead grass blades, attached at key points to the twigs around it and trailing loose ends below, among the pale green fountains of new oak leaves and catkins. Does the oriole construct its complex hanging nest like a spider, outlining the main structure and then filling in? If I had been laid up a few days sooner, I might have seen the whole process from the beginning—not that I'm complaining.

This afternoon I am out on the deck again, sitting in a chair and writing. As I do, a mourning dove has been making continuous whistling flights from a nearby pitch pine down to the garden below, which I managed to get turned over but not planted before injuring myself. There, on the disturbed earth, she pecks and pecks until she finds a suitable rootlet or twig or piece of mulch. Then, always with an air of being startled, she leaps up with it, revealing her white, scalloped tail border, and like some high-pitched helicopter in petticoats whirlies her way back up into the pine where she is also building a nest.

It is like every other dove nest I have seen, a ridiculously flimsy affair, built in an exposed, vulnerable spot, with an open weave of twigs so loose that you can see the large pink eggs showing through the bottom. A heavy rain or high wind often knocks down these nests, but doves are both persistent and prolific, and will re-nest several times during a single season.

This one has been flying back and forth from garden to pine for over an hour now, providing a pleasant, whistling shuttle to write by. But at some point I began to notice that she does not simply take the first stem or stalk that comes loose at her pulling, but sorts and picks over several pieces before making a choice. There seems to be some element of

evaluation in the process that I cannot account for. How does this bird decide which twig will fit properly next, if that is in fact what she is doing? Are there sense receptors in her beak or eyes that latch on to certain weight-shape-texture configurations, the way that certain chemical receptors in our brains "recognize" the right molecular configurations of proteins and enzymes? Is this a needlessly complicated and mechanical way of viewing it, or, alternatively, inadequately simplistic?

Perhaps I am more impressed by this seemingly deliberate process in a mourning dove because it is generally regarded as so remarkably stupid a bird. It may have received this reputation more from its relatively small head-to-body-size ratio than from any observed behavior (though doves are the only birds I hit with my car with any regularity), but it seems that we are always taken somewhat aback by any manifestation of conscious decision-making in wild creatures, for deliberate choice, as much as any quality, seems to us a peculiarly human talent.

There does not, however, seem to be very much basis for this distinction. Most of us, I would argue, as individuals or in groups, make few conscious decisions in our lives, and most of these are trivial in nature. Congresses, corporate boards, and scientific societies are said to make "carefully weighed" decisions on any number of matters, but the actual method of arriving at such decisions is still poorly understood and seem to involve largely unconscious, intuitive, and symbolic factors, including everything from body language to voice timbre to tie color. It is this, I think, that makes so many members of local municipal boards nervous about "open meeting laws," not because they have anything illegal or improper to hide, but because they are embarrassed by the rather sloppy and illogical manner by which they reach agreement on most issues. It is a perfectly natural process, but one at odds with our own dignified notions of "public deliberation." The art of rewriting history was first practiced by recording secretaries.

On the other hand, most cultures and individuals seem to enjoy the feeling of being swept on by the deep currents of their own history and lives, with the bulk of unconscious decisions consisting largely of minor adjustments designed to keep us in the middle of the stream. Most of the important people, events, and opportunities in my own life, for instance, seem to have floated down the river at me, despite a lot of back-paddling and exploring of side-streams on my part.

All forms of life, including our own species, appear to have designs imprinted within them that they seek to replicate almost endlessly—nests, tunnels, dams, DNA helices, court-ship rituals, wallpaper patterns, Rubik's cubes, Internet jokes—with very little variation. We may not be so remark-able for the overall structures we build as for the manner in which we go about building them. When given a free rein we tend to revise, hesitate, change course in mid-stream, take offhand hints, improvise on our mistakes.

This very deck I am sitting on, for example, was an after-thought. The space it occupies was originally planned as a storage closet off the study, and the slanting walls at either end were intended to be connected with sloping rafters, boarded over, and enclosed. Halfway through its construc-tion, however, a friend drove up, saw me banging away on the upper floor, and shouted, "What're you building up there—a deck?" "No, it's . . ." I started to answer, but then I thought, Well, why not? So here I am today, watching a dove building a nest instead of smelling mothballs.

The dove, on the other hand, is not likely to turn her nest into a birdbath on impulse. Yet doesn't her own method, mix-ing as it does serendipity and instant preference with instinct, represent a combination that most of us still largely depend on to get through our days?

Watery Love

I grew up along the Middle Atlantic seaboard and in the Ohio River valley, lands of muddy rivers, silty artificial lakes, and murky farm ponds, where so much of nature seems hidden, elusive, and ambiguous. My first contacts with fish were at the end of a hook, and these were usually sunfish, catfish, and yellow perch—small, bony creatures with sharp dorsal spines.

But hooking one of these common fish—generally using a lure no more sophisticated than a rolled ball of white bread—was always a sudden and thrilling mystery. The fight they put up was quite disproportionate to their size, enough to give a nine-year-old boy the sense that he might have hooked something strange, enormous, and memorable. The shadowy, wavering form of the creature being pulled from the murky depths *could* be anything, a notion I was not disabused of until the fish actually broke the surface. Nor did the fact that there was usually nothing more than a quarter-pound crappie or pumpkinseed on the hook ever diminish my expectations for the next cast. For what drew me, then and now, was felt contact with the unknown upon which my imagination might work.

On Cape Cod, where I have lived now for most of my adult life, the ponds are glacial, sandy, and by and large much clearer than my boyhood waters, revealing their mysteries more easily. Slough Pond in Brewster, for instance, despite its name, is a deep and lucid body of water, excellent for swimming, with a sandy bottom along much of its shore.

One afternoon in early summer I set off in a canoe and paddled the circumference of the pond counter-clockwise. A light breeze came from the south, and there were as yet no insects visible on the surface of the pond. Its western edge, though only a few feet deep, is clear, broad, and sandy. As I paddled over it, I began to notice small, shallow depressions, or craters, along the bottom a few yards from shore. They varied from a little over a foot to nearly three feet in diameter, and perhaps two or three inches deep. At first I wondered if some kids might have stirred them up with oars, but as these concavities stretched on in front of me, slipping under the gliding yellow hull of the canoe for over a hundred feet, their extent and number exceeded any casual human cause and began to take on the unmistakable appearance of a natural phenomenon.

This being a herring pond, I thought they might be random depressions caused by the "flurry" of alewives breeding along the shore. But then I began to notice bluegills hovering in place over most of the scoops. Clearly, then, these were fish nests, each one spaced from its abutters by a yard or more.

Bluegills are small, pan-shaped fish with dark vertical dorsal bars and a bright blue margin along the lower jaw and gill covers. They are part of the diverse family of sunfishes, the *Centrarchidae*, which includes both largemouth bass and tiny snail darters. Males of most sunfish species make nests, fanning these depressions in lake, river, and pond bottoms with their tails, and removing debris with their mouths. After attracting females to lay their eggs in the nest, the males fertilize and guard the eggs, then watch over the newly hatched fry for several weeks.

This is a well-known and common behavior, one I had seen on film and TV programs many times but had never actually witnessed before. I began to have one of those odd reverse recognitions so common in our image-shaped age. Here, I realized, was one of those many Disney "True Life Adventures" of the late 1940s and 1950s I had watched as a child (not so "true" as those of us naively indoctrinated to nature by faked Disney documentaries would later discover) now come to life, with a clarity and proximity that seemed rare to one raised among midwestern rivers and lakes. Here was, as Thoreau might have said, "the thing itself," unstaged, unprogrammed, solitary, and unexplored.

Peering over the side of the canoe, I looked down into the bottom of these watery scrapes, many of which had scatterings of pebbles in their centers. Some contained gelatinous masses of transparent fish eggs, shot through with tiny black yolk dots. The bluegill males guarded their nests very tenaciously. If one fish wandered into a neighbor's territory, he was quickly chased off. Only when I drifted directly over them would they leave their stations, returning instantly after I had passed. Their wonderfully patterned iridescent scales seemed brighter and more intense than I remembered, probably heightened during the breeding season; though by now my impression of them was colored by contact and memory, and perhaps by the sunlight that still sifted down through the clear water, illuminating them.

Further along the shore, on the east side of the pond, I found another, smaller area of these nests, this time scraped in an area of dark bottom debris, so that they shone clearly against the black bottom like golden bowls. In one I saw a breeding pair of bluegills, swimming continuously in circles within the small circumference of the nest. The female was considerably darker than the pumpkin-colored male. As they swam he stayed on the outside of her, pressing her close, as if to drive her into the very center. From time to time the female would lean, almost horizontally, out toward the male, showing a light electric-blue ventral surface, at which moments, I suspect, she was shedding eggs. One could sense the centrifugal-centripetal tension in their circlings, that conflict of attraction and antagonism at the heart of all sexual encounters.

His importunations were interrupted regularly by the presence of other males, causing him repeatedly to leave her side and chase them off. Whatever the quality of the experience was for her, it was clearly not one of passionate oblivion for him. Rather, it had to be more like that of a man constantly coaxing his mate back onto the nuptial bed while at the same time chasing off other men trying to come in through the bedroom door. Sexual ecstasy, one suspects, must be a somewhat peripheral experience in the piscine world.

As I paddled and drifted on across the pond, the quiet splendor of the spectacle touched me. I floated over a floor of golden dishes, in the centers of which jewel-like fishes hovered, motionless, like water-suns. It was immensely different from the raucous displays of gull and tern colonies, going on simultaneously elsewhere, where the harsh aggression and raw energies of communal nesting are shrilly verbalized; and yet these silent, subaqueous courtships and rivalries filled the pond with mute tension and the formal passions of art.

Dressing a Swan

One August a few years ago my niece, Andrea, then 13, and my nephew, John, 10, were visiting from Wisconsin. One afternoon we took a walk over to Mud Pond in East Dennis. Aptly named, Mud Pond is a small, very shallow, soft-bottomed pond that was created in the early part of this century by damming up a wet meadow. A modest stream, Bound Brook, runs from its outlet into Cape Cod Bay, and a small herring run has been built there.

As we walked on the path toward the run, we heard a great commotion along the shore to our right: deep hissings, whackings on the water, a general flurry. Swans, I told the kids. Each year, ever since I have known this pond, a pair of mute swans has raised a brood of cygnets on the far shore. These large, formidable, naturalized European birds dominate the pond, not only keeping off native wildfowl, but also chasing off human intruders into their territory.

It didn't seem likely they were reacting to us, however, hidden as we were by the thick foliage. When we came to the little landing the pair of white adults were swimming around near the shore off to the right about thirty feet away, obviously highly agitated over something. A few yards behind them swam three cygnets, each about two-thirds the size of the adult, and still grey and unfledged.

"They're ugly," said John, ignorant of Hans Christian Andersen.

"No, they're not," said Andrea.

Up against the shore, under some low, overhanging bushes, was the form of a fourth cygnet, seemingly inert. It suddenly raised one wing, then the other, in momentary struggle, and then relaxed. Its head appeared to be underwater.

My first thought was that it had become entangled in some fishing line or hooked on a lure. There was no way I could reach it without a boat, and I was not sure it would be wise to try with two agitated adult swans nearby. Leaving John and Andrea on the shore, I ran over to the Kelleys' house on the other side of the pond. I pinned a note to their door—"Have taken your boat to try to rescue a swan"—and set out from their dock in a tiny fiberglass punt.

As I rounded the point, I encountered the swan family swimming back, minus the one in difficulty. They ignored me, and I knew then that the cygnet was dead. In nature a dead child is a vanished child. When I reached the floating form, the head was still underwater. I lifted up the long, water-soaked length of neck. The head came up easily—it was not entangled. But one eye was gashed, and the black beak was almost entirely crushed.

Snapper.

This pond has bred some monstrously large snapping turtles, though I had never before heard of one taking anything as large as a nearly full-grown swan.

"What are you going to do with it, Uncle Bob?" asked Andrea.

"Well, I think I'll see if the Museum of Natural History might want it."

But as we walked home with the swan flung over my shoulder like a wet, feathered sack, my brain began to retrace a familiar path, a kind of cultural regression of my race that it had followed before—once when a ruffed grouse broke its neck against our picture window, and another time when I came upon a black duck in its death stagger along Route 6A. Like them, the cygnet had initially been a fellow creature in distress, spurring me to render assistance. Then, following its death, it became an object suitable as a donation for scientific and educational use. Now, upon calm reconsideration, it seemed to be revealing its true and unmistakable identity—as a generous amount of freshly dead meat.

When we got home Andrea said, "Aren't we going to the Museum with the swan now, Uncle Bob?"

"Um, no, I thought we might eat it instead."

"Eat it! You wouldn't do that, would you?"

"Why not?"

"It's disgusting!"

"You had chicken last night."

"That's different."

I went to the kitchen to consult *The Joy of Cooking*. In the past it had yielded me instructions for preparing and cooking such wild dishes as grouse, groundhog, and even whale ("Last but vast.") But there was nothing under "Swan." I called my friend Ralph, something of a connoisseur of wild meat, who said it would probably be delicious, especially a young bird. But in this weather, he advised, I would have to clean it immediately.

I set the swan on a plywood board on two saw horses outside and got a sharp, heavy knife and a pail. Andrea and John gathered around, staring. Then Andrea asked, "What are you going to do now, Uncle Bob?"

"I have to gut it and clean it."

"You mean right here, in the yard? Well, don't do it around me!"

Making a gesture of disgust she ran off with John down to the garden, where they stopped and turned, watching me with disapproving looks. Though my brother is a surgeon, his kids had apparently never seen anything, living or freshly dead, dissected before. Well, I thought, it should at least help prepare Andrea for Take Your Daughter to Work Day.

And so, opening *The Joy of Cooking* to the directions for dressing wild goose (the closest I could find), I proceeded to gut a swan. First, I plucked enough feathers from the breastbone to the vent to make a clean incision. When I opened up the peritoneal cavity, there were a lot of guts: yards and yards of looped, greenish-white intestines, seemingly full; large slabs of lean, red-brown liver; and a large, round, hard, red gizzard the size of an ox heart. There were long dark masses on either side of the lower backbone that I assumed were the kidneys. The organs were still warm. The bright red blood flowed readily when I inadvertently cut an artery. I had the distinct feeling I was handling, operating on, a living body.

As I worked, the kids gradually crept closer until, at last, unabashedly fascinated, they stood near and watched in silence. The membranes were tough, but eventually most of the organs came out cleanly—half a ten-quart pail of them. The lungs were last—spongy, strawberry-colored masses from far up in the chest cavity. I flushed out the cavity with a garden hose, and when I saw the ribs clean, it all at once looked like a turkey brought home from the supermarket. There was, surprisingly, almost no breast meat. Apparently the breast muscles don't develop until the bird fledges. But the legs were thick, heavy, and powerful, the size of drumsticks from a twenty-pound turkey.

It was now too late to think of preparing the bird for supper that evening, so I cut off the legs and put them in the freezer.* Then I drove the carcass over to Ralph's, where we tossed it into his legendary compost pile, an amazing mound

---

*Weeks later we roasted the swan's legs, seasoning them with ginger and pearl onions. They were quite succulent and tender.

of organic wizardry surmounted by a clay head referred to as the "God of Rot"—a kind of black hole of decomposition that would probably swallow a horse whole. (Several years later Ralph dismantled the pile and found a curious, shoe-horn-shaped object among the compost: it was the swan's bill—all that remained of it.)

When I got back both John and Andrea expressed disappointment that we weren't having roast swan for dinner. They were, it seems, my brother's children after all.

A Missionary Among Moonjellies

Recently I spent a day as a guest at a private beach, a thousand-foot crescent of white shining sand, flanked on both ends by public beaches with their packed hordes. Normally, I am uncomfortable among such privileged disparities, but this time I came not to comment, or even to observe, but simply to unwind and relax, to swim in the clear, warm, blue-eyed waters of Nantucket Sound, to lie in the white sun, and to read my beach mystery, Timothy Findley's *The Telling of Lies*.

I showed my guest pass, walked through the wooden pavilion out onto the pristine sand, which had recently been mechanically swept and smoothed by a beach version of a Zamboni. I spread my towel among the few dozen other beachgoers, and plunged into the clear seventy-six degree water. There were two sizeable rafts placed offshore, both crowded with the small bodies of children. Oddly, none of the children were jumping or diving into the water.

I swam out between the rafts and looked back at the colorful, brilliant scene of blankets, bathing suits, chairs and umbrellas on the beach, embraced by the long, curved arm of the bathhouse galleries. Atop a white lifeguard tower, a young, muscular woman sat cross-legged, holding a cellular phone. And then, as if the whole scene were a staged movie set onto which I had inadvertently blundered, a director's voice trumpeted from speakers mounted on the office building:

"ATTENTION, PLEASE. THE TIME IS NOW 4:30. THE OFFICE WILL CLOSE AND LIFEGUARDS WILL GO OFF DUTY IN FIFTEEN MINUTES."

I decided to swim over to the eastern float and take a dive off before heading in. As I did, I was struck more forcibly by the tenacity with which all of the kids remained massed on the raft, like boat people. I estimated some fifteen bodies, and none of them were in the water. They seemed excited and preoccupied with something. Most were gathered at one end, slightly submerging its edge and tilting up the opposite side, on which the ladder was mounted. Something was definitely going on.

Curious now, I climbed up the inclined ladder onto the tilted raft. The children were pelting one another with clear plastic bags partially filled with water. A couple of these bags lay in one corner of the raft. Heading over to get a closer look, I suddenly realized what was going on—and wished I hadn't. The bags were not bags; they were moonjellies, a common species of jellyfish found here in late summer. The kids were slinging small moonjellies and pieces of larger ones at each other.

The deck was covered with invertebrates: pale, pink, and yellow masses of gelatinous, glistening protoplasm. Now I could see that the waters surrounding the raft were filled with moonjellies, most them smaller than the ones on the raft.

"Here they come!" shouted one of the boys. "Push it down and they'll come aboard."

Several more bodies crowded to the lower edge of the raft,

levering it down into the water and creating a suction that swept several more of the sea creatures onto the canvas deck. As the jellies swirled around their young legs, they scooped them up, the boys with their hands, the girls in plastic pails, and began pelting one another again, screaming in half-feigned horror and delight, oblivious to the adult among them.

Great, I thought. All I wanted was a couple of hours of undisturbed relaxation, and now I had been drawn into the middle of a moral and environmental dilemma. What was I supposed to do? I was conflicted on many levels, not the least by some of my own words. In the past I had defended such casual cruelty by children in nature, arguing that it was a price we should be willing to pay in exchange for the tactile and imaginative bonding such play engendered. Most children, I maintained, grow out of such behavior on their own. In any case, was it *my* responsibility to reprimand them? Wasn't it the duty of their parents, who sat oblivious on the beach immersed in books and newspapers? Why didn't I have the sense to stay on the beach with them?

But here I was, the only adult among a dwarf forest of young limbs and bodies that were shouting and squealing, hurling living creatures, or bits of them, at one another, engaged in behavior I had defended in print, but which now repelled me—deeply, viscerally, unequivocally.

What should I say? What could I say? They didn't even seem to recognize the moonjellies as living creatures. For that matter, strictly speaking, they aren't true organisms, but colonies of semi-autonomous single-celled individuals, the most primitive form of cellular organization on the planet. Surely jellyfish exist in the nether regions of human sympathy. Does that make them less deserving of protection? Do they feel pain? Who knows? Who cares? I just wanted to dive back in and head toward the beach and my book, leaving the children to their perhaps-not-so-innocent, but, so I told myself, important and, in the long run, beneficial fun.

Fun? But the moonjellies *moved*—and the children *knew* they moved! I saw two young girls, perhaps eight or nine, gathered at one corner of the lowered raft edge, watching several small moonjellies—pulsing, fringed, supple vessels of grace—throbbing like transparent hearts through the water. I could see they were fascinated, full of awe and incipient admiration—and also a little afraid, watching these small extraterrestrials, terrible in their foreign element. Yet once the shimmering creatures had stranded on the rough surface of the deck or were scooped up and made captives, their mystery collapsed and they became fair game for their sadistic impulses.

"Jellyfish coming on board! Evacuate! Evacuate!"

It was no good. I could not stay outside it. I was already inside it, surrounded by a barbarism I could no longer believe would possibly lead to anything positive. I would have to step into it, or else have this stick permanently in my craw. Raising my arm, I spoke:

"Okay, now. Uh, listen up. Could I have your attention for just a minute?" They all turned, surprised, as if for the first time aware of me. I avoided their massed eyes. "Okay, now I don't want to spoil your fun [*the hell I don't*] but those are living animals you're throwing, and they feel pain just like you do." [*They do?*]

A ten-year-old girl in a polka-dot red-orange bikini gave me a sour look and said, "But they grow up to be the *bad* ones."

"No, no they don't. These are harmless. It's the others, the lion's manes, that have stinging tentacles. [*So what? Would I say go ahead, massacre the lion's manes?*] Anyway, these are living creatures, and they feel pain. Think about that the next time you're tempted to throw them." [*The next time? Do I think they've stopped?*]

Not waiting for their response I leaped off the raft, feeling suddenly ridiculous in their eyes, like some absurd middle-aged Superman, flying in to deliver a brief lesson on civic responsibility to a gang of young street thugs, then bounding off to fight for truth and justice. I dove gratefully down into the cool, clear water, welcoming the sudden silence and invisibility that embraced me, wishing I could stay down there indefinitely. When I surfaced, swimming, I heard an older boy's taunting voice behind me, "Okay. We will," followed by a chorus of giggles. I swam full out toward the beach, not looking back.

I climbed out of the water, spread my towel, and lay drying in the sun. Well, I thought, that was pretty ineffective. But I hoped, at least, I might have put a damper on their amusement. After a few minutes I turned over and looked back toward the raft. The boys all seem to have left the raft and were swimming over toward the other one, farther away, leaving the girls to continue scooping up the jellyfish in their pails.

No doubt on the other raft the carnage went blithely on, undisturbed by any adult missionizing. It didn't matter. I knew I would not go back out to try to convert the other island of barbarians. Who knows, I thought with cowardly consolation, perhaps the little bastards would pick some of the poisonous lion's manes and get a painful and well-deserved comeuppance.

"ATTENTION, PLEASE. IT IS 4:45. THIS OFFICE IS NOW CLOSED. LIFEGUARDS ARE NO LONGER ON DUTY. THANK YOU."

A Lower-case Walk

It was, as everyone observed at the time, a quiet Labor Day weekend. A downturn in the weather resulted in fewer cars, fewer celebrations, fewer arrests than usual. Clambakes on the beaches of Cape Cod Bay were held with windscreens and jackets, and a stiff northeast wind kept everyone huddled and subdued throughout a shortened afternoon. Bathers at the ocean beaches were kept out of the water by massive surf, a distant gift from Hurricane Emily. Helped along by the generally cloudy and cool weather, the diminished holiday weekend crowds seeped off-Cape early on Saturday and Sunday, like air from a leaky tire.

Monday was a pleasant surprise—a bright, sunny, still day that seemed a reward to those who had stuck it out, and a benediction to those of us who weren't going anywhere anyway. As though to reinforce my position as a resident, I spent Labor Day afternoon working in the garden: pulling up dry cornstalks and flowered broccoli plants, gathering another armful of tomatoes, digging up a few hills of potatoes that, during the last few weeks of neglect, had grassed thickly over like new graves.

By 6:30 there seemed to be just enough light left for a walk down Red Top Road before coming in for the day, a kind of end-of-the-summer walk, not so much to Take Stock of Things, or to Sum Up the Season, or anything so weighty as that, but more a lower-case walk, merely to mark the hiatus, to check one of the bounds of the year.

I am one of those people who think best while walking— as others do while eating or taking a shower or playing the piano—and I have found that the best walks, even if they lead nowhere in particular, usually come after periods of useful physical work, clearing both the blood and the mind of accumulated dross.

So, taking a mug of tea along for company, I started down the road. Considering the drought of the past month, it was less dusty than I expected, perhaps because of the cool, moist nights of late that have produced heavy dews in the mornings. Still, the oak leaves hanging over the road were all browned with drought, and the tall cottonwood stand off to the left was already considerably thinned, littering the ground with grey and yellow leaves.

As I continued down the road, however, its dirt surface bore a beaten-down look from weeks of summer traffic, which no rains had washed away. Along the shoulders and just off into the woods was strewn an appalling amount of summer trash—cans and bottles, bags of garbage, construction scrap, bits of underclothing and even some raw Polaroid prints of clumsy attempts at pornography that lay like pale fungus among the leaves—all emblems of that forcible domination without intimacy or responsibility that makes "rape" such an accurate, however overused, a metaphor for so much of our use of the land.

But this was to be, as I said, a lower-case walk. I did not want to think about the politics of litter, or the vulnerability of all locales to the world's carelessness—at least not at the outset. So I left the town road, taking to the woods along an old cart path that forks off to the left and climbs up a morainal hill toward the site of one of the neighborhood's original homesteads, now just an overgrown cellar hole.

In my walks through these repeatedly cut-over, third- and fourth-growth woods, I have developed a rough system of classification for unpaved roads that includes four categories. Red Top Road itself is an example of the first type, or primary dirt road: a public way, periodically graded and maintained by the town, used regularly and increasingly by vehicular traffic. The second type, or secondary dirt road, includes those old wood roads and cart paths on private property, no longer maintained but still clearly defined, still frequently used by pedestrians, horses, mountain bikers, and even an occasional car whose paint job is no longer a concern to its owner.

The old road I was now on was a good specimen of a tertiary road, also once a wagon path, but one so long abandoned and now grown over that it is not only impassable to vehicles, but no longer evident or even discoverable without some effort or luck. This one, in fact, I had walked by for years without noticing until one winter's day a light snowfall revealed its flat bed still curving its way up the flank of the hill. Even though I now know its location, I still have to look twice to see it. Young pines and oaks have sprouted up along the raised ridge in its center, and it takes a certain tactile as well as visual attention to keep its old contours in view as it snakes up the hill.

These tertiary roads gradually fade into a fourth catch-all and increasingly tenuous category that includes footpaths, game trails, the flight paths of birds, and shafts of sunlight. All of these roads are labeled by the town (with a dash of unintentional irony) as "unimproved."

As always, despite my best intentions, I found myself wondering how long this old road had left, what invisible property lines I was crossing, what subdivision plans were already recorded in the town planning board office, when all the new houses would inevitably come in and disrupt forever the integrity of the landscape, the web of old human thorough-fares, and all the subtle remains of local history—cellar holes, lilac bushes, bottle dumps, abandoned rusting farm imple-ments and rotting harnesses—that had accumulated like leaves for generations in this place. Most of all, I thought how impossible it is to explain to those who will determine its fate the value of walking along such a barely-discernible aban-doned old road up the side of some scrubby-oaked, rock-studded hill.

And yet, I had to ask myself in all honesty, did the old Cape Codders, whose tradition and history we seem to draw on so much in our attempts to preserve local landscapes, regard this countryside with any kindred appreciation? From most of the older natives I have talked with over the years, my sense is that they did not, at least not in the way most of us do today.

No, what they appreciated were its cultivated aspects, what they had *made with* the land: a well-ploughed field, a well-tended garden, colorful flower-boxes, planted trees, drained bogs and swamps, a barn full of hay and a woodshed full of stove logs. In other words, they valued thrift, order, security, and predictability among what was commonly per-ceived as the overwhelming profligacy, disorder, uncertainty, and anarchy of nature. They were certainly rooted in and deeply acquainted with their landscape, the old-timers, per-haps at times comfortable and even intimate with it, but by and large not appreciative of it for its own sake.

Still, walking up this old tertiary road, I had the sense of maintaining, albeit tenuously, a local tradition, though I could not claim much knowledgeable intimacy with it for myself. There are any number of common understory plants whose names I still do not know. I recognize only a few wild-flowers, mushrooms or insects, and several bird calls still elude me. I am like a waterbug skimming over the surface of its history, buoyed up by a certain tension between past and present.

As I reached the top of the hill I flushed a ruffed grouse, which went spiraling and weaving off through the oak and viburnum like a punted football. Here the tertiary road intersected with one of the secondary roads, which in turn ran back down toward Red Top. I followed its slow arc down the hill, passing several large morainal boulders, some ten feet or more in length. They sat comfortably by the side of the cart path, like huge grey armchairs, or their pale, settled occupants. Their wrinkled, cracked surfaces, washed and swept clean of leaves each winter, were disturbed only by dark tufts of moss and scaly coatings of lichen—slow products of decades of undisturbed growth, which I could easily have swept away with a casual swipe of my hand.

In these quiet, unlittered woods I seemed to be intersecting with a different time frame, one in which man was not so much absent as irrelevant. These glacial rocks, which seemed so immobile, were actually engaged in a process of transformation that I could only apprehend with geologic abstractions. Time seemed to go more slowly here, as in Einsteinian physics, where the physical processes of objects operate at retarded rates as they approach the surface of a large planet or other object of great mass (a principle that reaches its logical paradox at the surface of so-called black holes where time is thought to stop altogether).

It was as though the simple components of this hillside— the boulders, the brittle lichen, the thin crooked ranks of trees—rested closer than I to the gravitating heart of earth. No birds called. No leaves fell. The woods exhaled a sudden hushed stillness within which, to our eyes, "nothing was happening." Yet for them existence was no doubt going on at a perfectly normal rate. For them the glacier might have left only yesterday afternoon, and humans, unheld by any communal focus in their lives, flitted like blurs, half-real and unnoticed, across the landscape.

I reached Red Top Road and started back home, passing more of the debris of summer washed up along its sides. I had nothing but an empty tea mug to collect it with, and really no heart for it, this evening at least. There would be time enough, during the coming winter, to set our houses and our environs, if not our lives, in order. Summer was over, a wall of cricket sound fell in the woods like dry rain. Later on, the rocks might have more to tell me as the leaves fell and their grey shapes, washed by autumn rains, emerged out of the hills like bones. But for now I was comforted by the total indifference with which nature and her creatures seem to regard whatever desecrations we might choose to inflict upon them.

September Song

This is the season when the common black field crickets begin to come indoors. Crickets, it seems, come inside our houses to get warm, a trait that has endeared them to poets for centuries. But they can cause considerable damage by eating clothes, books, and even shoe leather with their powerful, sharp mandibles. And their song—that familiar, metallic three-note chirp that forms such an appropriate part of late summer's outside insect orchestra, or may seem so merry a solo on the proverbial hearth on a September evening—can, at silent midnight, detached and stridulous under the staircase or in a closet, reverberate with a maddening and unquenchable persistence. Still, despite these habits, I find myself reluctant to put them out as the nights grow cooler.

Field crickets may begin singing as early as May, one of nature's few springtime insect instrumentalists. Unless I deliberately listen for them, however, they do not usually make themselves a felt presence until late July, when a few hesitant chirps and trills rise out of the garden, and the heavy, curving z-ing of the cicadas presses down over the yard at noon like the bending weight of the sun itself.

The insect chorus begins imperceptibly in midsummer and grows unobtrusively like the grass. By the time the horse chestnut leaves begin to curl and turn brown along our streets and the sea lavender blooms on the marshes, the sound has swollen and fills the nighttime air like a many-textured fog, thinning but never quite subsiding by day. When I finally catch myself aware of it, I feel like a child whose wandering ear picks up some snatch of conversation between adults. I want to say, "What? What are you talking about? Start over again."

The actual mechanics of cricket song are well known and simple enough. Specialized ribbed-and-notched membranes on the inner edges of the forewings of adult males are drawn back and forth over one another, producing high-pitched pulsations of sound ranging from "low" frequencies in the upper registers of the piano keyboard to pitches of ten thousand cycles per second, beyond the hearing range of many people. Most of these sounds are not pure tones but slurs, and while they may seem unexpressive and monotonous to us, they are apparently capable of great variation, which is presumably detectable by the females. By changing the angle at which the wings are held during stridulation, and using the folded outer wing covers as dampers, crickets can make rapid and dramatic changes in the volume of their singing. This gives their song a striking ventriloquial quality, making it difficult for predators and sleepless humans to locate them. Grasshoppers have a more fiddlelike arrangement; they produce their songs by drawing small, pegged projections on their hind legs across the thick projecting veins on their outer wings. Cicadas, the loudest of the summer insects, are actually percussionists; located on their thorax, beneath their wings, are round, ridged, drumlike muscles that vibrate in and out to produce their sharp, cutting sound.

I value these "songs," these insect scrapings and tympanic vibrations, not only for the texture and acoustical shape they give to the season, but because they tend to bring to life my dulled senses, which so often seem to film over and go half-asleep by late summer. Like a storm of sound they can shake me into awareness and participation. They bring my ears back to life after what seems a long sleep.

Go out into the garden at noon on an early fall day, or on a warm, hazy evening. The cricket chorus is at its flood then. During the day their background chiming is like the spring-time peeping of the Hylas: from the garden come little, rasp-ing, zigzag figures and from the surrounding treetops, the high, cutting whine of the cicadas.

On a warm late summer evening the sound is much more—not so much louder as palpably denser. Like the peep-ers, the insect chorus is, from a distance, a fairly uniform sound, a constant background noise, like the smooth, unre-garded hum and static of electrical appliances running in a house. Once you go out and enter the sound and give it an informed ear, however, the fog begins to resolve itself into identifiable components. You begin to distinguish high lisp-ing trills, rhythmic bleats, and running ticks against a fainter bagpipe background. Among the evening soloists are the field crickets with their triple-noted chirps, and the katydids (a long-horned grasshopper) with their scraping, sawlike fig-ures. The ground crickets have high, metallic, bell-like calls, a running beat like the sound of a wristwatch heard next to your ear through a pillow. From the entrance of its burrow the odd mole cricket, an inhabitant of low, wet areas, adds his bass chirp.

At this time of year I begin to hear a gentle urgency in their voices, as though I were listening to a muted alarm clock: "hurry-hurry," or "retreat-retreat." They seem to be pecu-liarly connected to the concept of time, that impersonal measuring off of the universe. As I walk along under the power lines in late August, over the washed-out, gravelly ser-vice road lined with burned and dying sweetfern, bayberry, huckleberry, and gay clusters of goldenrod and blue asters, the various cricket cries fill my ears. They abound under every log, can, or stone I lift, springing out in every direction like the insides of a watch when the cover is lifted off.

The various voices heard together remind me of an old-fashioned clock shop I once visited in Lausanne, Switzerland, filled with hundreds of timepieces all ticking away at different tempos and timbres, the ratchets and gear teeth clicking, various ones slipping in and out of phase by chance, deaf to one another. It was a soft and pleasing cacophony, all the clocks keeping the same time, all the hands moving together in concert, despite the diversity of movement and sound.

So the crickets, all variations on a single theme, represent the year's clock winding down as they become manifest to our ears: first softly at night in midsummer, then during the day, growing louder and more imperative as the sun slants further south through September skies, articulated insect clocks that have no hope for survival themselves, but that seem to warn others—terns, geese, chipmunks, and people— to flee or prepare. Rising to an urgent, contradictory climax, they chant, "We are running down, running down!" then gradually sink, slow, come apart. The grasshopper, being most sensitive, shuts off at about sixty degrees. The katydid gradually dismantles his song, losing it syllable by syllable as the temperature drops—"katy-did...she did...did"— becoming silent at fifty-three degrees. The snowy tree cricket, the last to keep singing, slows to nothing at forty, the cricket zero.

Small as they are, these singing insects seem attuned to things much larger, universal, and indifferent. They are impersonal barometers and sing in a world apart from man. They listen and respond only to themselves or abstractly to the world around them, translating it into some high, hiero-glyphic code. They have no heat of their own, and their song is not, like ours, an expression of inner moods, but an automatic register of the season. Unlike birds, they are not so affected by small daily fluctuations in the weather. All day today it was cloudy, with a strong, steady wind out of the southeast that set people to talking of a storm. By dinner time the wind grew gusty and sent spits and tatters of rain against the windows. By 9:30 a heavy wet spell set in, pouring sheets of water on the eaves. Through it all the crickets sang with mirthless good spirits, ticking away like little waterproof clocks.

Now it rains, whipping and thumping on the roof, an earnest drumming and splattering, a real Cape Cod "tempest" that tests the snugness of our hiding places, mine and the crickets. Just before I fall asleep I still hear their calls through the rain and wind, dampened at last, but not silenced. Nothing will do that but the frost.

A Marginal Species

"I . . . am small, like the Wren."

EMILY DICKINSON

It was in early October, as I was lighting the first long fire of the year in the wood stove, that I saw a small brown bird in the yard maple tree, framed against a blazing fan of yellow leaves. I thought it was a brown creeper at first, or perhaps a kinglet, but it had a definite wren shape—squat, short-necked, and up-tailed—with a long, slightly down-curved bill and prominent white eye-stripes, a ruddy back with dark wing outlines, and a light-reddish breast.

After much preparatory fluttering on the branch, as though it were about to make its first flight out of the nest, it leaped down to the ground beside the back door, landing among the violets and a female towhee that was kicking up some of last year's leaves for insects. The towhee, a much larger bird, gave one flick of its outer white tail feathers and flew off, a brown and white blur.

The wren remained, poking among the plants, and because of the way our house angles around in back, I could stand beside the bay window and follow its remarkable progress. From the ground it leaped onto the foundation ventilation block, then up onto the rough cedar clapboards, where it thrust its sharp, curved bill here and there beneath them, working its way diagonally across the face of the house wall toward the bathroom window, where it hopped up to the window screen and then under the eaves. There, clinging upside-down to the rafter ends, it appeared to feed on several embalmed and web-hung moths, and perhaps on some of their spider captors as well; then, leaping around a jog in the wall, it began to work up the clapboards of the bedroom gable end, poking and hopping its way up to the second-story window. From there it moved onto the cedar rake trim, searching continuously beneath the trim overlap, then up to the very ridge of the roof, where it combed the grooved wooden shingles, and then down the other side, where it finally slipped under the eaves again and disappeared around the back of the house.

In all of these peregrinations the wren never appeared to actually fly; its short wings, buzzing in quick humming-bird blurs, seemed at most to aid it in its leaps. It was a veritable house-creeper, this little bird, and in those few minutes of watching it, it gave me a greater knowledge of the contours and textures of my house than I had gained while building it. Now no mere wooden covering, the sheathing was reanimated as the ridged and creviced skin of some great beast, a rhinoceros or alligator, whose bowels I inhabited and whose surface this small insect-hunter seemed to know so intimately.

This was my first real contact with the Carolina wren, *Thryothorus ludovicianus*. It was not the first one I had ever seen, but the first that had ever revealed itself as more than a brief "sighting," that had exhibited its personality to me in so unconscious and compelling a fashion that it put a new face on the day.

As its name implies, the Carolina wren is a more southern species than our other Cape Cod wrens—the house wren, the winter wren, and the long-billed marsh wren. It is also noticeably larger than any of these and the only one that is non-migratory. It is listed as an "uncommon permanent resident" here, at the northern edge of a recently expanded range. Like the titmouse, cardinal and mockingbird, the Carolina wren has moved gradually northward during the latter half of the twentieth century, taking advantage of a gradual warming trend and increasing numbers of human feeders. During periods of mild winters its numbers may increase dramatically, and it has bred irregularly on the Upper Cape as far down as Orleans. Unlike these other southern immigrants, however, the Carolina wren is almost totally dependent on insect food in the wild, and a series of harsh, cold winters can decimate local populations, especially when deep snow covers the ground for long periods. For this reason, it is unlikely to ever become a permanently abundant bird here and is still considered, like other organisms at the extreme end of their ranges, a "marginal species."

"Wren," in its various forms, is one of the oldest words in the English language, coming from the Anglo-Saxon "wraenna;" and "wrenlike" has become a metaphorical synonym for small. Yet the Europeans were familiar with only one species of wren, the winter wren, one of the smallest. All other fifty-eight known species of wrens in the world are found only in the Western Hemisphere, where the family is thought to have originated. When early explorers in eastern North America discovered the much-larger Carolina wren, they dubbed it the "Great Carolina Wren," which is something like calling the common domestic mouse the Great House Mouse because it is greater in size than field mice. When later explorers encountered such western giants as the cactus wren (at an awesome six and a half inches in length), they were disenchanted with their former wonder and the "great" was dropped from the Carolina wren's common name.

How astonishing this variety of New World wrens must have seemed to European eyes, which were so accustomed to their single example of wrenness that it was not only simply referred to as "the wren," but must have seemed the only possible type. I think American wrens must have added in no small measure to the idea of unlimited variety and abundance that has dominated so much of our country's history. Here the wren took on unfamiliar sizes, proportions, feathers, songs, and dwellings. Leaving behind its ancestral Old World caves or holes (its family name, Trogloditidae, means "cave dwellers"), here it sang in strange tongues and built its nests in marshes, deserts, canyons, thorny underbrush, and even human dwellings.

Throughout the late fall the Carolina appeared from time to time, ticking his way across the skin of the house or, more often, darting about the brush piles by the garden. I knew him for a male now, for the Carolina wren is one of the great singers of the bird world, and one of the few in our region that sing at all seasons. Unlike the house wren, with its constant bubbling and uniform warbling, the Carolina wren has a great variety of calls and songs, so many, in fact, that some ornithologists classify him as an "imitator," though this may simply be a back handed tribute to his versatility, as a writer who does not stick to one style is often accused of copying others.

The Carolina wren's most common song is a loud, warbling, descending triplet, similar in form and accent to that of the yellowthroat, but more liquid and musical. One afternoon, shortly before Christmas, the wren landed on the steps just outside the sliding glass doors and began uttering, with very proclamatory and forceful posturing, a series of loud, single, scolding calls, very similar to a blue jay's, though thinner in tone. After several minutes of this, he hopped onto the woodpile stacked against the house, where I could observe him closely from the kitchen window. At near range the white eyestripe had a yellowish tinge, and I could see clearly the fine barring on the wings and the tail. His back was a lovely, warm reddish-brown, like that of the wood thrush, and there were fine dark streakings along the sides of his throat.

He did not seem at all aware of me, but kept up his scolding calls, mixing them now with a clear, rapid, two-note sequence—*peet-peet, peet-peet*—introductory in quality, like the launching notes of the song sparrow, but faster, with the rhythm of the chivy calls of a roseate tern.

The Carolina wren was originally considered more "wild" than its domestic cousin, the house wren, preferring the more isolated and thorny underbrush of river bottoms to the haunts of men. It does seem more wary of actual human presence, taking cover at my approach and stealing away on foot in the underbrush, so that it is almost impossible to follow.

Nonetheless, it is a curious and alert little bird, and over time it seems to have adapted itself equally well to our proximity. Arthur Cleveland Bent writes that "Nests of the more domestically inclined wrens have been reported in a great variety of nooks and crannies in, about, or under buildings of various kinds...Almost any kind of receptacles left lying around, such as tin cans, coffee pots, pails, small baskets, pitchers, or empty boxes may be used...Nests have been found in mail boxes, bird boxes, old hornets' nests, and ivy vines growing over porches; and the nest is sometimes built in an unused cupboard or on a mantel shelf inside a house... I am told [of] a record of a successful nesting in a farm tractor that was in daily use."

When the house wren leaves in late fall, the Carolina remains and becomes even more intimately associated with its human neighbors, showing up readily at suet feeders and taking shelter in outbuildings, in pockets of clothes hanging on a line, or even occasionally inside inhabited houses. A friend of mine, not given to exaggeration, told me that one winter, during a prolonged hard freeze, a wren who was staying inside his garage leaped into his coat pocket when he went to get in his car.

Not only has the bird insinuated itself into our environs, our houses, artifacts, machine, and even our clothes, but more than most species it has mixed itself into our language. Few birds have produced such a wide variety of human interpretations of its songs. For its primary triple-note song, these include "tea-kettle," "Sweet William," "Richelieu," "Jew-Peter," "sugar to eat," and "witch jailer." Edward Howe Forbush reports one boy who expressed one of its songs with the phrase "kick 'er mother."

In an era of scientific description and Sonograms, the practice of making human analogies for birdsong has fallen into disuse and even disrepute. I think it is a loss, and perhaps no small one. It might be hard to make a case for this behavior as psychotherapy (as in the case of Forbush's boy), but its disappearance implies a loss of intimacy with our most visible natural companions, a kind of unwillingness or embarrassment of the imagination to entangle itself so unsophisticatedly into the lives and language of other creatures (though we may observe and record them more than ever). Of course, where anthropomorphism obscures accurate perception or interpretation, the cobwebs need to be cleared away; but when we know that what we create are fictions or metaphors based on our interactions with nonhuman creatures, we are, I think, the richer for them. I am not yet familiar enough with the Carolina wren's song to offer my own translation, but I am listening.

When the long cold spell of January arrived this year, accompanied by heavy snow, I put some suet and peanut butter in the log-feeder under our roof overhang. The next day I was rewarded to see two wrens show up at the feeder. They clung to the log bark rather than perching on the little wooden dowels I had set beside the feeding holes. As they fed industriously they braced themselves, as a creeper or woodpecker would, with their short barred tails. They are cocky, aggressive little feeders, pushing away chickadees and sparrows, and even large birds like titmice and cardinals. Only the yellow-rumped warblers, that seem to usurp anything around the feeder, can drive them off.

The wren seems to see better than many birds, especially on the ground. Once, when a yellowrump pushed one away from a suet bag I had nailed to an oak, the wren flitted to the ground and began pecking industriously about its base. Immediately the warbler flitted down after him, as though to say, "What's that? What have you found? Whatever it is, it's mine!" But the warbler never seemed to see what the wren had discovered, and the latter held his ground.

It is late February now. Ground patches are beginning to show again after this latest snowfall, welling out from around the bases of trees and over the septic tank in the yard. Salmon winter sunsets greet me at dusk driving home. The wrens have not been around for several weeks now, and tonight the temperature is due to drop into the teens again.

I think about the Carolina wren and its periodic pushes north. They are not like the seasonal migrations of other wrens, which are practiced, well-timed advances and retreats, like the dash of shorebirds up and down the slope of the beach before the rush and withdrawal of the pounding surf. Rather, the Carolina pushes against the limits of its own mortality, a strategy as opportunistic as any of the others, but more of a gamble. It exhibits a "wrong direction" migration, expanding northward primarily during the fall months, rather than in the spring or summer, as one might expect. If it finds a sufficient food supply and the winter is not too severe, it may establish a new, though generally temporary, foothold.

If it happens to expand on a longer cycle of moderating temperatures as it has over the past fifty years, it may gain a relatively permanent extension of range. The Carolina wren is a prolific breeder, sometimes raising two broods simultaneously, and it gambles its excess seed on unproven ground and the fickleness of the weather.

These small birds raise large questions. They remind me that no longer do we have the luxury, if we ever did, of enjoying or observing anything in isolation from ourselves. Just as we are now physically involved in every creature's existence, so I cannot follow the life history of this little bird without it eventually leading home. Sooner or later I feel my own hand tapping me on my shoulder, reminding me of my involvement in what I watch. This is not just a matter of putting out bird feeders. Wallace Bailey, in his *Birds of Cape Cod*, writes that, among the relatively few numbers of Carolina wrens breeding here, "Orleans continues to be the most regularly tenanted area. However, clearing, filling and building is reducing the suitable habitat in the favored Rock Harbor area." Thus the mere presence of those like myself who find joy in watching this bird may be reducing its ability to survive here.

It seems that the Carolina wren may always be, at best, a "marginal species" here, subject to the caprices of climatic cycles, not to mention human development. The wren has demonstrated its capacity for living in close proximity with us, even taking advantage of our many works, but just as there are two distinct sides to its personality—at once curious and shy, aggressive and retiring—so it still seems to need the wild environment with the domestic, a place to nest and a place to retreat unseen.

What is it worth to keep these bright, alert, industrious, wall-hopping creatures scattered across our increasingly altered countryside, trilling their varied songs in the winter landscape, showing us dimensions and textures to our own houses we did not know existed? What does it matter if a marginal species like this exists here or not? I know now, for instance, that the Carolina wren is one of those insatiable consumers of "harmful insects," especially caterpillars. But its value is not only as some minor cog in the ecological wheel, as an "environmental indicator," or even as an unmatched living ornament of our own dwellings. The Carolina wren has *eschatological* value, absolute worth solely for what it is, and as an opportunity for us to experience greater, fuller being in its presence.

Early in our history here, the wren took our closed notions of itself and ran away with them into the thicketed canyons, marshes, deserts, and high mesas of this continent, showing us what a species could become if given enough play and opportunity. We might have stayed in Europe and still come up with gene splicing, but would we ever have come up with the cactus wren, or the songs of the Carolina? The geneticists tell us that the old, slow process of evolution by natural selection will continue; as one put it, "There's no way to stop it," as if natural selection were just some backward culture allowed to persist in its troglodytic ways because it was too much trouble to exterminate, instead of the force that has driven life into its varied splendor. Will life become just another "design problem" for the genetic engineers of our brave new world? Will we, finally, reduce the majesty of creation and the odyssey of time to the technological jargon and cultural whims of the moment—and if so, what will that do to us?

Perhaps this is why I have come to feel such a close bond with the Carolina wren. Its migrations are like ours, gambled advances into unknown situations—some brave, some foolish —following the wake of glaciers or beckoning continents, building our homes on unstable geologic formations and our futures on untested articles of faith. We are all, in different places and in different times, marginal species.

Dark Visions in a Field

I am pedaling home at sunset, a cold wind aching in my throat, pangs in my unaccustomed legs. Already the purples of November are becoming prominent in some of the far-turned oaks, the sumac, the cranberry leaves. As I ride the bike across the marsh, things begin whispering to me: the soft rustle-whispers of the tawny marsh grass and cattails, the feather-whispers of the tall, dust-grey, phragmites seed heads; the clatter-whispers of the drooping clusters of bleached canoe-paddle seeds as I pedal beneath the ash trees; and the dry whispers of the crumpled grape leaves in the viburnum, faded and closed for the season. Even the silent cranberry bog beside the road seems to whisper.

I stop at the old Dugan farm stand, boarded up these many years. The single white Getty gas pump still stands in front of the barn, like a forlorn sentinel. Fragments of empty wasp nests cling to the metal nozzle, and the price of gas is frozen forever at forty-one and four-tenths cents per gallon.

All of a sudden the sky above the old barn fills with starlings, a whirl of black ashes thrown into the wind against the moving blue sky and white clouds. At one point a great mass of them breaks up into several diverging groups, so that it seems as if starlings were materializing out of thin air, through some entry for black antimatter. They have a look of going about them, as they gradually disappear over the trees and into the old field behind the greenhouse.

I lean my bike against the old barn and follow them to the edge of the field, now overgrown and unplowed. I hear them, a massive, dense sound in the trees just out of sight—impersonal, but purposeful, intense, like a great field of static electricity with a few peripheral chirpings. But most of all they sound like a torrential rain at night on a large, invisible lake.

At my approach, a few flit away into staghorn sumac, wild grape, viburnum, and other shrubs, but most are perched in the stunted black cherries growing all around the edge of the field. Decades ago this field was a private airstrip, and I fancy that perhaps it is the vanished aeronautical history of the place that draws the birds here in such numbers. But more likely it is the fruit of the cherry trees that brings them, each fall, into this field. They have already stripped most of the stems bare.

All at once the vast inanimate din ceases, and a thousand starlings rise out of the black cherries with a great *whoosh*, like the sound of a single, immense wing beat. They fly in a rush toward a stand of tupelos that grow west of the field, and, after gathering critical mass in this new perch, begin their crackling din again.

I follow them across the stubbly field, full of tall, blackened mullein stalks and the nubbled dry husks of milkweed seed pods, and into the tupelos. The flat-topped, downwardly crooking limbs of tupelos always seem under duress, as if someone had forced some rigid hardwood into the shape of a willow. Now they are in their autumn glory, and I stand beneath them under a canopy of spangled leaves bathed in rich gold-and-red light as though under a ruined cathedral of stained-glass domes flecked with the black shapes of the birds.

Starlings are a discredited, even a despised species in our landscape. Imported into Central Park a century ago as part of a bizarre and ill-conceived Anglophile dream to introduce all of Shakespeare's birds in the New World, they have naturalized themselves across the continent, displacing many native songbirds and, in places, reproducing in such numbers as to have become serious pests and health hazards.

Starlings were first reported on Cape Cod in December 1916. When Henry Beston wrote *The Outermost House* in the late 1920s, he speculated that the flocks he observed on the Eastham moors might "ultimately mingle to form one enormous and tyrannous confederacy." But their numbers have never grown to anything like the size of mainland flocks, probably due to our decreasing open field habitat. Still, each fall, deprived of their ancestral European migration patterns, they stir and gather in our skies with the instinct of ancient restlessness.

As though someone has snapped a switch, they suddenly launch themselves outward again with another huge *whoosh* and head southwest across a field that is filling in with young junipers. This time they land in a stand of pitch pine, where I follow and find them congregated around a yellow kite, which is caught like some giant sunbird in the branches.

From cherry to tupelo to pine they go, blossoming suddenly as black fruit in each one. Other groups must have joined them in the pines, for when they take off again, the size of the original flock has doubled. This time they come straight at me, two thousand strong, and when they veer and bank, the uniform black of their upper sides changes to the pale grey translucence of their stubby bat like wings. Now they fly with the precision and synchronicity of shorebird flocks.

The mass uniformity of the flock does not hold, however. It breaks up into a half-dozen smaller groups, diverging, then melding momentarily again, flowing back toward the earth with a casual grace. Yet even in this divergence and breaking apart, each of the smaller flocks exhibits a cohesiveness and grace within itself and in relation to the other flocks, forming a series of swirling, related, dark galaxies, manifesting a communication and order that no human crowd of its size ever possesses.

As they flow over me, swinging back across the field, settling into the cherries again, occasionally some inner group tension or external event, such as a plane passing overhead, provokes a group to explode out of a tree, spraying hundreds of birds into the sky, sizzling and crackling like black fireworks.

This is a diminished landscape, no doubt: an abandoned field full of stunted trees, prickly underbrush, gouged and eroding soil. Its days are probably numbered, if not already surveyed, and I suspect we will soon displace even such modest multitudes of starlings into the small, contemptible bands that bully other birds at our feeders.

Yet for now, this field still possesses the breadth and rich receptiveness to host such impressive stirrings and gatherings. Whatever our anthropocentric prejudices against them, the starlings remain one of the great metaphoric birds of our remaining fields and open marshes. Therefore I must seek out such places and follow these wild presences across the landscape while I can. I have no choice but to try, in the light of the late October sun, to etch these dark visions into permanence within myself.

Leaffall

There is a rough pattern or sequence to the going of the leaves, which over the years I have learned to recognize but not expect. In most years the relatively few red maples in my neighborhood are among the first to go. I see them blazing here and there through the woods like scattered wildfires. Then the pignut hickories that stood anonymous all summer among the oaks turn honey-hued and flow clear and distinctive in their falling. Then the beech grove just below the yard, each leaf turning yellow at the outside edges first and gradually spreading and deepening toward the center to a rich, uniform, butterscotch tan. This process is repeated by the trees themselves, for a beech tends to lose its foliage from the outside in, harboring a cluster of coppery leaves close to its trunk all through the winter like a mound of coals kept covered on the hearth through the night.

The oak leaves are generally the last to turn, and hold on longer than the others once they do. If there are no autumn gales, not a single oak leaf may fall until November. The white oaks in particular will hold on to bunches of crabbed brown leaves throughout the stiffest winter winds, refusing to let go until they are pushed off, it seems, by next May's buds.

In some years, however, the sequence gets hopelessly scrambled. A few years ago, for instance, the oaks went first, while the Virginia creeper was still burning in the cedar trees. The maples and hickories were in full color, while on the town's main street the locusts and horse chestnuts, normally the first to turn and go, remained fully leaved and green. There were almost no acorns that year, and on the 15th of December my neighbor's forsythia bloomed. What do we know about seasons anyway?

Two years ago we had a very strange fall. After a while I began to think there wouldn't be any. A cold but wet October, the wettest in over a decade, kept things green throughout most of the month. By the 20th the green wall of trees at the edge of the yard was still standing, nearly intact, having barely grown perceptibly paler and scattered a mere handful of leaves across the lawn.

During the last week of that October, it turned dry, windy, and quite warm—Indian summer. Surprisingly, the mild wind brought all of the oak leaves swamping down in a rush in a matter of days. Like overripe pumpkins they collapsed in orange and brown heaps at our feet. The young maple tree in the yard, which usually seethes in reds and yellows as the bright October winds fire and tear it away leaf by leaf, fell literally overnight, so that we woke one morning to find a perfect pool of pale yellow leaves beneath its wiry branches. By Halloween all the leaves were gone, like carnations after a homecoming parade, leaving only the bare, grey superstructure and the distant rim of Berry's Hole in view.

This fall, during the long-awaited rains of October, I sat before the glass doors of the dining room and watched the oak leaves drop dark and heavy, with almost metronomic regularity, from the trees. The big ones flopped wetly down and lay scattered like dead birds across the grass, which was green for the first time since last June. By the first of November they lay evenly everywhere, like a brown blanket over the landscape. In places they were more than a foot deep, obscuring old wood trails and gathering into new ones. Eventually, swept from lawns by the wind or from the sides of roads by passing cars, they piled into drifts, as snow does. And like snow, although more slowly, the leaf drifts melted away unnoticed. In gusts of wind I sometimes mistook them for darting birds or small animals scurrying across the yard, until they blew off into the bordering woods and caught on their lobe bristles somewhere, unclenched, and sank at last to flatness, stacking themselves in ever more compressed layers to form a black, moldy pastry on the forest floor.

Now, on a November evening at dusk, I stand at the brink of Berry's Hole, the large, round glacial bowl behind the house, looking across the maze that stretches out nearly leaf-less below me, a field of bent and knotted stems, a grey sea of branched fretwork. Something about the steady, measured, passive fall of leaves over the past several weeks has drawn me out to see what has become of it all, this, the earth's true harvest.

For the past two days it has turned mild again and is now absolutely calm. I look up and see that, of the remaining leaves, curled and brown in the topmost branches, not the least bristle-tip moves against a colorless sky. They look glued to the twigs. The air is at slack tide. Nothing breathes. And then the dark form of a small bird comes winging over the house, going fast, alternately flapping its wings and holding them close to its sides. Threading its way through the laby-rinth of motionless trees at the edge, the small creature sails out over the abyss of the dark basin. My heart leaps after it as it disappears from sight halfway across, winking out like a star against the cloudless, pale-yellow sunset.

I step over the edge of the bowl and shuffle a few yards down the path that leads to the bog. The path is now a brown river of leaves, and I have to be careful not to lose my footing as they slip and slide over one another under the weight of my passing. Every year the same leaves, and none, not even the tough oaks, keep their identity more than a year, or at most two, on this relatively dry forest floor. In a few seasons they disappear, like tidal streams that peter out into the sand before they get anywhere. They also seem like a rehearsal for something, I'm not quite sure what.

At the bottom of the kettle hole at the bog's edge, it is already night, too dark to make out anything. So I turn off the path and stop by a large red maple. I stand ankle-deep in leaves, waist-deep in huckleberry twigs, while a pool of blackness slowly wells up out of the hole. I stand quietly, swaying slightly back and forth in the currents of the evening like the stand of pitch pines on the far ridge, listening intently. But all I can hear is the sound of a few remaining leaves falling, ticking, and clicking against twig and branch as they rock, tumble, and bounce to earth like so many slow-motion velvet pinballs.

Leaves are like us that way, I think, only briefly individual, commanding some attention in their dying, but in death anonymous. Like the seasons, we are preoccupied in youth with content, motion, color, and sound, and only in age begin to focus on the underlying form of things.

The carpet of oak leaves spreads out all around me, still freshly fallen, burnished and uncrumpled, making the bare oaks look strangely divested, as though caught with their pants down. On the ground their various lobes interlock in a kind of seasonal mosaic or giant jigsaw puzzle. I recognize most by name: post oak, white oak, black oak, scarlet oak, and scrub oak, along with an indeterminate number of variants and hybrids. Some leaves lay face up, smooth and dark, while others have their lighter undersides exposed.

They are all, at this point, some shade of the basic oak-family brown, but like sand grains on the beach, remarkably individual in color when looked at carefully. There are tan leaves, bronze leaves, light buck-suede leaves, leaves beginning to turn white and greenish-black with mold, leaves still fresh with yellow and pink hues, leaves with streaks of red shot through their veins—all the complexions of the human race.

Saving the Whales

On Monday morning I got a call from Kathy Shorr, who works at the Center for Coastal Studies in Provincetown, telling me that sixteen pilot whales had beached themselves on the shore just east of Sesuit Harbor in East Dennis, about a mile from my house. These were the same whales that had tried the day before to beach themselves in Truro, some twenty miles to the northeast across Cape Cod Bay, but members of the Cape Cod Marine Mammal Stranding Network had managed to push them off before they got in.

I am not a member of the Stranding Network—volunteers who are trained to help out when these strandings occur—so I wasn't expected to help, and in fact wouldn't be allowed to, but Kathy asked me if I would see what was going on and report back to her. I drove down and found the whales, mostly in one clump, with several dozen cetologists and volunteers already tending to them and several hundred onlookers behind yellow ribbon barriers the police had staked up on the beach. Two or three of the whales had already died, but the rest had been covered with sheets and blankets and were being kept wet with buckets, and later by salt-water pumps brought down by the Department of Public Works. Shallow pits had been dug around the whales so that water would seep in and help keep them wet and partially buoyant.

The whales had first been spotted about 6 A.M. by a fisherman on the jetty. It was now about 10 A.M., dead low tide, and there would be no chance of refloating them for several hours. I asked a man who seemed to be in charge if anyone from the Center was here. He said, "Not yet, but you can help us turn this next whale." So, just like that, I was pressed into service and spent the next twelve hours tending whales.

I was taken over to two whales off by themselves near the harbor jetty, a young eight-foot male and a larger fourteen-foot female who was possibly pregnant. She was very active and obviously uncomfortable, thrashing about and wedging herself deeper into the puddle. She had already vomited a couple of times and from all her thrashing was cut in several places by the rocks below the sand. The smaller one did not seem to be in very good shape either, was having trouble breathing, and remained pretty quiet.

This was the first time I had been near live stranded whales. I have a lot of ambivalence about the whole practice of "rescuing" pilot whales. No one yet has a clear idea of why these whales strand. Most appear healthy, yet even when they are successfully gotten off a beach, they more often than not try to strand somewhere else, as these had. A lot of time, effort, and expense is spent in these efforts, with no clear way of determining their value. Scientists justify the exercise as a way of learning more about the whales and how they function. Certainly it is interesting and exciting to be working with these animals close up, and there is, of course, a kind of generic satisfaction that comes in any group effort with a clear goal and limited time period in which to accomplish it. But it bothered me, not only whether or not we were actually *helping* the whales, but also that we seemed to be doing it with the same kind of complacent certainty with which we used to drive them ashore only a couple of generations ago. Some people who would give generously of their time and assets to help whales, or spotted owls, or cats, could care less about homeless people, poor children, inner-city youth, or third world hunger. Was what we were doing worthwhile, or were we just making ourselves feel good while having an undeniably interesting time?

I had had these doubts for some time, but actually working with live stranded whales changed my perspective a bit. For whatever reason they stranded, they were obviously in distress. Some had already died. One female had given birth to a stillborn fetus and then had died; I saw the bloody placenta hanging out of her genital opening. People who work with stranded whales know that they respond to care (whether or not they are "grateful"), and will regroup and go off if given sufficient opportunity, though they strand again. In the absence of hard evidence that these efforts are actually *harming* the whales, it seems to make sense to err on the side of compassion. Besides, the "bonding" that takes place with the whales on the part of the volunteers, even if one-sided, or misplaced, may induce compassion for other groups, even human ones.

I spent the next few hours with our two whales, walking out to the edge of the tide for buckets of water, carrying them several hundred feet over the flats, trying to keep wet sheets over the animals, digging out the puddles around them or shoveling sand under their heads to prop them up. During this time the whales were all measured, blood-sampled, and identified by punching small holes in their dorsal fins and attaching numbered plastic tags that are designed to rust off in a few weeks. The whales kept their eyes closed, which made it easier to work around them. At uneven intervals, they breathed through their blowholes—black, three-inch-wide ribbed holes that go deep into their head cavity, with a tight-fitting operculum, or cap, that closes between breaths—in great puffs of air and water vapor. A few times I got a faceful of whale-breath, and, surprisingly, it smelled clean and fresh, like the smell of ozone in the air after a storm.

It is hard to think of whales as fellow mammals; they are so artificial to the touch—cold, wet, slick, and rubbery. Yet once, when I was digging sand out from around the larger whale's tail, I accidentally nicked a fluke lightly with the shovel blade. Bright red blood began to flow from the cut and pool into the cloudy water around her. (The tail apparently acts as a heat exchanger, so that the blubber is thin there and the blood close to the surface.) I felt awful, and sick.

As the tide began to come in, I walked off the beach to go back to the truck for my waders. In the dunes between the beach and the harbor I came upon an unexpected and amazing sight. Several hundred iridescent blue-green tree swallows flocked among the bayberry and goldenrod, buzzing, perching, then taking off in mass bursts of flight, only to turn around and group again in a kind of constant dynamic cohesiveness, their white bellies flashing, morning light glinting off their shiny backs.

It is a cliché of nature: vibrant, fecund vitality going on indifferently side by side with helpless, pathetic mortality. But I was held, mesmerized. It is at such times I feel not that nature has no values, or that ours are superior, but that hers encompass ours and go beyond them, to realms of meaning we cannot yet begin to comprehend. All we have are our humanity and affinities, and the hope that these may be enough in this world.

As the tide began to reach the whales, a decision was made to try to move as many whales as possible off the beach and inside the harbor to a calm, deep-water situation, giving them a chance to reorient and recover before letting them go. This was done by slipping large plastic stretchers, specially made with holes for flippers, underneath the whales, then threading long aluminum poles through the stretcher sides and attaching the stretcher by chains to a front-end loader that would carry them off the beach and over to the boat ramp beside the pier, where they would be lowered and released into a holding pen.

This was not easy, especially getting the stretcher under a two-ton whale that is liable to start thrashing around when disturbed. But we managed it. Our two whales were among the first to be taken off. We followed them to the harbor, and when the large whale was lowered into the water, about six of us held onto the stretcher to contain her until she became acclimated to her new surroundings. As soon as she got into the water, however, she seemed to sense the other whales nearby on the other side of the pier and began to get excited, vocalizing with whistles and clicks, and struggling to get out of the stretcher. (Whales are extremely social animals, and the strong herding instinct is suspected to have something to do with the mass stranding behavior.) We realized there was no holding her. She surged forward and dove, swimming beneath a yellow oil slick boom that had been roped around the penning area. We thought we had lost her, but she immediately came back under the boom and joined the other whales in the pen.

The transportation of the whales off the beach continued throughout the afternoon. As this point no one knew how long the whales might have to be kept penned. Stormy Mayo, a senior research scientist at the Center, thought it might be all night. No one had ever had whales in this situation before. For the time being, people in wetsuits stayed in the water with the animals, three or four to a whale, trying to hold them upright, to keep them calm and together, and waiting for decisions. Since I had no wetsuit and wasn't trained in in-water care anyhow, I drove back to the house to get a camping stove with some water, pots, coffee, and hot chocolate.

When I got back I went over to the Center's van, which had just arrived with more suits. The Center's director, David

DeKing, asked me, "Do you want to put on a Gumby suit?" Not having the faintest idea what that was, I said, "Sure."

A "Gumby suit," it turns out, is a bright orange, one-piece, foam, dry suit—so called because it has oversized feet, attached mittens, and a hood, and wearing it one really does look and move like the famous eraser character played by Eddie Murphy on the old *Saturday Night Live* show. I staggered down into the water and joined the other people and whales. By chance I was assigned to #46, whom I recognized as the large female I had cared for on the beach, along with two young students from the Massachusetts Maritime Academy. Three people were assigned to each whale, one holding onto each flipper and a third at the tail. We now had nine whales in the pen. High water prevented the front-end loader from carrying the last three off the beach, so they had been let go in the rising tide in the hope that they would make it on their own.

The whales seemed to have calmed down and were kept in a rough circle with their heads together, occasionally vocalizing. Gumby suits are buoyant, made to swim and float in rather than to dive, and several of the lighter volunteers were having trouble keeping their footing without weights. I had no such trouble since my left leg had a leak in it, and the bottom half of my suit was soon soaked. At intervals people were asked if they wanted to be relieved, and at one point a woman waded among us feeding us pieces of fudge as we opened our mouths, like baby birds receiving worms.

It was dusk now, and Stormy Mayo decided to make an attempt to let the whales go. Two of them had temporary radio transmitters attached to their dorsal fins, and all had been fitted with those plastic glow lights they sell at fireworks displays, in order to track them out of the harbor at night. On signal, we released them slowly and stepped back. When we did so, they began to act like a bunch of drunks, bumping into one another, turning over on their stomachs and swimming upside down, etc. Novices like myself were distressed, but apparently this was expected behavior for stranded whales. One thing stranding does is screw up their balancing mechanisms (we were told it was like hanging a human being by his feet and spinning him around fast), and so an initial reorientation period was normal. Some recovered sooner than others, and it was clear that these whales were making an attempt to aid those still confused. Gradually, though, they all seemed to be swimming normally and began to circle together in a clockwise direction. A plastic net hanging from the boom kept the whales from swimming under it, and the rest of us stood in the shallow water, pushing them off if they tried to come into shore.

I say "pushing them off," but a whale of that size will do what it wants to. ("Where does a two-ton whale swim?" is the cetacean version of the 500-pound gorilla joke.) *Guiding* them off would be more accurate. It was then I began to think of them as horses, large animals that we fool ourselves, and them, into believing we can control. They moved like a herd of horses in slow motion. They even sounded like horses, with their heavy, throaty bursts of breathing. It was quite a sight, nine large black shapes with carnival lights attached to their fins, swimming inside a circle of brightly colored human erasers. It really did look like a circus, and there was a festive and anticipatory sense as Stormy gave the order to move the boom away and let them go.

A line of boats had formed across the inner harbor to keep the whales from going farther inshore, and they gunned their motors as we splashed the water in front of us to encourage the whales to head out. At first they continued to circle, not going beyond where the boom had been (Stormy surmised they seemed to have "learned their containment"), but gradually the two large males began to lead the others out. We all started cheering, but after a hundred feet or so they seemed to become disoriented and began to swim to the sides of the channel. We regrouped and kept them off, but they seemed more confused and a little panicky.

After a while it became clear they were not going to go out. It was now totally dark, and the tide was beginning to ebb again. I had been in cold water for several hours and my bladder was about to burst. I slogged up onto shore, where I had to ask for help to unzip the top of my suit; then I waddled back out of the glare of the spotlights to relieve myself. When I returned, a decision had been made to close the boom again and let the animals regroup inside the pen. I asked David DeKing what the thinking was, and he began to explain the options, then stopped and sighed, "Oh hell, we don't know what we're doing. Nobody's ever had whales in this situation. We're making it up as we go."

But those in charge agreed that the whales should be kept overnight and a release tried again at first light. Wet, cold, and tired, I decided I had had enough. Reinforcements had arrived from the Maritime Academy and elsewhere, so I climbed out, shed my soggy "dry" suit, and handed it to an unsuspecting volunteer. My pickup by this time had been commandeered as a general canteen for making coffee, soup, and sandwiches, so I left it there and called Beth to pick me up. It was now 9:30. A warm bath and a can of Dinty Moore later, I felt very pleased with myself and slept well till 6 A.M. when Kathy Shorr showed up at the door to ask if I wanted to come down to see them let go. I did.

For a while it looked as if the whales wouldn't get the idea again, but then they began to move out purposefully into the channel and toward the bay. This time we withheld our cheers and followed them apprehensively out to the end of the jetty. A crew from the Center trailed them in a Zodiac raft until both whales and boat were out of sight. We walked back with a sense of finality and accomplishment, but the most we would say was, "Keep your fingers crossed." Later that morning the Zodiac radioed in that the three that had been released from the beach the afternoon before had rejoined the pod, and that they were all swimming off into deep water.

That was Tuesday morning. Since then the pod, moving west, has stranded three more times, twice in Yarmouth and once in Barnstable. Six more have died. The volunteers and staff are strung-out and exhausted, but they feel they have to keep trying as long as there is a chance for a viable group to survive. The remaining six were pushed off a marsh at Old Wharf Lane in Yarmouthport yesterday. So far this morning there have been no further sightings.

Brave New World

Shortly before Thanksgiving I spent a couple of afternoons on the bay shore at Point of Rocks landing, gathering eelgrass in order to put the garden rather belatedly to bed. I had been lulled into putting off this annual chore by the extraordinarily mild and prolonged fall and by the lack of much eelgrass on the beach. But a northeasterly blow in mid-November piled up windrows of the long, dark blades of this underwater grass in thick tangled masses along several of the town landings, and I took two truckloads out. Hauling the grass over the sand to the landing in a garden cart, I gained a new appreciation for the value of horses on a beach.

So now at last the garden lies once more beneath a shiny, six-inch, black-green comforter of eelgrass, kelp, and deadman's-fingers, with strips of marsh grass laid in the pathways just for contrast. I notice that there are almost no plastic tampon applicators in this year's haul, a sign, perhaps, that the cleanup of Boston Harbor, thirty miles to the northwest, is beginning to show results.

I have a long history with eelgrass, going back to my first summers on the Cape in the early 1960s when I worked at a

sailing camp on Pleasant Bay. Eelgrass was then merely a nuisance, something that had to be raked out of the swimming
area each summer. Later I learned that these same beds of eelgrass in Pleasant Bay had been rare survivors of a blight that
killed off almost all of the eelgrass on the East Coast during
the 1930s. The Pleasant Bay beds played a vital role in the
survival of populations of brant, those smaller cousins of
Canada geese that grace our winter waters and depend on
eelgrass for winter forage. In fact, some ornithologists believe
that the traditional spring migratory routes of brant actually
changed during this period, shifting east in order to take
advantage of this remaining food source.

In the decades since, both brant and eelgrass have recovered to the point where a flourishing brant hunt continues at
this season, and the grass in many places is so thick it is once
again considered a nuisance by bathers and boaters, not to
mention quahoggers trying to rake through the long, tangled
strands on the flats. On the other hand, autumn and winter
storms conveniently rip the dead strands from their moorings and deposit them on our beaches, where, with stranded
marsh grass, they provide complementary mulches for our
gardens. Eelgrass, rich in trace minerals, provides excellent
winter cover and breaks down quickly in the spring. Marsh
grass, on the other hand, persists as spring mulch for weed
control. And, of course, being saltwater plants, both are
weed-free themselves. It was from such serendipitous useful-
ness that the old, fallible belief in a nature designed for man's
material benefit was fashioned.

After I loaded the second truckful of grass, I took a walk
east along the curve of the long beach past a line of waterfront condominiums to a row of a dozen or so old cottages.
Here, for many years now, the owner has been maintaining
an elaborate system of snow fencing, beach plants, and
removable stairs in an admirable but probably futile effort to
slow down the erosion of the bank in front of the structures.

Trusting I would not be undermining his endeavor significantly, I cut a few sprigs of an enormous tangle of bittersweet
growing at the base of one section of bluff. As I snipped them
with my pocket knife, I was joined by a very curious blue jay,
who screamed at me as if in reprimand.

The sight of any blue jay on a beach is moderately unusual,
but this one was odd in both appearance and behavior. It
looked immature, slightly smaller than an adult, lacked the
crest, and the head and shoulder plumage was generally grey
rather than blue. I wondered if it might be a scrub jay, wandered down from Canada, but later the description of fledged
juvenile blue jays in Bent's *North American Birds* confirmed
my first impression. It was a young blue jay, likely the off-
spring of a very late summer clutch.

The jay seemed oddly tame, flitting about me, landing on
different parts of the snow fencing and occasionally on the
sand, where it picked nervously at it. I finally stepped inside
the snow fencing and went over to where it was perched on
the fence. I found it would let me put my hand to its mouth.
Then I offered it my finger as a perch—something I have only
been successful in doing with chickadees—but it hopped onto
it without any hesitation. From time to time the bird uttered
a small, soft, *aahnt* call, nothing like the adult jay's strident
cry, as if its voice, too, were still unformed. Where did it come
from, I wondered, and where were its parents?

The jay looked at me forthrightly and vigorously explored
its perch, drumming at the fingernail on my extended forefinger as if it were a nut it would crack. Then it grasped the
finger itself in its black bill and wagged it back and forth, like
a dog worrying a rag, as if my digit were a caterpillar on a
twig that it might wrench loose and swallow. Finally it tugged
at the loose skin between my thumb and forefinger as if it
were a piece of frog membrane it might tease off. The bird
was going through all the right instinctual motions, it seemed,
but without any common sense of recognition. Perhaps, I

thought, the jay had been abandoned early by its parents, or had fallen out of the nest, before its behavioral conditioning was finished.

It did not perform any of these actions forcefully enough to hurt me. It was only when it moved fearlessly back onto my wrist and began pecking hard on my knuckle that I shook it off. But it only dropped to the ground at my feet and began pecking at nothing again in the sand. I wondered if it ate bittersweet, and as if it had read my thoughts, it pecked at a couple of weathered orange berries that had fallen onto the sand, but rejected them, disappointed.

If ever there was a bird that looked as if it needed guidance, this was one, and yet I could not help but admire its fearlessness and evident curiosity about the beach and me. It reminded me of Miranda in *The Tempest*: "O brave new world, that hath such people in't!"

And then another inland bird, a flicker this time, landed on the high beach a few yards away and began pecking on the sand as well. Was I observing the beginning of a seaward adaptation, an incipient colonization of the beach by some of our land birds? After all, they had watched us at it long enough.

The jay then startled me by flying up and landing on my bare head, where it began tugging familiarly at my front locks. Again, it was not hard enough to hurt, but since I have gotten to the point where my hair needs no external thinning, I brushed it off—whereupon it flew up the sandy slope and landed on the peak of the cottage above, staring out over the calm, silk-blue waters full of ducks, geese, and brant, surveying its wide, bright, strange world.

The Times of Their Lives

Earlier this month, before the cold wave came in and locked the ponds, a series of drenching rains fell that finally put some water back in Berry's Hole, the deep hollow behind our house. The small bog at the bottom had been dry since late last spring, but one morning about a week after the rains, I went down into the hole to find a good-sized puddle in its center. A patch of newly greened grass floated on the water surface, rimmed by a narrow collar of recent ice.

The rest of the bog was brown and grey. Ranks of maple, oak, beech, and pitch pine rose up the slopes and carded the wind through empty or needled branches, as thin, wispy veils of white cloud floated overhead.

Yet the dead grass stalks, the bare shrubs, and the branches were busy and alive with a handful of industrious chickadees, the only animals in sight on this winter morning, aside from one elusive jay. I watched these cheering little birds darting and pecking away like the embodiment of optimism, finding and extracting life where I could see none, uttering their woody tinkles of warning or association in the bright, thin sunshine.

I wondered, as I often do when watching birds, what consciousness or awareness of their own lives they possessed, if any. Obviously they were highly alert and responsive to their environment, but did they have any sense of themselves, any feeling—good or bad—about their individual lives? Can a chickadee "have a good day?"

We are a welfare-oriented society. We talk a great deal about "quality of life," yet seem unable to agree wherein it consists. This does not, however, stop us from regularly compiling lists of cities (and why, for that matter, only cities?) where we are most likely to find it. But these fiercely alive little chickadees—what did their bird-brains say to themselves as they flitted from one branch or vine or stalk to another, with no apparent hesitation or indecision, as though their entire morning's itinerary were laid out, programmed for them in advance?

We are familiar by now with the notion that other organisms possess senses we do not: bees see ultraviolet light, snakes sense heat from warm-blooded prey at a hundred feet or more, birds somehow use the earth's magnetic fields to navigate and may be able to hear low-frequency sound waves made by the ocean surf a thousand miles away. But recent research suggests that animals may possess not only different sensory perceptions of the environment, but also a different sense of existence itself, different apprehensions of the scale, pace, texture, and—well, yes—the quality of the lives they lead.

Harvard evolutionist Stephen Jay Gould, for instance, has suggested that the humpback whale's amazing ability to repeat complex thirty-minute songs without error might in part be explained by the possibility that a half-hour is a *short time* to a whale. At the other end of the mammalian scale, a shrew, possessing one of the fastest metabolisms in nature, may experience as much life, internally, or biophysiologically, in its short, brutish dart through existence as we do in our seventy-odd allotted years.

A broader and more dramatic version of this idea of different "life senses" was explored on public television's *NOVA* program a few years ago in an episode that demonstrated new experiments with time-lapse and slow-motion photography, one means by which we may actually experience some sense of the world as perceived by nonhuman beings. The footage shown suggested that there are forms, processes, and sequences in nature never apprehended on our time scale. In one scene, a time-lapse film of blow-fly maggots devouring a mouse carcass over a twenty-four-hour period revealed the maggots acting like a single organism, *hiving* in a swirling mass over the carcass in a purposeful, effective progress from eye to tail, exuding digestive juices as they went.

Such alien time scales can work the other way around as well. At one point the program suggested that a hummingbird may not only move rapidly, but lives and perceives at such a fast pace that it may not even be aware of certain slower processes, such as the movement of a human photographer. That is, the bird may not recognize some of our movements as movement at all; we may not *go by* fast enough for it to see us as other than stationary objects. In the same way we may not register the progress, say, of a walking starfish, though it may seem all too rapid to the clam it is heading toward.

One of the researchers called the world revealed by these photographic techniques a "fairy-tale land," but it is hardly that; rather, it is a reality to which we are ordinarily blind. Nonetheless, it is possible to intuit such a diversity of apprehension in nature without technological aids. Watch a swallow chasing a midge across a marsh. Think not only of the unparalleled ability and expertise necessary to follow and capture such a small, fast prey, but also of the *pace* of it: the constant, split-second reorientations and readjustments involved, the total involvement and concentration (or maybe lack of concentration) such maneuvering requires. Such an intense and unremitting pace of life might be too swift to bear if the bird experienced it at the same rate of apprehension that we do.

Think of plants extending their rootlets, micron by micron, through the soil; think of generations of bacteria living and dying in a day, of glaciers advancing at a rate of one foot per century, the plates of the earth's crust colliding at a breakneck speed of one inch per millennium.

How many more processes, physical and organic, inhabit this planet, of which we are only dimly aware, or not at all? Who needs to travel to Mars or the Crab Nebula to encounter alien life and novel viewpoints? Who needs to wait for the next Big Bang to experience a new heaven and new earth? Only study the hummingbird, which, as D. H. Lawrence wrote, "We look at...through the wrong end of the telescope of Time,/Luckily for us."

It would seem that the "otherworldly" look of wild animals is precisely that: the vision of another world. And yet, these little chickadees darting about me in the bog at the bottom of the kettle hole undeniably share the same physical world with me. Moreover, they often seem as curious about my viewpoint as I am about theirs. One fellow came over and alighted on a bud-nubbed maple branch a few feet above me, looking directly down at me with his coal-black eyes, cocking his head. I held very still. The next second, before I was aware of it, he flew behind me and landed on top of my blue wool hat. I could feel the weight and clutch of him as he perched there for several seconds, pulling at the yarn with his sharp little bill, perhaps in search of bugs. Not finding any (I trust), he flew off again. I felt my beard crack in the cold and realized I was smiling.

When I turned around the chickadee was on the ground a few yards away, pecking at a fallen oak leaf, or some fuzzy pink growth on its underside. I hated to interrupt his breakfast, but I went over and picked up the leaf to find that he had been picking at a half-round insect gall the size of my thumbnail. Later I examined it more closely and found that he, or some of his companions, had extracted every one of the dozens of insect eggs that had been deposited inside it the previous summer.

A Visigoth in the Study

This morning my study, unheated for two days, was down to twenty-five degrees. The stove roared for two hours before getting the room up to seventy. A little after ten I went in and found a small brown bat flitting about. For a second I thought it was a wren or a junco, but it flew so softly, so utterly silent of flight and voice. A flute sonata was playing on the speaker, and the creature seemed an embodiment of that pure, delicate, continuous line of melody.

My immediate impulse was to open the sliding door to the deck and let it out, as I would have a trapped bird, but two things made me hesitate. First, I suspected that the bat had worked its way into my study under the wood shingles at the onset of last week's cold snap, intending to hibernate for a spell. It had probably been awakened by the sudden warmth of the stove, stimulated, perhaps, to come out through the unfinished ceiling and fly about the room looking for non-existent insects. If I simply let it out into bitterly cold weather, could it survive the shock and rehibernate? Furthermore, it seemed in absolutely no danger of banging into things in my study and injuring itself, as a bird might. Even in panic, a bat's sonar navigation system seems to function flawlessly.

I stood for several minutes watching the tiny brown silent blur circumnavigating the room in a lilting flight, looping under the desk, around the stovepipe, through the bookcases, toward the windows and the doors, never hitting them, as trapped birds will, but banking softly as it approached, stalling, and swinging deftly away. At last it came to rest on the wall next to the stove, hanging from a pine board in a haphazard manner from one leg—a dark brownish creature not quite three inches long, including its tail, the tip of which protruded beyond the wing membrane. It was slightly lighter in color on its underside and fuzzy, so that it resembled a dustball with wings.

I reached for Godin's *Wild Mammals of New England* from a nearby shelf and turned to the section on bats. I was surprised to find that there are nine species of bats whose range includes Cape Cod. I had never keyed out a bat before, and many of the species seemed very similar in appearance, but I decided that it was either a little brown myotis or an eastern pipistrelle, both fairly common here. I leaned toward the pipistrelle, partly because of its slightly smaller size and lighter coloring below, and because Godin says that the pipistrelle "is sometimes found hanging singly in abandoned buildings," but also because I liked to say its name: pipistrelle. Today I had a pipistrelle in my study. How delightful.

The name derives, in fact, from the Italian word for bat, *pipistrello*, which is even more charming, and which in turn is a derivation of its Latin antecedent, *vespertilio*, where we see its origin in *vesper*, the word for evening, the time when bats fly. And if we take one additional etymological step backwards to its Indo-European root, *wes-pero*, we find that it springs from the same source as west, the place the sun goes down, and, somewhat unexpectedly, Visigoth, one of the barbarians who invaded the Roman empire from the *west* in the fourth century A.D.

Then, suddenly, as if bored with my meditations on its identity and name, the bat flew again, and this time landed on the back side of a cardboard box full of computer paper under my desk, clinging to the top edge with one extended rear foot. Here it stayed, seemingly at home, scratching and biting itself, more like a miniature fox or dog than the rodent it was. I thought to let it spend the morning there with me if it wished, and then to release it after the day had warmed up.

But I heard our cat scratching at the study door to be let in near the stove, as is his wont when I work; so I decided to trap the bat for its own protection. I went for a fish net, thinking the cat would not spot the bat where it was. I was gone for only a minute, but when I returned the cat was on top of my desk, looking up at the bat, which he had apparently flushed, and which had now taken refuge on the shelves above.

After two tries I trapped the bat in the net against a wall and transferred it to a large jar, turning the net inside out and leaving the portion with the bat on it dangling inside the jar, with the top placed loosely over the opening. It began emitting small clicking noises (like that of miniature silverware being tapped against miniature crystal glasses), as it disentangled itself from the net in the jar, but it continued to hold on to one of the net loops with both its rear feet, from which it has hung, upside-down, for the past half hour.

It appears to be a male, with a tiny pink penis protruding from the lower belly. He has typical long, curved, translucent bat ears and a small, blunt inconspicuous nose, with none of the odd fleshy leaflike nose growths found in more southern species. He licks himself with a long pink tongue, like a cat, and "preens" like a bird, drawing his claws and wing edges through his mouthful of tiny sharp teeth.

But most of the time he hangs quite still, with only intermittently perceptible breathing, his dark leathery wings cupped up around his sides, so that he appears to hold himself in his own hands. He looks like a dark brown pupa, and as still; or like the dried cup of some large flower, that of the tulip tree, perhaps, or butterfly weed, the raised wings as dark bracts cupping a cache of downy seeds, as yet unflown. He seems content, dormant again, as if withdrawn into a dream of death. On the floor next to the stove the cat sleeps, curled away from him, and only I am mindful of either, or myself.

Big Bone Lick

Thoreau claimed that "we need to witness our own limits transgressed, and some life pasturing freely where we never wander." It's a nice sentiment, but we don't really believe it. Most of us like our wildness contained, like a good story that we can pick up, get involved in, then put down and go mow the lawn.

Last week there was a story on the radio about the federal government shooting buffalo that had wandered off their winter feeding grounds in Yellowstone National Park onto neighboring ranch lands. The killing was done out of a fear of the remote chance that a bovine disease sometimes carried by bison might be transmitted to cattle. There is no record of this happening.

The buffalo story made me think of a trip I recently took through the winter hills of north-central Kentucky. I had just dropped my daughter off to look at a college in Ohio and was driving toward Louisville along U.S. 42, the winding two-lane highway that parallels the loops and bends of the Ohio River. It is a landscape I love to travel through this time of year, with its alternating farmland and forestland, thick mist lying like cotton candy on the ridges, swollen rivers and little waterfalls running beside them, grey birches shining in the winter light, and dark silver-edged clouds spreading out before me.

Between Florence and Carrollton I passed through a stretch of rolling horse farms, large old river houses, enormous sulphur-belching, coal-burning power plants, new industrial factories, and sprawling trailer parks. Then, near the confluence of the Kentucky and Ohio Rivers, I saw a sign for "Big Bone Lick State Park—5 Miles." Well, now, there's an irresistible place name if ever there was one. I pulled off the highway and followed the signs.

Like so many "colorful" rural names, Big Bone Lick turned out to be descriptively accurate. It contains a number of natural salt deposits, or "licks," scattered among extensive sulphur springs into which hundreds of this continent's prehistoric mammals wandered and were trapped—a kind of eastern version of the La Brea Tar Pits. In fact the state park hypes itself as "the greatest graveyard of ice-age animals ever found." It is a ransacked graveyard, however, for most of the mastodon, great ground sloth, giant bison, and other skeletons were carted off to museums and private collections elsewhere in the U.S. and Europe during the eighteenth and nineteenth centuries.

In a touching if somewhat misguided gesture to a vanished past, the Commonwealth of Kentucky has imported a small herd of bison into the park, heralding it as "The Return of the Buffalo"—though of course they are western plains bison and not the original eastern woodland race, and are kept caged in a large fenced wooded enclosure of some twenty acres.

I was the only visitor in the park that grey, drizzly, winter Sunday's afternoon. After some searching I found the buffalo herd at the rear of the enclosure, gathered in their feed yard. There were nine bison, including a suckling calf, and although, behind their fences and among piles of hay and feed troughs, it was hard not to see them as large, shaggy cattle, there was also something alien, if not exactly wild, about their presence.

It was a strange sight to see these prairie animals walking, rooting, nursing, feeding, and resting among eastern oaks and hickories. A map mounted on the fence showed that bison once inhabited forty-four of the lower forty-eight states (all except Arizona, Vermont, New Hampshire, and Maine), although the last one east of the Mississippi had been killed in 1825. Still, the migration routes of woodland bison created many of the original "traces," or paths, followed by Indians and early pioneers through the eastern hardwood forests.

I stayed and surveyed them for a half hour or so, trying to think them more wild than I knew they were (they were, after all, domesticated animals bred from domesticated stock). But I was nonetheless glad of and affected by their presence here. The great thing about bison, of course, is that they are so front-heavy, as if all the mass and muscle of their bovine bodies were squeezed forward from their legs and shanks and rump to create that formidable humped-up back, like a cresting wave, and the enormous, horned block of a head, held always low and wary, so that even at rest they look as if they are charging.

Their enclosure showed me how far we have to go for genuine restoration of our wildlife, but they were real enough, evocative enough, that I could think of them ranging hundreds of miles north and south of here, crossing swollen rivers and gorges like wildebeests, rubbing their shaggy, wet hides against the rough bark of hickory and ash trees, stumbling ox-like into the pungent, sulphur-colored muck of the springs, while others of their kind licked nearby, unaware of their slow deaths.

The bison, in their turn, paid little attention to me, except for one old bull, with a broken right horn and a light shawl of thick curly hump fur, almost golden in appearance, who shadowed me as I walked along the fence. He stood at least five and a half feet high at the hump and was nearly nine feet long. He wandered away from the rest over toward the entrance gate, where there was a separate feeding yard. There he paused, aware of me, but eventually paced across the muck of the open enclosure to a feeding trough and salt lick right at the edge of the fence.

I moved cautiously toward the fence until I was less than five feet from the huge head. I watched, fascinated, as the strange, pointed tongue of the beast—long and flexible, light grey in color, with a bright pink swath up the middle of the underside—slid out and licked the bottom of the nearly empty feed trough clean of a few last kernels of corn, then licked the red stone salt block. The tongue was remarkably agile, almost prehensile, curling and sliding around the edges and crevices of the trough, slithering in and out of the beast's mouth like a flounder, as the square jaw crunched sideways. The head nodded massively, like some inanimate counter-weight, and its bovine eye kept a steady, wary gaze on me. The old bull's head was so enormous and disparate in its parts that it seemed not to belong to a single animal, but to comprise a community of different entities: tongue, jaw, cranium, eye—loosely coordinated, but with separate awarenesses.

I made my way slowly up to the fence (which I now noticed, with some apprehension, was stapled to the *outside* of the posts) and reached carefully through the wide wire mesh in an effort to touch, to make contact with that head. But when I got within an inch or two of the broken horn, the bull, which had only moved with the slowest and most deliberate speed, suddenly flinched back three or four feet from my outstretched hand so fast that I did not see it move.

In that instantaneous, unregistered withdrawal—faster

than any cow could ever dream of moving—I felt more contact with the beast than if I had managed to actually touch it. And in its removal from me it asserted its inviolateness, its hidden and unpredictable potential, its claim to privacy and wildness, however much we had fenced it in.

Snowplow

My neighbor, Dave Williamson, is an insurance agent with Mutual of Omaha. He lives next door with his two children—Jennifer, eight, and son, J.P., six—and his wife, Jane, an intelligent and level-headed woman who works for a local children's services program and who manages with good grace and a healthy cynicism such things as "suggested" company courses in "career helping" for agents' wives.

Dave is a Cape Cod boy, born and raised in West Barnstable. After getting out of the Navy (a picture of his submarine hangs on their living room wall), he shuttled around for a few years in a variety of local jobs, including vacuum cleaner salesman and bank clerk. Eventually, on the advice of a friend, he enrolled in Mutual's agent training course and thus embarked on a career that he, like most of its practitioners, hardly envisioned for himself in the dreams of his youth.

But he took to it with an adaptability and a talent that surprised no one more than himself. A good-looking young man with a likable personality, he possesses a knowledge of the territory and a genuine interest in the concerns of his clients (many of whom have backgrounds similar to his) that pro-

pelled him in a few years from a local agent to assistant man-
ager of the entire Cape district. I like him because, during the
years we have lived next to one another, he has never once
talked insurance to me, let alone tried to sell me a policy.
Good reticences make good neighbors.

Last fall he was offered a district of his own on the North
Shore. After a period of family agonizing over leaving the
Cape, they have finally closed on a house in a suburb north
of Boston and plan to leave here in the spring.

Like most physical neighbors in this mobile and selective
society, Dave and I have seen relatively little of one another,
although we are on friendly enough terms. Children remain
the great democratizers of any neighborhood, and if ours had
not been roughly the same age, we would likely have
exchanged no more than a few polite words. We do not, as
they say, move in the same circles. Though we hail one
another from time to time, pushing lawn mowers or raking
leaves, across the broken stone wall that forms the property
boundary between us, we have never broken bread in each
others' houses, nor discussed anything more weighty or personal than the property tax rate.

Also, in modern self-sufficient fashion, our mutual neigh-
borly assistance has been pretty minimal. Because Dave
strives to be a model property owner as well as father and
husband, his house and possessions are always in much
smoother working order than mine, and therefore I tend to
ask the bulk of the favors. When I was building my foundation he let me hook up a hose to his sill cock, and several
times I have called on him to help me jump start my balky
VW bus with his Audi. When our water pump failed two days
after we moved in, we used their washing machine.

Only twice has he directly looked to us for help. The first
was last spring, when he won a sales prize of a week's vacation with Jane in Bermuda aboard the company yacht and
asked if we would baby-sit for J.P. and Jennifer. Even this he

seemed to regard more as a duty than a pleasure, explaining that it would be more business conferences than sunbathing, though Jane would be pleased to get away.

The second time was earlier this month, during the snowstorm that knocked out power in our neighborhood for thirty-six hours. The first night, about 2 A.M., with a mad wind whipping snow around the corners of our house, I heard someone outside cursing to himself and moving things about. I decided that a burglar deserved anything he could get on such a night and went back to sleep. The next day Dave came over and explained with some embarrassment that he had borrowed some of my stove logs to burn in his fireplace to keep his family from freezing.

The following day, a snow holiday, the Williamson kids were playing in our yard with my own, while their parents slept in. By late morning snowmen, snow forts, and sledding had all lost their appeal, so I proposed that we might try clearing off some of the frozen bog down in Berry's Hole for skating.

J.P. ran back to his house for shovels and skates, shouting that he would ask his father to join us. I suggested that he would probably rather not be disturbed yet and slogged down to the bog to begin clearing. About fifteen minutes later a buoyant J.P. came bouncing down the slope, trailed by his father who seemed to sink rather than walk down the path. His face was bleary-eyed and drained, and there was wordless proclamation upon it that snow-shoveling and ice-skating had not figured in his plans for the day.

Nevertheless he dug in doggedly with a large snow shovel that had a hardened steel edge and was far more efficient than my cracked plastic $3.99 Mid-Cape Center Special. The children pitched in, too, J.P. with his smaller shovel and Jennifer with an old broom.

At first Dave was silent, snapping at the children when they got in the way or got bored and started sliding around in their boots. But as we scraped more and more of the old snow off the bog, a change slowly came over him. After a while he began to shovel more with a will of his own and less as a fatherly duty to which he had resigned himself. At one point he paused and remarked, more to himself than to me, that in the eight years they had lived on the rim of Berry's Hole, this was the first time he had ever walked down to the bog.

After we cleared an area about twenty-five feet across at the northern end of the bog and a track around the entire perimeter (most of which was cleared by Dave), we all put on our skates and the kids and I began tentative forays around the ice. Dave, however, continued clearing the ice, shoveling the powdery snow to the sides, leaving exposed an ice so clear and smooth that the kids kept falling down on it. I continued to scrape, too, but on my weak ankles I was slow and awkward beside him.

Dave was wearing a pair of oversized black figure skates, size ten (he's a seven and a half), that looked brand new. His parents had bought them for him when he was a high school sophomore, sure that he would grow into them. But he wielded the shovel with the confident grace of a hockey player, dancing with it in short straight runs, flinging away the snow with sharp turns, coming to quick stops and turning to make another sweep back. Faster and faster he seemed to work, clearing the snow right up to the edge of the banks, turning it from drudgery into a form of snow-play that none of us could have managed.

When he had cleared away just about all the smooth ice, my own son Christopher arrived with his skates, and with some self-consciousness (it was only his second time on ice) slipped into them and out onto the bog. Dave put down his shovel and began to play with all three of them, teasing J.P., zipping by Jennifer and picking her up as he passed, making her squeal with delight. He let them all push him backwards, pretending to stumble and lose his balance, though he never once fell (the only one of us who didn't).

Then he would go off on his own, racing low and fast around the perimeter path he had made, his feet crossing and recrossing in that smooth unconscious rhythm of the polished skater. He would go sailing off among the flooded dead pine trunks. Then, hidden by the center island of debris, he would come round and sneak up behind the kids, shouting like a banshee. Every now and then he stopped to pick up his shovel again and clear off some more snow, as though by sheer effort and exuberance he would make the bog even bigger than it was; and in a way, he did.

As he shoveled, he talked about skating as a boy on his grandparents' cranberry bog in West Barnstable: "Sometimes sixty of us—well, thirty or forty—would come with shovels and clear off the whole bog—it was a big one, too, several acres—and then play snap-the-chain and snowplow all day long. You don't know snowplow? One kid stands in the middle and a chain of fifteen or twenty try to get by him, plowing right over him without breaking the chain. One by one they're caught and have to stay in the middle with the first one, forming a chain of their own, until only one is left on the other side. When that last guy can get through, that's really something."

We stayed down in the bog for nearly two hours, shoveling and skating, skating and shoveling. How we made that old overgrown kettle hole ring with our blades and our laughter! But at last the golden bowl of sunlight burned slowly up the east slope to a thin shining ring at the top, and we followed it reluctantly up the hillside and back into our respective houses.

That evening Christopher said to me, "I didn't know skating was such wicked fun. Me and J.P. and Jennifer are going again tomorrow." The next morning we were asked over to the Williamsons' house for a Saturday breakfast of pancakes and sausages. We stayed most of the morning, learning most of the things I now know about them. For the first time I felt as if I would really miss them as neighbors. I don't know how Dave will make out off-Cape, but I'm willing to bet that, no matter how strong a chain they form around him, he'll get through.

The Once and Future Cape

As a nature writer, I have always felt that my primary purpose was to celebrate the natural world—"celebrate" not only in the familiar sense of extolling and publicizing the delights of local environments, but also in the religious sense of performing ritual observances, and perhaps even more in the oldest etymological sense: that of simply being acquainted with a place or thing (from the Latin *celebrare*, "to frequent").

I began doing so, publicly, in 1975 in a series of weekly columns that ran in local Cape Cod newspapers. These were not so much "nature columns" as personal essays describing my own adventures with the land. Thanks to tolerant editors and sympathetic readers, I eventually wrote myself into an off-Cape audience, then off-Cape publications, then a book, and finally out of the local papers altogether.

But I continued to think of myself primarily as a celebrant of the natural world, preferring to keep whatever environmental debates or activities I was involved in out of my "real work," or at least to allude to them only indirectly. Celebration, I believed, was the most effective way to change people's thinking about nature, by conveying its possibilities in a way that could be felt, rather than argued. As one reviewer of my first book commented, "It's so good to find an *unburdened* nature writer." It was, apparently, a successful fiction.

Lately, however, I seem to be seeing myself more and more not as a celebrant of living nature, but as a eulogizer, a writer of epitaphs for moribund places and creatures, one who speaks well of the dead, or dying. Leafing through my old columns I am depressed to see how many of them celebrate things that no longer are, or have become distorted out of all recognition.

One of my earliest pieces described a tract of typical scrubby pine-oak woods across the street from where I used to live as "vintage Cape Cod woodland, impossible to improve, beyond improvement, unique only in its dwindling representativeness of a native landscape almost unrecognized because so characteristic, speaking mutely to us, asking only, like us, to fulfill itself." Today that patch of woodland has fulfilled, not itself, but some developer's ambition, has been "improved" into final unrecognizability with paved roads, houses, cars, lawns, dogs, cable TV—not, it must always be said, that these things are bad or undesirable in themselves, but spreading as they have relentlessly across a native landscape, they leave no room for any presence other than the human one.

I wrote once of a small landing at one of the herring ponds in our town, an unaltered piece of low shoreline that had for generations been used informally by fishermen and now serves as a private beach for a nearby subdivision. I praised "its extraordinary plant and animal diversity, which flourishes in unredeemed heathen health; its cup of life runneth rank and over. Here, on its shores, a man may still stand and put the electric human summer at a distance, the spirit may go out and claim such pools of peace for its own." Recently I stopped at that landing and saw that it had deteriorated sadly within the last year. Erosion at the end of the subdivision road has gotten so bad that soil runoff has covered most of the low beach vegetation and is now silting into the pond itself. With such natural degradation, license for human abuse seems to have increased. Tires, plastic buckets, and other refuse litter the shore and shallows. The landing has become, in essence, a slum, ugly and insulted, and I realized that I wanted nothing more to do with it. A few yards offshore a rusty oil drum, remnant of a homemade raft that has deteriorated, rested half-submerged in the water. Two boys, twelve or thirteen, rode their bikes down the eroded cartway and out into the pond, beating on the drum to scare frogs.

I have always regarded the extensive clam flats in our town as not only a source of chowder and tasty hors d'oeuvres, but also a kind of spiritual sanctuary, a refuge from the burgeoning human presence. "Out here," I wrote several years ago, "there is still space enough for all of us. How well used these long, low flats have been! And how remarkably unscathed they have remained, even today, despite the increasing intensity of human activity." How naive these words sound now, as each month seems to bring notices of more closings of swimming beaches and shellfish beds due to pollution, more evidence that we are poisoning with our own excrement, in insidious and often untraceable ways, the generous bounty of the ocean.

One would like to think that the ocean beach, at least that portion protected by the Cape Cod National Seashore, would be exempt from such debilitating change. Last March, in a bracing northeaster, I walked for the first time in months along the Outer Beach in Truro. I did not see another soul during the entire afternoon, yet the beach itself was slathered with an appalling amount of plastic debris—bottles, jars, fence sections, tampon applicators, whole rafts of plastic milk cartons tied together with plastic twine—an endless wrack line of enduring junk. At high tide I constantly had to watch my steps to keep from tripping over some half-buried piece of trash. I was more aware of the smothering presence of human consumption and waste than if the entire beach had been plastered with the bodies of summer sunbathers.

In fact, as I look back upon the local places I have described over the past two decades, about the only one that has remained essentially unchanged is the little cemetery next to my house, a place for burying things.

Change in itself, of course, is not bad. It is, as I have asserted many times, one of the chief attractions about a place like Cape Cod. "Change is the coin of this sandy realm," I wrote at the beginning of my second book. What is destructive is change that bears no relationship to its setting, change that is merely directionless, visionless exploitation. What scares me is the way we seem increasingly to accept such change as normal, or at least unavoidable. Last winter, in a neighboring town, a twelve-acre tract of pine woodland simply disappeared overnight, topsoil and all, creating an instant and utter wasteland of denuded, blowing sand—the site of yet another mammoth shopping center. In the aftermath there was no general outcry of rage at the arrogance, the total disengagement from the environment that such an action, however legal, implies—merely some complaints from nearby businessmen about the effect of the resultant dust storms on new autos and motel windows.

What I fear now is perhaps the most dangerous change of

all, a change in our own regard, or sensibilities, for the land we have defiled. There is a point, a very definite and noticeable point in our relationship with a place, when, in spite of ourselves, we realize that we do nor care so much anymore, when we begin to be convinced, against our very wills, that our neighborhood, our town, or the land as a whole is already lost, that what is left is not some injured yet still viable and salvageable entity, but merely a collection of remnants no longer worth saving. It is the point at which the local landscape is no longer perceived as a vital *other*, a living, breathing, healthful counterpart to a human existence, but something that has suffered irreversible brain death. It may still be kept technically alive—with sewage treatment plants, "compensatory" wetlands, shellfish reseeding programs, lime treatments for acidified ponds, herbicides for hypereutrophic ponds, beach nourishment programs, fenced-off bird sanctuaries, and designated "green areas"—but it no longer *moves*, or if it does, it is not with a will of its own. Many of our Cape Cod towns have already passed that point; the rest are fast approaching it.

It was not that I was innocent, even at the beginning, about the magnitude of the forces threatening this once-lovely peninsula. In an early column I wrote, "The capacity for human change now rivals, and on the surface surpasses, natural process itself, so that the earth seems to shift under our feet. Land itself becomes little more than abstract patterns on a developer's plans or the assessor's map, coordinates for profit or taxes."

No, I was not innocent, but I may have been proud. Perhaps I thought too much could be done by writing, believed that language really did have some magical incantatory power, so that what was captured in words good and true would somehow be protected from the forces of greed and indifference. If I ever thought so, I have been disillusioned once and for all.

❀

In the end what hits hardest is what hits closest to home. Nothing has shown me so clearly which way the winds of change are blowing over this unsheltered land as the slow but steady demise of the dirt road I live on.

When I first wrote of it, nearly twenty years ago, it was a soft, winding, country road, overarched by the bordering oaks, lined with banks rich with tapestries of lichens, mosses, and small native wildflowers. I loved it for the way it discouraged speed and encouraged observation, for its close relationship with the surrounding landscape. Birds' nests could be found in the bordering shrubs, and tree seedlings, flowers, ants and wasp nests would occasionally show up on its surface. I loved the way its soft and yielding surface recorded the passing of the seasons and the passing of local wildlife, the way it offered unexpected encounters with animals: a glimpse of a deer or a fox, the slow peregrination of a box turtle, a hawk pouncing on some unlucky vole or chipmunk, a woodcock performing its mad vernal dances and songs in a locust clearing just off the roadside.

Gradually all that has changed. For several years now the local highway department has been grading and "improving" the road, spreading a thickening layer of grey gravel and stone dust on its sandy surface. Though the original road could become an inconvenient muddy mire during wet times of the year, it generally maintained itself pretty well, following as it did the natural contours of the land, using natural drainage, and requiring grading only twice a year. With the new surfacing and increased traffic from a new subdivision at the other end, a typical pattern of "washboarding" has developed, chronic potholes and ruts that have required more and more frequent grading, more and more loads of hardening, which in turn create more and more gullies, bumps, and holes, which in turn...

One portion of the road, a wide curve around a natural depression, was straightened out a few years ago because it lay off the official town road layout and, in the modern world of economic paradoxes, the town engineer found it cheaper to move the road physically than to relocate it on the paper layout. Consequently the hollow, where scarlet tanagers used to nest in an old cherry tree, was filled in, the woodcock courting-ground was wiped out, and a constant runoff of grey slurry onto a small piece of conservation land was set in motion.

Then, two years ago, partially to correct some of the drainage problems created by the straightening, and partially at the request of the subdivision residents at the far end, one half of the road was paved—a full-fledged highway with twenty-two feet of asphalt and ten feet of scraped, denuded shoulder on either side. After it was put in, some of the residents commented, "We didn't know it would look like that."

Recently, the owner of the woods on the remaining unpaved portion of the road died. Her family had owned the land for almost two hundred years, sharing it with deer, grouse, box turtles, and whippoorwills, all species that disappear with even modest development. Now the land has been surveyed and subdivided by her heirs, the first of the lots has already been sold, and houses will soon come, and I am sure that the request to widen, pave, and straighten the rest of the road, in the name of safety and convenience, will not be far behind.

Already the traffic has increased noticeably. For a while I tried to hold the road's beleaguered rurality intact in my mind, denying the changes that appeared, making excuses for each new vehicle I saw, as if each were only some temporary or special case. But they are too many for me now. The old dirt road, though not completely altered or built up yet, is no more; what was a back road is now an artery, and the twentieth century has at last arrived on my doorstep.

Even though our end of the road still retains more semblance
of what it was like when I first moved here, I am reluctant to
walk down it these days. It is too much like cataloging what
will soon be gone. The actual trees, shrubs, rocks, birds, and
other presences at times seem already indistinct, less than
real, existing only in memory, while the as-yet-unbuilt
houses, driveways, swimming pools, and other accouterments of suburbia loom with the intensity of the inevitable.

But one night this spring, at dusk, after cleaning some fish,
I walked outside and found the evening air so soft and the
dying light so sweet that I could not resist their call. I set off
down the road in a light sprinkle and the gathering dark to
see if, perhaps, the woodcock had returned this year, though
he has been gone for three seasons now. Once again the
magic, the soft solitude of this road in early spring, engulfed
me, full of unexpected possibility as of old, cruelly mixing
knowledge and desire. In spite of myself my spirit went out
into its still leafless hollows and slopes, like pond ripples
expanding into hidden coves. I suddenly knew that it would
not be possible for any car to appear along the road that
evening. None did. Where a pair of old cartways veer off into
the woods to the east, I heard what I first thought was an
early wood thrush, but it proved to be the song of a hermit
thrush—a clear, single, initial note follow by short, rising
trills that vanished upward into ethereality. It is such a fragile, vulnerable, beautiful, and intricate song that the heart
contracts with its poignancy. I walked off the road onto one
of the cartways and followed the faint notes for several minutes, not actually hoping to see the bird itself, but simply to

follow it and let the song etch itself permanently into my memory: *Once here, on this road, in late April, a hermit thrush sang out of the darkness*—a gift that asked nothing in return but attention.

A little farther down the road, just before the paved section begins, behind an old homestead that is now part of the new subdivision, I heard a whippoorwill, tentative at first, but then, like a balky motor coughing and settling into a steady run, confident and regular, the birdsong opposite of the thrush's shy, tender aria, yet complementary. I stood listening in what was now true darkness, as the bird ranged wide with its song over the oak woods, loving and requiring its solitude as well.

Whippoorwills and hermit thrushes, songs heard on a spring night, what are they against the tides of moneyed self-interest that wash ever more insistently over this land, changing it, despite our best efforts, into something poor and undistinguished?

Yet in spite of what I know is good for me, in spite of the palpable risk in loving something so vulnerable, I know that I will continue to walk out along this road and over this land, as I know the birds will continue to sing, the fox to hunt, the shy arbutus to bloom, the frogs to congress and clamor, undampened and undefeated, until the bulldozers arrive. After that, well...

We all adapt to change, like it or not. Some of us do it by changing our manner of living, reducing expectations, others by changing location, migrating. Some simply disappear. Oaks shade out pines, starlings and English sparrows evict bluebirds, gulls push out terns, dogfish replace the overharvested cod, houses dispossess meadowlarks and screech owls. It is called succession. Some of it is natural, some of it is not. But if I have learned anything as a writer, as a chronicler of this extraordinary, doomed place, it is this: There is only so much fascination in watching something beautiful die.

A Town Ghost

As I drove through Brewster the other evening at the coming of darkness, the streets of this town seemed suddenly full of ghosts. It was a winter's night, the streets lightly covered with new-fallen snow and empty of traffic, the people of the town invisible inside their lighted houses. Yet despite that, or more probably because of the absence of human movement, the terrain, thoroughfares, and structures of this community were densely and richly inhabited with voices, faces, images, and events of the past—a past both borrowed and accumulated through the years.

I began to see this place where I lived for over twenty years with the mind's eye, with what Barry Lopez calls "memory moving across landscape." This is not hard in a town like Brewster, where so much of its history is still visible in the form of old houses, churches, gristmills, windmills, herring runs, and venerable public buildings like the Brewster Ladies Library, the First Parish Unitarian Church, and the Old Town Hall.

When I first moved here, there were still a few places in town that were said to be haunted by actual ghosts, deserted houses where horses shied and balked when they had to pass them, or where townspeople claimed to have seen a mysterious hand draw aside a faded curtain in an upstairs window, and the ghostly, sad face of a woman stare out at the street.

But the kind of ghost I mean, the ones that seem now to populate these streets and fields and woods and beaches for me, are not disturbing supernatural presences, but real figures and images from local stories, reminiscences, and personal encounters. As such they are benign or even good ghosts, and like so many Cape "washashores," I used them to borrow a sense of history and tradition, of belonging, to my adopted town. But these stories have done more than give a veneer of history to my life here. They "haunt" me, in the old French meaning of the word: they "frequent" my life, they inhabit my imagination and dwell there unbidden, like the melodies of old songs.

Some of these are "public" stories, shared as part of the community's common lore, such as most old New England towns possess. They have either been set down in books, or adhere to well-known places or historical structures in town. But there are other tales and anecdotes, not so well-known, that still survive only in oral memory, in the communal conversation of the town. Many of these are about people or places in town that now exist only in our minds, and even then often as stories heard from those who are no longer alive. Such stories can change the way we see a familiar, present landscape, giving it a depth of layering in the mind's eye.

Near the center of town, for instance, on Long Pond Road, there is a twenty-acre tract of woods that is now town property, a piece of unmarked conservation land that I suspect few people in town even know exists. For me, however, these twenty acres are indelibly and forever known as "the Elephant Field."

The property was donated to the town over two decades ago by Mariette Gervais Arthur, a lifelong resident who lived in an old house across the street from this property. One afternoon, as a member of the Conservation Commission, I was speaking with Mrs. Arthur about the terms of the gift. She told me that when she was a little girl the land, now a wooded tract, was an open field. One day a circus train came down Cape, heading to Orleans where they were to perform. Since there was no place for them to pasture the animals overnight in Orleans, they asked her father if they could use his field. He agreed, and so that evening there was a strange parade of circus animals from the Brewster train depot about a half-mile down what is now Route 137 to her uncle's field. They left the next morning, but the animals, and particularly the pachyderms, left such an impression on the field and on the local people (not to mention a powerful olfactory legacy) that it was known thereafter as "the Elephant Field."

Today I know of no one alive who remembers that spectacle, but when I pass those woods I still see, through the eyes of an old woman now long dead, a field of ghostly elephants, munching on the long grass of a vanished Brewster pasture.

Most of the stories I gleaned here were gathered in West Brewster, in the neighborhood where I built my house on Red Top Road in 1974. I think that is probably true for most of us. Local stories grow up in neighborhoods, or used to, and are rooted, or should be, in a particular landscape. For the first several years I lived there I listened to stories about former inhabitants of the area, gathering them like a sponge, from the few old natives who still lived in my neighborhood—Jenny Baker, Lillian Scott, Charlie Ellis—or from other long-time residents.

There was, for instance, the story of "Miss Newcomb and her pen pal," which I heard about from my friend John

MacKenzie. John's family lived in several old houses in town, which his father would buy in a dilapidated condition, fix up, and then sell. One of these houses was the old Newcomb homestead on A.P. Newcomb Road—a small square, Federal-style house dating from the 1700s. The previous occupants— A.P. Newcomb's spinster daughter and a woman friend —lived there for many years by themselves, and apparently never threw anything away. When John's father acquired the house in the early 1950s, they found the rooms piled shoulder high with newspapers, magazines, letters, cards, even cardboard milk-bottle tops. Some of the rooms had only a narrow open path to walk through them.

One of the packets they found contained correspondence dating from World War II, when the two middle-aged ladies volunteered to write "pen-pal" letters to Navy men. The letters from one of Miss Newcomb's correspondents, John said, became increasingly familiar, even racy. One day the sailor came to call on Miss Newcomb. Several days later she received the following letter: "I'm sorry you had gone to Boston the day I stopped to see you and that your mother and aunt had to entertain me."

Some of the stories from our neighborhood have left visible legacies. There is a tall spruce tree that grows on a small traffic island at the intersection of Stony Brook and Setucket Roads next to the old Grist Mill. During the Christmas season the tree is illuminated with lights, providing a colored spire to cheer homeward-bound commuters on dark December afternoons. The tree is now maintained by the town, but few people, I suspect, know the story behind those lights. I learned it after I had lived here a few years. Bill was an electrician neighbor of ours whose son had drowned one day several winters before while playing on the ice on the pond behind the Grist Mill. Following the accident, Bill wired that spruce tree and strung it with lights each year in remembrance of his son. Bill himself died several years ago, but that gesture lives on, and each December it brightens the spirits of those who see it, whether or not they know the human story behind it.

I missed, by only a few years, one of Brewster's most powerful storytellers. The poet Conrad Aiken spent over thirty summers on Stony Brook Road, a short distance east of my house. He died in 1973, but he had storied our neighborhood in many poems, letters and novels, and his presence there was still strong when I arrived.

Aiken's writings contain a number of satiric, and sometimes biting, portraits of his West Brewster neighbors, so I suppose it is only fitting that one of the most colorful neighborhood stories I heard not only is about "the po't" (as he was called by the locals) himself, but also produced a bit of enduring local doggerel.

Aiken was, by all accounts, a notorious womanizer. One summer during the 1940s, when he was in his fifties, he came back from England, leaving his wife abroad. He brought with him a stunning redhead named Alma, with two young children of her own in tow. The bus let them all off at the bottom of Stony Brook Road, and the four of them paraded in full view up the street with their suitcases to Aiken's house, an old saltbox known as "41 Doors." There, as the neighbor who told me this story put it, "Conrad and Alma had a high old time of it all summer," until early one morning, one of Alma's boys took Conrad's false teeth and put them in his training potty and peed on them. Conrad was furious, and the next day, as the neighbors watched, Alma and her children, carrying their own luggage, trudged back down Stony Brook to meet the next bus out of town.

Later the "Alma incident," as it came to be known, was fittingly memorialized by a local versifier, who composed the following quatrain:

Infants, looking for adventures,
Did a job on Conrad's dentures;

Said Conrad, muttering through his gums,
"With Alma, one must take what comes."

Brewster is one of the few Cape towns without an official history. With its bicentennial coming up in 2003, there may be
plans in the works to rectify that omission. Part of me would
welcome such a history, but another part would be concerned
about its effects on the town's ghosts, that is, its legacy of oral
history. The danger is that the stories in such a history
become the history, the story of a town. They become fixed,
like a photographic image, and many of the ghosts are left
out, shut out, in a way, from ever coming in.

Real history, haunted history, is never finished, never over,
never merely in the past or in a book. It keeps an open door
through which the ghosts enter, leave, and are transformed
by each succeeding generation. In so doing it becomes a part
of us, as much as the ongoing natural forces that constantly
reshape the land through tree succession, wildlife introduction, beach erosion, hurricanes, climatic changes.

Thus I am of two minds about setting down in print a
town's unofficial or unrecorded history. Of course in the very
writing of this essay, in the setting down of these few examples by way of illustration, I become complicit in the process.
Nonetheless I strongly believe that not all history should be
documented, written down, or even taped—any more than
every part of the natural landscape should be an officially
designated conservation area with signs and labels marking
every, plant, tree, animal and rock. Every town needs a certain amount of unfixed history, an outback of the mind, just
as it needs a certain amount of undesignated and unmapped
hinterland. This is especially true for its young people, who
have such a strong need to discover things on their own. After

all, isn't that what we all value most in our lives: those things about ourselves, our landscape, and our community that we have discovered, or re-discovered, on our own, rather than what we been shown or presented with in some finished or "authentic" version? History, human and natural, must have room for mystery.

I know this, believe this, and still the ghosts crowd in on me, insistent, asking me to give them voice, to rescue them from oblivion...to tell you about the woman I knew who came to Cape Cod in the 1950s, married a Brewster man, and for her honeymoon was taken to Skaket Beach in Orleans where they shot seals and cut off their noses to take into the town hall for a five-dollar bounty...or about the West Brewster man who chased his wife with a butcher's knife down Stony Brook Road into the yard of a neighbor who confronted him at the head of the driveway, his hands raised, intoning "Sanctuary! Sanctuary!"...or about the carpenter I worked for who, during the 1930s, went to Camp Monomoy, a boys' sailing camp on Cape Cod Bay in East Brewster, and who, at the age of thirteen, was "picked out" by the camp nurse who slept with him every night, "in canoes, tents, everywhere," and who told me that "after I got back to school that fall I found that I had respect for all women, that I could take them out and have a good time and not worry about seducing them—God she was a good woman!"...or about the dinner party at my neighbor's house where an elderly woman from Dennis told of a time, years ago, when she was fourteen and visiting the Lido in Paris for the first time with her mother and got onto an elevator where there was a trained boxing kangaroo who accosted her and, when the doors opened, pushed her onto the stage of the nightclub where she had to defend herself from the kangaroo with her parasol as the French audience cheered wildly, "Merveilleux! Merveilleux!"....

The most vivid ghosts I have, though, are those of my own memory, of my own living here. On that clear winter night, as I drove through the center of town feeling ghosts everywhere, the shadows of a vanished spiderwork of lacy, graceful branches arched over Main Street. I remember that summer of 1975, when Brewster's majestic elm trees, planted over a hundred years before, were all taken down in a matter of months. I chronicled their demise, measured the girth and the breadth of their fallen torsos. I still have the list somewhere. It was as if giants, or gods, had fallen. I had only lived here a few years before they died, but their central presence along our main thoroughfare had already lodged itself so strongly in my mind that I can still feel their spectral shower of leaves shading and protecting the houses beneath them.

As it is with these trees, so it is with the individuals who nourished, protected, and were part of my life there. The old burying ground I lived next to for so long, Red Top Cemetery, was initially a place of some historical interest to me, where I could read the faded and broken epitaphs as fragments of mute stories whose gaps I was free to fill in. In addition, the graveyard provided a buffer of privacy, a place to hide Easter eggs or to stage treasure hunts on my children's birthdays. But gradually the little cemetery gained a more personal meaning and human resonance for me as three or four acquaintances, one close friend, and our family's pet, all came to be buried there. Over time it became populated, haunted, in a way it had not been before.

Not only are so many of the figures and structures in the stories I have heard here gone, but so are an increasing number of the people I heard them from. More and more of those who made my life in Brewster a rich one, individuals who gave color and vitality to my neighborhood and to the town, exist only in the memories of those of us who knew them. In a few instances I may be the only one left who still remembers them clearly. From living where we live, we all of us become receptacles for the ghosts of those we shared that life with, carrying with us those who told us stories, retelling those stories, and now telling stories of them—and so we ourselves become history.

Now things have come full circle. Five years ago I left Brewster for another town, another life, and so I myself have become one of its ghosts. But I lived there in earnest for over two decades, built a house, helped to raise a family, planted gardens and trees, built stone walls, buried a cat and a father. I engaged in the life of the town: went to town meetings, voted for new schools and against new roads and streetlights, joined civic action groups, attended school concerts and my children's ball games, scratched the tidal flats for quahogs and netted alewives at the herring run, served on local boards and committees, took elementary school classes on nature walks, picked up beach litter on Earth Day, participated in library book sales, town parades, Memorial Day services, and Founders Day celebrations.

As a result I have left more than a few ghosts of my own in the town, some of which will haunt me, I suspect, as long as memory holds. But perhaps there may also be, for a while at least, some stories told about me. I hope there will be, and that at least some of them will be good ones; for I would like to think that I, too, have become a good ghost.

WELLFLEET

Barren Ground

*"Perhaps it is best approached in misery of soul, because
then it stands out in all its cryptic mystery as the raw room
that owns us, the desert without illusion."*
JOHN HAY, *The Great Beach*

One day last month, before the rains fell again, I thought to
escape the darkness of the afternoon by taking a walk on
the Outer Beach. I drove to a spot in South Wellfleet near
LeCount Hollow and headed toward Marconi Beach, about
a mile and a half south.

For some reason, this is a stretch of beach I rarely walk.
The bluffs here are largely unvegetated and notably level in
height, averaging about fifty feet. The scarp showed signs of
recent, severe erosion. Its face was a steep slope of intersecting facets composed of thin horizontal layers of very sandy,
light, varved clay, with seams of iron oxide, the color of dried
blood, running through it. The steep angle, the faceted patterns and the rusty stains gave it the aspect of an ancient sand-

stone wall, Jerusalem's Wailing Wall, perhaps. Its sand layers looked momentarily stable, but when I walked up to it and looked closely, I could see that the entire face was alive with trillions of minute sand grains flowing down its face, like multitudes of tiny mites.

About a half-mile south of LeCount, I passed beneath the site of the Marconi Station, where America first sent a wireless message to England in 1903. Since then half of the site has eroded into the sea, and the massive square concrete foundation of one of the four original transmission towers lay exposed, cracked, but still remarkably intact, on the sloping sands of the beach.

Offshore, beyond the breaking swells, several dozen black scoters bobbed in the shoals. Farther out, hundreds of yards offshore, I could see the large, white forms of gannets feeding actively, closing their streamlined bodies like umbrellas and plunging like javelins into the dark sea, sending up sprays of water as straight and narrow as themselves, as if their unfocused reflections had emerged from the water as they entered it.

As I continued south, the composition of the bluff changed from glacial drift to pure, homogeneous, wind-driven dune sand, with here and there a long-buried log protruding from it. It was beginning to grow late now, and so, at a place where the angle of the cliff face gentled out, I climbed to the top of the bluff and began to walk back along the flat and curiously barren shelf of land that borders the beach here.

Though still in Wellfleet, this part of Cape Cod is geologically in the northern part of the "Plains of Eastham" that Thoreau described as "an apparently boundless plain, without a tree or fence," when he walked across it 150 years ago. At that time most of the Cape was a treeless landscape, but this particular area has long been recognized by Cape Codders as unusually barren. For reasons that are not clear, this stretch of the Outer Cape is covered with inland dunes, thick layers of sand overlaying the glacial deposits and extending over a thousand feet in from the beach. It was traditionally referred to as "Goody Hallett's Meadow," a reference to the quasi-historic "Witch of Eastham," exiled by the good people of Eastham to this barren stretch of ground, where, it is said, she lured unwary sailors to their death or, in some cases, fates worse than death.

Whatever the cause, long after most of the Cape has reforested or at least revegetated itself, this fringe of tableland remains curiously stark in appearance. Its flat sandy surface is mottled with thousands of small stones, most undercut by the wind and perched on miniature sand pedestals, with tails of sand stretched out behind them, driven by the north winds of winter. This time of the year it is a waste of darkened humps of poverty grass, with small stands of bare bayberry and beach plum twigs, an occasional bright green bristly eyebrow of a pitch pine hugging the ground, withered grey seaside goldenrod with blown cottony seedheads, and the drooping sculptures of dusty miller that stand like melting ghosts.

As I trod this ground, a chorus from Brahms' *German Requiem* came unbidden into my head: "*Denn alles Fleisch es ist wie Gras...*":

> Behold, all flesh is as the grass, and all the goodliness of man is as the flower of grass; for lo, the grass with'reth, and the flower thereof decayeth.

I had been rehearsing the requiem with a local choral group for several weeks past, and I realized that the rhythms of this chorus, stately and insistent, were those of the sea beating endlessly against the shore.

At one point I spotted something green and black emerging out of the top of the dune. I thought at first it was a piece of upholstery, but as I got closer I saw it was an article of clothing. The fabric was quite rotten and tore easily as I tried to extricate it, but one swatch was unmistakably the right front section of an army fatigue jacket. There were still four heavily rusted metal buttons down the front, and another button held shut a flap pocket. Above the pocket, on a sewn white canvas strip, were the faint but legible block letters: "SOUZA."

This unexpected artifact brought to mind an aspect of this place's past I had temporarily forgotten, an era not as old as Goody Hallett's legend, or even the Marconi site, but one that had more of an effect on the local populace than either. During World War II, this featureless plain was part of Camp Wellfleet, an antiaircraft emplacement, and, after the war, an off-shore firing range. Souza is a common local name on the Cape, and most likely this jacket belonged to one of the dozens, perhaps hundreds of local boys who spent all or part of the war here. It was tempting to think that this was some old bivouac site, or gun emplacement, but more likely it was just one of the numerous small dumps that pocket the area.

Now, half a century later, nearly all of the visible signs of Camp Wellfleet—the watchtowers, bunkers, gun emplacements, and barbed wire fences—have vanished. Instead, a benign blue water tower looms over the beach, and, to the west, the outlines of the faux-Colonial buildings of the Cape Cod National Seashore headquarters. The few remaining corrugated metal barracks, now used for storage, are hidden from view.

It is curious that, while the nearby Marconi site and its remaining artifacts have been carefully preserved, labeled, and memorialized, there is nothing to point the casual visitor to the more recent and less benign uses to which this place was once put. One needs a certain knowledge of local history and a willingness to weave the past out of such tattered threads: a patch of stained fabric, some corroded buttons, a faded name strip. But they stand for a life lived here, or, perhaps, one put on hold, depending on how its owner viewed the war and his part in it. A child of luck and timing, I have no personal knowledge of war, but like this anonymous soldier, I, too, have stood in desert places, waiting for something to jump-start my life again.

A Night on the Slopes

The first snow of the season fell on the evening of December 13, a light coating of sea snow, the sea's breath blown and congealed upon the land. In the morning it left a cover of snow dust as thin and ephemeral as the lining in a lint filter after a heavy wash of whites. At 9 A.M. we drove out to Cahoon Hollow. The air was calm, the sea leaden and overcast. With snow squalls predicted for later in the day, I was surprised to see several fishing boats plying the waters on the horizon. The tide, now ebbing, had licked the lower beach clean of snow during the night, leaving it scalloped and bare. But at its farthest reach it had left that characteristic ice highway that forms on the upper edge of the beach in winter: a serpentine swath of frozen sea wash, which, with its light covering of snow, provided firm and sure-footed walking.

We walked a half-mile or so north, encountering small mysteries everywhere. The wrack line, for instance, was littered with frozen clumps of marsh grass, as if a hay wagon had passed along the beach, spilling its cargo as it went. The beach here is nearly ten miles from the nearest salt marsh—how did these plants arrive?

But the most extraordinary thing, as we walked between cliff and sea with snow-gathering clouds massing overhead, was the face of the glacial scarp itself, an 80-foot-high slope which, along this stretch of beach, is fairly smooth and unvegetated. Everywhere it was a tapestry of strange, delicate hieroglyphics traced into the thin and undrifted fabric of sea snow that covered its face like a bridal veil. A complex and lovely embroidery of lines ran down the whitened slope, some threadlike and continuous, others thicker and broken, like intermittent stitches. Some ran straight down the scarp, while others curved slightly to right or left, crossing the paths of the straight ones. Still others traced wide, graceful parabolic arcs or tightening spirals, like emerging tendrils of plants, in their descent to the bottom.

Whatever their shape or course, there was, at the bottom of each of these lines, a single stone, or pebble, or sometimes a frozen clump of clay—like a lure on a fishing line at the bottom of a deep pond. The mystery seemed to be not that the causes of these cliff hieroglyphics were hidden, but rather that they were so openly and consistently revealed. It amazed me, though I am not sure why. Perhaps it was because we so seldom find anything at the end of a set of tracks, or really expect to. In each case, as we traced the lines from the top of the cliff to the base, it was like following a set of animal footprints and miraculously finding the animal itself, sitting there and waiting for us to recognize it: slate, milky quartz, blue clay, iron oxide, garnet, agate, chert.

There were, in a few places, the prints of real animal visitors—the single-file tracks of a fox, or the larger separate footprints of a dog, or perhaps a coyote—instantly distinguished from the stone tracks by their paths, angling upward across the snow-covered scarp, gestures against entropy. And once, at the base of the cliff, there was an ecstatic profusion of overlapping wing prints running eight to ten feet up the slope. They were gull-sized, and many were perfect impressions, so that we could pick out the individual feathers. There were no other tracks or prints with them, no feathers or bloodstains to indicate a violent encounter. It was as if a gull, having forgotten what snow was like, had been suddenly seized with a passion to make snow angels.

But it was the stone tracks that held us. Like different species, each track had its own character, course, and pattern, determined by the size, shape, angles, and hardness of each stone. As a rule, the larger the stone at the bottom, the more intermittent the track as it bounced down the slope. The largest seemed to be about three inches across, and these often leaped down the cliff face in three or four foot jumps. The most remarkable of the tracks, though, were those left by the smallest stones, sometimes pebbles no bigger than my fingernail. Yet these, too, had all made the entire journey down the slope, leaving continuous linked lines, like the finest of gold chains, across its white breast.

Most stones came to rest within a few feet of the base of the slope, but the momentum of some of the larger ones carried them twenty feet or more out onto the beach, as if they were kids on sleds, trying to set records for distance. In fact, from the perspective of the lower beach, the entire snow-veiled cliff resembled in miniature a steep mountain slope covered with the random tracery of ski and sled tracks, the record of a night of alpine recreation.

This slow ticking of the erosion clock on the outer beach is like a light snowfall itself. It is a process that goes on at all hours and seasons, though we are usually aware of only its more violent leaps and changes following storms or moon tides. A rare set of conditions must coincide to produce a record as clear, complete, and intact as this. There must be a covering of snow sufficient to record the tracks of the stones and clods, yet not so deep or dense as to impede the descent of even the smallest pebbles. The snow must fall in calm air, and remain undrifted; and beneath the snow the unconsolidated cliff face must be frozen hard to provide a smooth and slippery surface.

All these conditions had been met for a few hours that morning, not only to record the continuity of change in this land beside the sea, but also, it seemed, to remind us how alive, how quick with active beauty, even an empty beach in winter can be.

Seeing the Light

On Wednesday—a cold, clear winter's day—I finished work at three and went for a walk with my dog along the Herring River. The tall grass by the river's edge is blanched and sere now, the path along the bank padded down by the hunters of autumn, the river itself full and black, swollen by winter rains, drowning thin birches beside the lower bank, its deep current indicated only by little whirlpools and kinetic wrinkles in its otherwise smooth skin. It seems to run like a highway, gently curving, slick black, and about the width of a newly paved road.

To my left is the rising, wooded slope of Merrick Island, like a forested version of the eroding ocean bluffs; to my right, the river, a constant waterway, like the sea, ever changing, from stretch to stretch, season to season. At this season, and this time of day, Ollie and I walk directly into the lowering sun, so that my vision of things is occluded, fragmented, blinded, and double-sunned by reflections in the water. It is like walking through a visual bramble, or maze, with my hand held in front of my eyes for protection. All is back-lit and glaring, so that I can get no hold on the landscape. The elements are all familiar: overhanging, twisted oak limbs, the worn path, the black ribbon of water, but everything is splintered and incohesive to my sight, and so to the mind.

This doesn't bother Ollie, of course, for whom sight is at best a peripheral sense. He snorts and sniffs, pees and poops, shoots his blond shaggy body along the path, lags behind to investigate a novel smell, then bounds ahead to wait, like a small lion in the path, ready to pounce.

There is little life on the river today—only a single small duck, which through my glasses I make out to be a female bufflehead: dove grey with a dark band on her back, white smudge of a cheek patch on each side of her head. She skitters and shoots down the river ahead of us for a hundred yards or so, then comes to rest again. I know this will happen again and again as we continue along the river-course, like the bird in Robert Frost's poem "The Woodpile" that similarly flies on ahead of him, refusing to undeceive himself about the poet's intentions, "like one who takes/Everything said as personal to himself."

As the river bends and heads south toward the bay, the hills of Merrick Island seem to veer away to the east, leaving a wide plain of brown wet meadows studded with patches of shrubs, willows, and chokecherries. Then, across the river, the larger bulk of Griffin Island begins to slide nearer, moving in from the west. The bufflehead, who has disturbed herself several times fleeing ahead at our approach, finally tires of the game and flies overhead back up the river, unaware that we are about to turn back ourselves and thus unintentionally putting herself in a position that will only increase her paranoia. But it is a mind that is used to being thought of as prey and so is probably comfortable with its fear.

When we do turn back, the fragmented, Cubist landscape I walked through coming out is transformed—as I knew it would be, counted on it being—into a sudden unity of form. What was broken is now whole, what was obscured is now revealed. Cacophony has become harmony. The hillsides are bathed in a golden flood of light. The grey tree trunks stand out with breathtaking clarity. Their stark and twisted forms take on a comeliness—no, more than that: an idealization of form that belongs to Greek statues. The warped, scaly trunks are redeemed. They vibrate and sing with incandescence. The whole island, bristling with its head of tough, twisted oaks, now stretches before me like some kind of revelation, like an idealized form. But of what?

Of a bare hillside with leafless oaks in late sunlight on a winter's afternoon.

In other words, like a perfection of itself, a thing come into its own. And all because of a simple change in the angle of light. And at the same time I feel as if some great clarification has taken place within myself, as if my own life, as Frost says elsewhere, had been "too much like a pathless woods," but that now I saw things clear.

Now this is the curious thing: for several minutes after turning back, I felt as if some profound illumination had taken place within my own life, as if I had come out of some brambly, dark passage and emerged into clarity, had come through and into my own. But even as I experienced this sense of revelation I knew that no such thing had happened. I had not walked out here under any personal cloud, deeply troubled or lost in any way I was aware of. Nor had any question I carried with me been answered. There *was* no question. I was simply on a walk with my dog.

But the emotion—the sense of things unexpectedly opening up, the rush of suddenly pushing through, beyond confusion, into knowing and seeing without obstruction—that was real. And what was more, it was identical to the feeling at those times when I really *had* experienced such a clarification in my life. The scene, in other words, provided me with a *pattern* for such revelation, an external template for internal emotions, a way of recognizing, giving shape to, an inner process.

I had had these experiences of outer weather triggering inner weather before—on the beach, inside watching spiders in my study, in a pine woods—but rarely had there been such a clear separation and wide gulf between the emotional experience and my actual psychological state. It seemed to suggest strongly that the physical natural world might in fact be the source of our emotional, psychological, and even spiritual lives.

The earliest civilizations interpreted natural events— floods or good hunting—as signs of divine favor or retribution. The ancient Greeks, Plato in particular, gave us the notion of natural objects as imperfect incarnations of Ideal Forms. Christianity, especially the Puritans who settled this narrow peninsula, took up this idea and saw the natural world in terms of "signs" or "types," reading God's will and intent in astronomical portents and the suggestive shapes of plants, finding the Devil's abode and his minions in wilderness and its "wild men." More recently, Romanticism and Transcendentalism conceived of nature as a storehouse of images, metaphors, and symbols reflecting and illuminating the inner life of man: Wordsworth's cloud, Blake's tyger, Shelley's west wind, Keats's nightingale, Emerson's rhodora, and Thoreau's beloved pond ("Walden, is it you?").

But my walk that afternoon seemed to suggest that the main historical thrust of understanding the "meaning" of nature might be misdirected—might in fact be 180 degrees wrong. Nature, rather than being seen as an imperfect manifestation of ideal truth, or a symbolic system of divine intent, or even a set of correspondences to psychological states or aspects of the human mind, might be more accurately regarded as the source, the very building blocks, of human identity.

A bird, say, or a duck, fleeing ahead of us, allows us to understand a type of human behavior by giving it a physical image. A moldering, abandoned woodpile, or a light-fractured landscape and its subsequent restoration to visual wholeness, provides us a moment of self-revelation—or if not actual revelation, at least the pattern for it, part of a multifarious guide we have constructed from its materials for being human in this world where we must live both within and without nature.

Whether such experiences in nature are firsthand, or are culturally learned, or whether they actually relate to our immediate state of mind, does not matter. The psychological reality of the experience is true and reflects an evolutionary heritage and connection with our natural surroundings that go far beyond biological, behavioral, and perceptual links. It suggests that we are directly dependent on nature for the raw materials of our inner lives, and for the cultures they generate. Put another way, our souls may be created both individually and as a species by what we experience through our senses. If this is so, then when a society increasingly lives without direct access to natural experience, does it run the risk of literally becoming soulless?

None of this, of course, matters in the least to Ollie, who barrels ahead, bounding through the bleached white fire of winter's grass, into spring.

Outer Beach Endgame

Few places along Cape Cod's outer shores have undergone such striking changes over the past thirty years as Eastham's Coast Guard Beach. The most dramatic of these occurred during the Great Blizzard of February 6–7, 1978. During that memorable blow, most of the beach's dune line was flattened, the National Seashore's six-hundred-car parking lot and bathhouse were completely destroyed, and all but three of the dozen or so remaining beach cottages were swept out to sea.

Over the years I repeatedly revisited Coast Guard Beach and watched and meditated on the fate of the three remaining structures, now all gone. None attracted my interest as much as a small one-room duck-hunter's shack that belonged to a gentleman by the name of Fiske Rollins, who died several years ago. Fiske was already elderly when I first met him nearly three decades ago, when we worked together restoring the Old Meetinghouse in Orleans that now houses that town's historical society.

Fiske was a small, feisty man whose pugnaciousness did not diminish with age. Over the years he and I argued, both privately and sometimes in the pages of the local newspaper, about the nature of Coast Guard Beach. I, as a young upstart columnist, had described it as a classic, retreating barrier beach, one that over time was moving steadily landward. He, who had observed the beach for many years from his cabin, insisted that it was no such thing. Fiske was a strong advocate of beach buggy rights. During the late 1970s, some of us expressed concern that use of the sand track by ORVs on the inner, marsh side of the dune line might be preventing the beach from retreating naturally, thereby narrowing the beach and making it more vulnerable to storms. Fiske argued fiercely that human impact had nothing to do with it.

The 1978 storm left his cottage standing, but inflicted heavy damage. He never repaired the structure and, as far as I know, never stayed in it again. This didn't keep him from maintaining his opinions, however, which over the years seemed to grow stronger. I, on the other hand, continued to visit the beach and occasionally to write about it, sometimes, I suspect, with a half-conscious intent to tweak his nose.

A curious sort of reversal developed. As Fiske abandoned his cottage, I began to take a more proprietary interest in it. For one thing, after the 1978 storm, frequent overwashes posed the threat of marooning anyone who, like myself, walked down to the end of the barrier spit at high tides or during storms. It pleased me to think that, if I ever became stranded, I could take refuge in Fiske's cottage. I even thought from time to time of clandestinely spending a night there, during a storm perhaps—but I never did.

Once, in the winter of 1983, I visited the cottage and found that the remaining dunes that had protected it were now virtually gone. Only a single, rounded, unvegetated rise of sand still hid it from the beach, and even this showed signs of having been recently breached by a storm surge. One of the cottage windows had been completely knocked in. Sand had drifted in and was everywhere, beginning to drown the interior. Sand sifts slowly, like age, over everything, softening, obscuring, and finally obliterating each distinct thing into a semblance of itself and the next thing. In this sense, sand is the ultimate progressive poet, whispering, *This chair is like this table, is like this bed, is like this sink—and each thing is, more and more, like all the others, until finally they are all— like me.*

The mattress bunk bed was still there, and the elaborate grated Victorian Franklin stove, flued into a crude asbestos chimney. But someone had thrown red paint over it all since I was last here, so that it looked like the scene of some cheap Hollywood murder. The roof remained intact, however, and I thought that a night here was still possible, though unlikely.

The last time I saw the cottage was six years later, in 1989, again on a winter's day. It was now completely open to the beach by way of a large dune blowout. The old iron stove had been thrown outside, its hearth plate broken off. The windows were gone and a portion of the roof was missing. Sand had swamped the floor to a depth of one or two feet, as if dry forerunners of the ocean swamping to come. The sink was full of sand, as was a small icebox that lay upended on the floor. Sand was piled up in the corners, so that I could walk up on it and peer into the small sleeping loft. The mattress, however, remained on the bed, and I thought that one could still spend a moderately comfortable night here providing it did not rain—though I knew now I never would.

There was thick irony here; it seemed to coat the place as the sand did. The fate of Fiske Rollins' cottage was itself proving the retreating nature of Coast Guard Beach; though I knew, of course, as in any position held so long and argued for so often, that he would not change his mind because of mere events. I had an ungenerous, but irresistible image of the old man himself, living out here, denying the very processes around him as they gradually buried him, like some solitary figure in a Samuel Beckett play, in the clean aeolian detritus of the ocean's implacable force.

But the ocean was also foreclosing on my long procrastinated plan to spend a night out here, filling up and obliterating the shapes that might have contained it. Seen from outside, the cottage had a touching air to it, vulnerable and exposed, continuing to offer an increasingly meaningless, implausible promise. A song sparrow perched on the roof peak and sang tentatively as I left.

Today the cottage and its stubborn owner are both gone, and I find I miss them both. We love what gives us refuge, or the promise of refuge, but we also love a good and unbending adversary, when nothing vital is at stake. The cottage, I realized, had been my "storm home," a place I had designated to seek safety in, should I have ever needed it. Now I will never stay there. Now there is only a flat sandy washover and a strange, empty space in the air where it stood for so many decades, like the socket of a decayed tooth that has been removed. Now it, and its owner, exist only in my mind and the memories of others who knew them—shelters from oblivion as precarious and ephemeral as any beach structure. The ocean itself finally stepped in and ruled our long-standing argument in my favor, but today it seems a hollow victory.

On the Killing Fields

Recently I witnessed two rituals of death. On the surface, they couldn't have been more different, but I sensed in them an unexpected subterranean plane of intersection, somewhere in that mysterious area of the nature of human love.

The first was a ritual of killing. I did not witness it firsthand, but viewed it in a documentary filmed on the icy killing fields off the northeast coast of Newfoundland: the annual harp seal hunt. The Newfoundland seal hunt is the largest wild mammal harvest left on the planet, and to many outsiders, it is a barbaric, repulsive practice that, if it was ever justified, is long past its time. Each year a few hundred Newfoundland sealers go out in longliners and other modified fishing boats to the Front, a massive river of pack ice, studded with icebergs from freshwater glaciers, that is carried down from Greenland by the Labrador Current. In late winter and early spring, a major portion of the estimated five- to six-million North Atlantic harp seals climb up onto the leading edge of the Front and whelp their pups. The "whitecoat hunt," during which thousands of two- to four-week-old seal pups in pure white coats were bludgeoned to death in front of their mothers, has been outlawed since 1983. But a legal adult harp seal harvest continues, with an annual quota that has been raised in recent years to over 300,000, a number that few have contested represents a sustainable harvest under current population dynamics.

The continuing controversy over the hunt, both within and without Canada, is not about ecology but about ethics. Many countries, including our own, have banned the importation of any seal products—but with an inconsistency of policy toward other wild animal commodities that seems to have less to do with ecological reality than with politics born of the vagaries of human sensibilities regarding nonhuman life. (Deer-hide slippers, for instance, can be legally sold in the U.S., but seal-hide gloves cannot.)

Newfoundlanders have been hunting seals commercially for over 150 years and regard the harvest as a traditional and fiscally necessary activity in a chronically depressed economy. They do not deny its bloody nature, but assert that it is no more objectionable than what goes on in any slaughterhouse. At the other end of the sensibility spectrum are the animal rights groups, which in the past have argued and protested for a complete ban of the hunt on humanitarian grounds. More recently, though, they have adopted seemingly less radical agendas couched in legalistic arguments.

In 1997, for example, the International Fund for Animal Welfare (IFAW)—whose North American Headquarters are, coincidentally, located on Cape Cod less than a forty-minute drive from where I live—filmed the previous spring's Newfoundland seal hunt and produced a twelve-minute documentary entitled *Canada's Seal Hunt: It's Not Just Cruel, It's Criminal.* The documentary, filmed by a crew that pretended to be working for a hunting magazine, claims to have found "at least 144 violations of Canada's Marine Mammal Regulations and other rules meant to control abuses in the sealing industry." These violations include the use of illegal

and unnecessarily cruel methods of killing the seals, the taking of protected baby harp seals, and the abandoning of seal
carcasses on the ice.

Though the film purports to be making a legal case for
increased government regulation and enforcement of existing
laws, its none-too-subtle subtext remains an emotional
appeal to ban the hunt outright. It contains numerous
graphic scenes of seals being killed and butchered, as well as
clips of the sealers themselves, some of them talking in a quite
candid, offhand manner about their work, which they clearly
felt would be seen and heard by a sympathetic audience.

Some viewers might question the journalistic ethics of the
deception IFAW used to gain the confidence of the Newfoundland sealers, while others, IFAW among them, would
no doubt argue that the end justified the means. One might
also criticize the documentary for its heavy-handed and often
misleading elements: a loud and menacing musical under-
score, the apparent overdubbing of separate sound tracks
onto video footage, and, of course, the editorial leeway
involved in reducing eight days of filming to twelve minutes
of finished footage and labeling it "uncensored."

All that granted, the film is painful to watch. Even though
in recent years I have become friends with many Newfoundlanders and have defended the principle of the hunt
against knee-jerk protests that too often seem based in the
self-deceptive conviction that cruelty in nature is a purely
human invention, something in my gut wrenched to watch
these child-sized mammals with large, soulful eyes being shot,
gaffed, and hammered to death, their graceful forms writhing
in agony on the boat decks, their all-too-familiar-looking
blood spreading out onto the ice pans like giant rose blossoms. The laughter and banter of the sealers on the sound
track may indeed have been overdubbed in places, but it was
nonetheless repugnant and frightening amid such scenes of
willful slaughter, suggesting that certain enterprises may

demand the coarsening or dulling, or at least the distancing, of sympathetic impulses if the participants are to retain a sense of their own humanity.

The emotional impact of these sounds and images not only overwhelmed my own intellectual impulses to defend or at least justify the killing of the seals, it also ironically undermined IFAW's own arguments about the illegality of the hunt. For instance, while watching a gaffed harp seal being repeatedly whacked on the head as it hung over the side of a skiff, I was informed that the sealer was using an unlawful device, in this case a simple pole, instead of the legally approved tool, described as "a steel implement with a wide hammer head with a spike protruding from it." Would anyone but a government technocrat have looked upon the scene with less discomfort if the "legal tool" had been substituted?

Even if one acknowledges the intrinsic cruelty of the hunt and the inevitable violations of the sealing regulations (though not necessarily as widespread and chronic as IFAW claims), it is still possible to argue that Newfoundlanders have some cultural or residual political right, or at least an economic imperative, to engage in the seal harvest. Newfoundland has a long history of subsistence hunting and gathering; it was an independent nation before joining Canada only fifty years ago; and it has the highest unemployment rate of any province in the country.

The argument for cultural tradition, however, is undercut by the fact that little of the seal meat or fur today is used by the sealers or their families. In fact, most of the meat is sold for food for other fur animals on farms in neighboring Nova Scotia. The hunt's principal legal market is for seal pelts that are processed in Norway and sold primarily as luxury fashion items; many (if not most) of the skinned seal carcasses are simply tossed overboard. Even more damning, hundreds of male seals are killed only for their penises, which are sold on the black market as aphrodisiacs in Asian countries.

Since the collapse of Newfoundland's traditional cod fishery in the 1980s, the annual seal hunt has undeniably helped, however minimally, to alleviate the plight of cash-strapped fishermen. Ultimately, though, whatever cultural or economic defenses one is tempted to mount out of sympathy for a hard-pressed people, and whatever charges of duplicity or distortion one might wish to throw at the IFAW filmmakers themselves, all these evaporate like water spots on a hot griddle before the searing images of butchery on the ice.

Shortly after viewing the tape of the seal hunt, I attended a memorial service here on Cape Cod for a good friend's son, a troubled man in his mid-forties who had fought alcoholism for years and seemed to have won the war, but whose damaged body gave out prematurely. I had never met the man, but I knew how much the loss meant to his mother, and I attended because of my connection with her.

Memorial services, usually held after the funeral and a period of initial mourning, are increasingly common in our society, more and more often replacing the traditional church services and offering nonchurch members a place and an opportunity to give grief a public and ritualized form. I have been to a number of them in the past several years, including my own father's, and I think they make sense for the way our society and its structures of family and friendship have changed. In most cases, these circles of family and friends no longer reside in a single parish for whom the local minister represents a common voice. Increasingly, family, friends, and acquaintances of the deceased are far-flung and unknown to one another, and the delayed memorial service gives this attenuated web of people a momentary nexus of unity.

The intent of most of these services seems to be to "celebrate" the life of the deceased, primarily by evoking his or her presence through tributes, recollections, anecdotes, music, artifacts, and other means. They celebrate not only the life but also the individuality of the loved one in a way that the more traditional religious services often did not. But the intent of the older rituals was different from ours today: it was, in part, to strengthen the unity and identity of an already cohesive community.

During my friend's son's service there was open grief as well as laughter, acknowledgment of anger as well as love, and always some testament to each speaker's personal knowledge and connection with the dead man, whether it was through a story, the choice of a poem or a piece of music, or simply the imitation of a gesture or phrase of the deceased that had particular meaning for the speaker. Whatever cathartic or healing value the event may have had for family and close friends, I found it unexpectedly moving, even though my emotional ties to my friend's son were more vicarious. Others seemed similarly moved. After the service, at the reception in the parish hall, another friend of mine said, "You know, I never met David, but I met him today."

Only later did certain strands of these two powerful but extremely different rituals of death began to interweave unbidden and disturbingly in my mind. Thinking about the film of the seal hunt, I wondered what the effect would have been if the same narrative rhetoric and cinematic techniques had been applied to a documentary on commercial fishing instead. After all, fish bleed, too, and their blood is red. Fish, when hooked or gaffed, squirm in what can only be pain. Fish, when killed, are often put to less-than-necessary or dignified uses, such as pet food and fertilizer. I have often been bemused by the protest against the dolphin by-catch in tuna nets, whereby many organizational and political tears have been shed for the dolphins but scarcely any for the tuna. Few voices are raised against the "cruelty" and "outrageous abuses" of fishing on humanitarian grounds, though the potential environmental effects of commercial overfishing are far greater than those of killing dolphins or seals.

The rhetoric of animal rights is laden with loaded words that mask unacknowledged assumptions. One of these is that when we say "animal rights" we mean primarily, on an emotional level at least, "mammal rights," or at most, "warm-blooded vertebrate rights." Much of our humane sensibility, when applied to wildlife, is not only speciesist, but what might be called "evolutionist." That is, the closer a species is to our own—in appearance or behavior, or on the evolutionary scale—the easier it is to evoke support for its protection.

This is not a new idea, but in recent decades it has been refined and elaborated somewhat by cultural anthropologists, evolutionary theorists, and other scientists. One concept that has gained widespread credence is the observation that the presence of what are called "neotenic" characteristics—that is, features characteristic of human infants and children, such as large eyes, large round heads, round plump bodies, short squat noses—evokes the strongest protective responses in human beings. In a 1979 article in *Natural History*, Stephen Jay Gould illustrated this cultural bias quite effectively by demonstrating how the "evolution of Mickey Mouse"—the change in the cartoon character's body shape and facial features from his early, more lifelike, more ratlike appearance to his later, universally popular incarnation—followed these principles of neoteny to increased commercial success. (As with much of human behavior, the scientific documentation of neotenic response has been anticipated by poets, at least since 1941 when Ogden Nash observed that "The trouble with a kitten is that/Eventually it becomes a cat.")

Seals, and particularly seal pups, are ideal illustrations of this principle, which offers an obvious explanation for the success of the movement to ban the seal pup hunt in the early 1980s. Squid are also taken in Newfoundland waters, and by means no less "barbaric" than those used on seals, but somehow they, and numerous other ocean species, are less under the umbrella of "animal welfare" than seals, whales, and other marine mammals.

Like most principles of human behavior, however, evolutionary bias is often affected and even overridden by other cultural biases or perceived benefits and threats. Thus we find a much greater amount of personal and public support for the preservation of old-growth (read "large, Western") forests than for, say, the Michigan jack pine; for timber wolves than for the Nantucket beach vole; and for monarch butterflies than for the Southern California Delhi Sands fly— just to give a few examples. Such discrepancies have little or nothing to do with a species' perceived evolutionary position, its resemblance to human infants, its endangered status, or even its environmental importance, and everything to do with myth, cultural standards of natural beauty, economic priorities, and human comfort.

Attempts to establish absolute moral or logical bases for our innate inequality of preference in the area of animal rights have led some very intelligent people into very absurd positions. David Quammen's 1984 essay "Animal Rights and Beyond" discusses the Australian philosopher Peter Singer, author of *Animal Liberation* (1976), generally regarded as one of the seminal texts of the modern animal rights movement. Singer asserts that an organism's perceived capacity to suffer is what entitles it to moral protection. This line of reasoning eventually leads Singer to the extraordinary statement that the evolutionary cutoff line for animal rights falls "somewhere between a shrimp and an oyster"—a conclusion to which Quammen wryly replies, "Moral philosophy, no one denies, is an imperfect science."

It is, of course, no science at all, and such exercises in logical absolutism in the arena of highly charged emotional and ethical issues are inherently futile. This is not to belittle the thorny questions surrounding animal rights, which are undeniably significant and complex, with real consequences to living creatures. Still, in our attempts to resolve them, wouldn't we do better, rather than positing some absolute standard of humane behavior toward and human sympathy with all life, to admit at the outset that our sympathies are unequal and that our behavior is based on irrational grounds; in other words, that our compassion and protective urges (or lack of them) toward other forms of life stem not from logic or science or dogma but from emotions, cultural norms, and personal experience?

After all, aren't these the sources of our feelings of love, sympathy, loss, and grief in our own lives? Aren't these what I responded to at the memorial service for my friend's son? I was genuinely moved, not (in Donne's abstract sense) for the loss of a clod from the continent of humanity, not even out of sympathy for the suffering of a friend for whom I had deep feelings, but by witnessing expressions and manifestations of loss and sorrow from those for whom this person had a private and individual significance, those who had suffered some kind of particular loss by his death.

Human love, though we may wish it otherwise, is largely particular and partial by nature. This may be obvious, but its implications, I think, are often overlooked. Few of us—only saints, perhaps—can truly love all humanity, let alone all of living creation. But then, most of us would not wish to be married to saints, for then we would be just one of a loved multitude. We crave to be loved as individuals, for our own personal selves, and we give our deepest love the same way. The most profound human relationships—marriage and parenthood—are based on an exclusivity which, at least in the first institution, is regarded as a supreme virtue, and in the second is defended with an unmatched ferocity. Rather than criticize this exclusivity of preference as prejudiced, narrow-minded, or inhumane, we praise its practitioners, sanction it by law, and hold it up as a standard to be emulated. We call it faithfulness, commitment, family values.

Yet at the same time, in political and ecological arenas we are increasingly urged, expected—nay, charged—to embrace the broadest, most inclusive forms of sympathy and kinship: to think of the entire earth as our mother, of all humanity as her children, of all creatures as brethren.

What are we to make of these seemingly contradictory standards and desires? What do we do with the disparity between personal or cultural preferences, which we praise in the private sphere, and growing social and political pressures to extend protective rights to those outside the traditional circles of human sympathy?

Aldo Leopold gave us a useful and hopeful context in which to view this problem with *A Sand County Almanac* (1949), a landmark work of environmental ethics, published in 1949, the year after his death. In his chapter "The Land Ethic" Leopold argued for what he called "the evolution of a land ethic." He traced through history a gradual cultural broadening and extension of human compassion and protection for larger and larger groups, and for increasingly *unlike* groups. This he saw as a slow but steady and salutary expansion of the concept of community. He even gave us a concise yardstick for measuring our cultural progress, gauging it by "the increase in the number of things which we are unwilling to kill." In this context, the controversy over the Newfoundland seal hunt, though bitter and complex, can be seen as part of an inevitable dialectic leading to a more compassionate treatment of all life.

This notion of an innate, inevitable, historical growth of human sympathy—something like an ecological version of Marx's historical dialectic—has been a popular one and a central source of encouragement for environmentalists in the last half of the twentieth century. It has been taken up and given various other expressions, including E. O. Wilson's idea of "biophilia," which he defines as the innate human attraction to and preference for living things; Stephen Jay Gould's belief in the ability of cultural forces to override genetic imperatives; and Lewis Thomas's concept of the human body, and even the individual cell, as a symbiotic community of formerly independent organisms, including bacteria and mitochondria.

But Leopold's proposition, though hopeful and attractive, is also vulnerable. For one thing, its inevitability has hardly been confirmed in the half century since the publication of *A Sand County Almanac*. As with Christianity, the idea may have been paid more lip service than life service. Still, it gives one heart, and in a less threatened world we might have the luxury to wait and see if it is true, might continue to look with hope and patience and detached curiosity for evidence of the historical evolution of compassion and the gradual extension of moral rights to other groups of living creatures.

But even Leopold did not foresee the acceleration of environmental degradation that has taken place since his death in 1948. The issue of human compassion toward other species has been redefined by an urgency that goes beyond ethics, that may have become more pragmatic than philosophic. Our situation now may not allow for a "natural" or unforced development of biological sympathy, even if such a trait is inherent in our species. In the face of impending global ecological disaster, we may *have* to learn to love faster than we would like, more broadly than our natures are fashioned for. The song says "You Can't Hurry Love," but on the killing fields of earth, the only choice left may be, in W. H. Auden's words, to "love one another, or die."

Mind in the Sky

Robert Frost once watched a tiny insect crawl across a manuscript page and, recognizing intelligence in a thing so small, uttered what must be a universal sentiment for any teacher who has ever read student papers: "No one can know how glad I am to find/On any sheet the least display of mind."

Last week I had two encounters with another class of animals that caused me to reflect upon the nature of intelligence, or rather, the relationship of human intelligence to the rest of nature. Both occurred on Eastham's Coast Guard Beach, the first on a day of heavy wind and rain. The sky was still clouded over but breaking through from time to time like silver-grey blossoms to the southeast, throwing a kind of daytime equivalent of moonlight over the white, tumbling surf.

To the west, the vast, sere, stubbly plain of the marsh, like a flooded, burnt-over prairie, stretched under the wind and lowering skies. The wind had turned slightly northeast, and a cold mizzle raked against me as I headed back to the inner side. As I did, a flock of dunlins blinked on and off as they banked and swerved over the marsh in that synchronized flying they have mastered so well.

I am in an old and long line of beach walkers who have been perennially fascinated and mystified by the coordinated flight of shorebirds, by how, without an apparent leader, they seem to fly with one mind. In recent decades the science of animal behavior has made many fascinating discoveries about how animals respond to their environment and to one another, but I have yet to read a satisfactory explanation of this particular behavior.

That day, however, it was not the dunlins' group behavior, but rather their individual actions that caught my interest. As I walked up the inner side of the beach, the dunlin flock landed ahead of me at the edge of the marsh. They were feeding together, and their psychic and spatial relationship had changed. They were more spread out, for one thing, and much less coordinated in their movements. They still seemed aware of one another, but much more loosely so. They were behaving, I realized, more like individuals in a group, like the crowd watching the parade rather than the lockstep marchers themselves.

I wondered, in what sense are such flocks of birds (or other groupings of animals) aware of one another? When we see shorebirds flying, or alewives schooling, or bees swarming, we tend to say that they move "like a single organism." But watching these shorebirds feeding, it seemed to me that perhaps the metaphor, like so many natural metaphors, has been used backwards. Perhaps it is not so much that a flock of shorebirds moves like one organism, or an ant colony seems to possess a single mind, as it is that we, as individual organisms, are like these flocks or schools or colonies. Could it be that we are, literally, not of one mind, but many?

Dr. Marvin Minsky, an artificial intelligence researcher at MIT, has hypothesized that what we think of as the conscious "self" is really an amalgamation of separate units, what he calls a "society of minds." Our individual personalities, it may be, are really like colonies of social insects or birds, or, more exactly, perhaps, jellyfish—physically connected, but not really a single organism. If he is right, then perhaps we are only truly connected, or of one mind, when we are awake, like a flock of dunlins flying, blinking to and from attention. When we sleep it is as though the different minds of our Mind alight to feed, breaking step and acting independently, though remaining loosely connected. This might account for much of what seems to happen in dreams and sleep.

The second encounter occurred a few days later, in almost the same place. This time it was a bright, sparkling morning. Large gulls stood pecking desultorily at the loose marsh edges, eyeing me, it seemed, as an oddity. As I walked along the inner side of the beach, I saw a large flock of brant pass overhead. There were more than two hundred birds, heading north, uttering their frog-like calls. In flight, brant hold no strict formation; rather, they maintain the shifting cohesiveness of rapidly moving clouds.

The brant flew to the northern end of the marsh and hovered there, circling one spot for thirty seconds or more, then moved on around the rim of the marsh several hundred yards to another spot and hovered there, still not landing, then moved on again. I watched them repeat this pattern for ten minutes or more before I finally lost sight of them far to the south.

I realized that, while watching them, I was thinking of the brant's behavior as "indecisive." But how do brant "decide" anything? How, for instance, do they decide, as a flock, whether or where to land? They have no discernible leader, as their larger, Canada goose cousins do. They do not even seem to have that strict and uniform shifting motion of shorebirds in flight that suggests a kind of psychological uniformity. They seem, even in flight, more like communities of individuals with common tendencies. But who "decides," and how? Or does it even make sense to ask such a question of brant?

It occurred to me that their behavior did not so much *express* indecisiveness, as *suggest* it. They provided, as it were, a natural external correlative action to an inner human process. Perhaps it is from watching such sights in nature that we originally derived the abstract notions of "decisiveness" and "indecisiveness." Our minds may have developed certain ideas about how we think through the observation of certain natural phenomena such as this. We may have taken notions from nature to suit our psychological needs, much as we take lumber from trees.

Of course, it remains a question whether we actually make conscious decisions in life any more than brant do, or simply yield to certain currents of events—shifts in wind or passions—and try to make up reasons afterwards. But whether we do make conscious decisions or not, we certainly like to think we do. And brant hovering over a marsh help us believe we live in a world where decisions, if not made, are at least contemplated.

Trickle-down Ecology

I have never been more than a casual, careless, and inconstant feeder of birds, and my present practice has not veered from that pattern. My current feeder is a single, cracked plastic tube that I hang each winter from the clotheslines strung across the small deck outside my study. I think the feeder came with the house when we bought it a few years ago, or else I found it at the swap shop at the town dump. Surely I have never bought one new. The plastic sleeves have come off two of the four perches, leaving bare-metal, threaded, three-sixteenths-inch bolts for the birds to risk freezing their claws on during cold snaps, but I have not bothered to recover them.

As for food, I keep it simple and cheap. Once or twice a winter I go to the Bird Watchers' General Store and, for $7.95, load a twenty-five-pound sack of Black Oil Sunflower Seed, none other, into my van. Sunflower seeds are the meat and potatoes of bird food, guaranteed to attract a steady, if not terribly diverse, array of birds. I get mostly chickadees, maybe 80–85 percent, maybe higher, along with a regular titmouse or two, a nuthatch, an occasional goldfinch, a rare cardinal, and, inevitably, a pair of bullying house finches with whom I am ashamed to share a name.

But it is the chickadees that are my constant companions. Having grown accustomed to me, they almost do not wait until I have gone back inside and closed the glass slider before they swoop down to their newly filled feeder. In a sudden flutter of wings and tail feathers they arrive. Each chickadee perches for only a second or two, reaching in one of the feeder openings and plucking out a seed, before it flits up to a branch on the nearby pitch pine, and, holding the seed between its claws, cracks it open with its tiny bill.

Occasionally, if all the perches are taken, or perhaps simply to check things out, a chickadee will alight first on one of the clotheslines, and perhaps give a call or two, before dropping down to the feeder. In any case, the whole process of arrival and retrieval takes no more than three to five seconds, though each bird may spend up to a minute or more opening and consuming a single seed.

In their landings and takeoffs, the chickadees exhibit a remarkable, instinctive understanding of avian air traffic control. On some days I have counted nine or ten of these pert, handsome, energetic little birds landing and taking off in rapid succession, barely waiting for the runway to clear. One particularly cold day I had let the feeder supply drop down to where only the bottom hole gave access to the seed. The chickadees seemed quite hungry, and there was a frenzy of half a dozen birds, a blur of wings and tiny bodies, swarming around a single perch. Yet though they seemed to be desperate to get to the seed, there were no collisions or even obvious confrontations. Never did the one at the feeder seem pushed or intimidated from its post, though some took longer than others. There seemed no true queue or order of landing; one might flutter around the feeder for a few seconds, then retreat to a dead pine twig above, letting another take its place. It was that same seemingly random, shifting, yet unchaotic harmony that prevails among migrating alewives when crowding and jockeying for position in a stream, an urgency combined with what seems an innate or natural courtesy, a common concern not to ruffle feathers, or scales.

Lately, I have begun to fancy that the chickadees also think of me somewhat proprietarily, and even considerately. In the past weeks I have noticed that, instead of swooping down as soon as I fill the feeder, they seem to wait until I am ensconced in my chair, notebook out, pen in hand, before they begin feeding.

What I marvel most at, however, are their legs—those tiny, delicate, toothpick bones, scaly feet, and tendril-like curved toes, no longer than an eyelash—with which they secure their foothold in the world. (I remember reading a story once, perhaps the most terrible story in the world, in which a boy or a man, I forget which, deliberately breaks the legs on crows or some such bird and then sets them loose to fly off into a world where they can no longer find rest.) When, occasionally, I coax one of them onto my finger to take a seed from my unfolded palm, that light but determined pressure encircling my knuckle reminds me of my infant children when they first grasped my fingers—so tactilely different, but so similarly trusting and vulnerable. The birds' legs make me think of Ollie's legs, which, though much larger, also seem impossibly slender and fragile, thin kite sticks bowed with ligament and muscle (I can feel the whole anatomical structure of them between my fingers), which I could snap with one hand, and with which he so recklessly explores his doggy world. They are like Kathy's thin wrists that I can encircle between my thumb and forefinger, wrists that anchor the hands and fingers with which she writes her poems and rubs my neck. On such slight and breakable foundations does life stake its wholeness and happiness.

I was pleased to find—though I did not intend or expect it—that the placement of the feeder in the center of the plastic-coated clothesline seems to have protected it from the usual marauding by squirrels. But then, perhaps the squirrels have learned that they don't need to reach the feeder. The chickadees and other birds are not particularly careful eaters, and after a day of active feeding, the deck boards below are littered with a substantial pile of seeds, many of them still unopened. Sometimes one of the chickadees will dart down to the deck to retrieve one of the fallen seeds, but more often they attract a second tier of feeders, groundfeeders like mourning doves, towhees, juncos, and the occasional Carolina wren, but primarily grey squirrels, who sit up wrapped in their tails, feeding their motor-mouths with tiny, incredibly dexterous paws, until Ollie, somehow sensing them in the middle of his usual morning-long nap, leaps off the bed and flings himself futilely against the glass doors. Lately the squirrels have not even bothered to leave, unless I let him out for a minute to run around the yard and bark out his aggression, while the squirrels wait, contemptuously it seems, in the branches above him.

But the rain of food, I have gradually learned, does not stop at this level. Some of the seeds and seed hulls fall, or are pushed by the squirrels and groundfeeding birds, or are simply blown by the wind through the cracks between the boards and fall into the open storage area beneath my study. A few times this winter, having occasion to go down there, I've noticed that this seedfall has collected on a spare piece of linoleum I had thrown over some second-hand cabinets.

I did not think any further about this until one day recently, when I went down to the space below the study to cut some boards on the table saw I keep there. This part of the storage area is open at both ends but protected from precipitation by the rooms above, and has a south wall composed of glass slider panels that were scavenged from the dump by the house's previous owners. I was going through the stacks of boards stored on suspended racks when I noticed a cat curled into a small bundle on top of a pile of outdoor chair cushions stacked up against the glass panels for the winter. It was such a small, fuzzy, grey ball that I thought it was a kitten, curled up, its sides heaving rhythmically in the sunlight coming through the glass.

I had no idea how long it had been there, or where it came from. It wore no collar. I thought at first it might be sick or injured, so oblivious did it seem to my noise and commotion. But when I went over to it, it stretched out, revealing itself to be a full-grown adult, meowing softly and reaching out its paws toward my outstretched fingers with that complete self-possession and instant proprietariness that cats have. It looked healthy enough, and when it rolled on its back to allow me to scratch its stomach, I saw it was a female. I felt her belly; she seemed well-fed. She was just taking her ease on a bed in a sunroom she had happened upon that no doubt seemed made just for her.

Well, at least I hadn't seen her around the bird feeder. Live and let live, I thought—though that is hardly what cats think. Still, as long as I didn't catch her stalking the local wildlife, I would be willing to harbor one transient for the rest of the winter.

I began to select the boards to cut and the cat went back to her nap in the sun. I pulled back the piece of AstroTurf covering the table saw, and there, in the space created by the guide bar, was one of those small, round, downy mouse nests that seem to be made out of laundry lint. Our house has been free of mice for a few years now, ever since I cleared the initial infestation by setting out cardboard wedges of D-Con. Again, in a spirit of magnanimous coexistence, I thought that as long as these rodents remained outside of the house walls, I could tolerate their using inactive spaces. Still, it was my table saw, so I carefully lifted the weightless nest to set it down on the dirt floor. As I did, I noticed that beside it, on the metal table, was a small clutch of—unopened sunflower seeds.

Suddenly, in one of those instant floods of connections, I knew what these creatures already knew: that there are no random presences or isolated actions, that all of them—birds, squirrels, mice, and cat—were part of a connected chain of relationships that were a direct result of my desire to see feathered forms moving outside my study windows. The sunflower seeds, initially placed by me in the cylindrical feeder, had been dislodged onto the deck by the feeding birds, then had sifted downward again through the action of other birds, squirrels, and the wind, collecting onto a piece of linoleum covering, where they provided a reliable and steady grain supply for an invisible family of mice, which in all likelihood were contributing to the plumpness of this feral feline, now lying in such comfort on my summer chair cushions.

So, it seems, we create new worlds with as much casualness, ignorance, and lack of intention as we destroy existing ones. If I were still interested in speculating on Divine Intention, I might be tempted to wonder if our own world, which we take so seriously, might not also be merely an unintended consequence of some trifling amusement of the gods.

So the chickadees continue to come with their quick flutterings to the column of sunflower seeds and, as a result, several layers down, beneath the chair where I sit writing this, a lazy, well-fed cat licks her paws and lies dozing in the glass-filtered sunlight. Why, she probably doesn't even have to risk getting wet to get a meal! It is as if I were delivering mice pizza to her—not that she would ever think of thanking me. Room service, after all, is only her due as a cat.

And there was the end of it—or so I thought. But nothing ever ends; we just stop looking. Sometime in April, when the weather began to warm up, the cat left for parts unknown, and shortly thereafter I stopped refilling the bird feeder until next winter. Then one day in mid-May I went down to the open storage area to unpack the bicycles for the season. I looked at the linoleum-covered cabinet and decided it was time to clear off the winter's accumulation of seeds. It was then I noticed several small sprouts—infant sunflower plants with a pair of tiny oval leaves at the end of each hair-thin stem—that had germinated in the moist bed of seeds and were struggling up toward the slats of light falling through the deck boards overhead. I paused for a moment, then went to get several small potting cups, carefully rooted the seedlings in them, and carried them up to the deck to set out in the sun.

Fishing on the Common

There I was, less than a week after Boston's record April Fool's Day snowstorm, sitting on a bench on the Common in seventy-degree sun, the last small piles of snow hiding in corners of shade like yesterday's discarded newspapers. I had been walking for hours and had just sat down to rest on one of the benches facing Tremont Street. It was noon hour and Boston's business workforce was swimming by in coatless shirts and floral skirts on its way to or from lunch. I began to read the paper, when a large barrel-chested man in striped overalls, carrying a covered yellow wastebasket in one hand and a large black umbrella over his head in the other, sidled up to the bench and lowered himself with a sigh next to me, an iron armrest between us.

He was a tall, powerfully built man, with grizzled stubble on his face; but though his general demeanor was that of a street-person, his appearance was nonetheless neat, that of someone concerned with his overall impression to the world, and his eyes, which almost seemed to bounce on the shiny rounded tops of his cheeks, were not glazed or vacant, but alert and darting, predatory. He walked with a slow, rhythmic lurch, like a wide-hulled ship in heavy seas, and when he came to rest on the bench, he carefully closed his umbrella, as if a large vessel had made port and was slowly furling its sails. He had a regal, if eccentric, bearing, and might have been a character out of Melville. Yet I was exhausted myself, physically and mentally, and was not looking forward to having conversation with anyone right then, however intriguing.

I need not have worried. He took no more notice of me than if I had been an unlit lamppost. Rather, he arranged himself on his half of the bench, laying his wastebasket on one side of him and his umbrella on the other, as if they had been his orb and scepter, and placing a red cassette player (turned off now) on his lap, as if he were about to hold court.

Almost immediately he began to address young women as they passed by in a deep, rich voice and an unaggressive, even kindly manner: "How are you today, m'dear?" or "And how are you m'dear?" and other slight variations. So full-hearted and fresh was each salutation that he almost invariably received some response, sometimes cursory, but more often with a certain noncommittal friendliness returned—"Fine," or "Fine, thanks"—usually accompanied by a smile.

I could see why they found him attractive and unthreatening: the rich, heartfelt voice, the kindly and avuncular demeanor, and the vast bulk that seemed to anchor him to his seat with cables of inertia. His overtures seemed to go out to all females under forty, regardless of race or pulchritude (an equal opportunity womanizer, he), whether they were alone or in pairs, on foot or on bicycle.

Watching him interact with them, I gradually realized that there were far fewer women going by at lunch time than men (perhaps an average of one young female every fifteen to twenty seconds). All males, however, he ignored as completely as he did me. "Ignored" is probably too active a verb. I think he actually did not *see* any of us, any more than a fisherman on a stream bank pays attention to the dragonflies hovering over the water. I think one of us would have had to come up and speak directly to him before his concentration would have been broken.

For he was fishing. As soon as he evoked the slightest reply, or even a glance, he patted the empty seat next to him and said, "Why don't you take a break, m'dear?", "Sit down, darlin'," or similar invitations, all spoken in that same unhurried, unaggressive, affectionate, and seductive voice. Then, it seemed, the women suddenly became aware of the potent masculinity that lurked beneath his amusing and casual eccentricity, his deceptive sedentariness. His line was older than he was, his lure thrown out with a graceful, effortless motion, landing lightly on the ears of those he addressed, seamlessly followed by his trolling manner.

But these were not fish, they were women, urban women. Without exception they turned him down, sometimes (if in pairs) with mutual giggling, sometimes with a few lines of banter, occasionally with cold silence. The most common responses were, "Oh, I've got to get back to work," or, "I'm late now" (though it was still early in the lunch hour), to which he would usually reply, with undiminished friendliness, "Well, come back later, m'dear!" and without missing a beat would turn to cast his greeting to the next one coming by.

He gave no visible response to being turned down; but once, after a series of cursory "I'm late" replies, I heard him utter what sounded like a sarcastic assent under his breath. Some of the women seemed to recognize him, as if he were a familiar fixture and this a daily ritual, which perhaps it was. I began to wonder whether he ever got a positive response, as you sometimes wonder whether anyone ever purchases some of the more ludicrously extravagant items in junk mail catalogues, though you think that *someone* must order them if they keep on advertising them.

But then, perhaps he didn't really *expect* to land any of

these women, though his whole manner suggested that he did: his careful concentration, the darting predatory eyes, the careful voice as smooth and practiced as any actor's in a long run, so that his invitations never sounded mechanical or rote, but always fresh and personal and offered especially, particularly, to *you*, m'dear.

After twenty minutes or so, I stood up, turned to him, and said, "Good luck." He blinked, noticing me for the first time, and replied, "Thank you," in a surprisingly ordinary and unaffected voice. I crossed the street and turned as I reached the other side to see him casually reach over the armrest for the *Globe* I had left on the bench for him.

Not biting today.

Dancing with Lights

Earlier this spring I spent several days and nights in one of the dune shacks deep in the Provincelands. At night I would go outside and look to the southeast where, because of the shack's position in a hollow between the two outermost ridges of dunes, the only earthly lights visible were the stately, measured, double flashes of Highland Light some three miles to the southeast and, on clear nights, the fainter flash of Nauset Light some fifteen miles farther down the coast. Looking at them, I thought, Two giant steps backwards for Cape Cod lighthouses, two small but significant steps forward for our human connections with this landscape.

Now, in October of 1996, both lights are temporarily extinguished during a massive relocation project to save these historic structures from the relentless encroachment of the ocean on the Cape's Atlantic shore. For a while it seemed as if the sea might win the race, especially for Nauset Light, which has only thirty feet of glacial bluff left between it and oblivion. But this summer, years of technical planning, political maneuvering, public fundraising campaigns, complex cooperative efforts between private preservation groups and the Cape Cod National Seashore, and the engineering wizardry of the International Chimney Corporation (the firm moving both lights) finally coalesced to preserve these buildings for posterity—or at least for the next several generations. Groundbreaking for the moving of Highland Light, the larger and older of the two, began last May, and Nauset Light is expected to reach its new site by mid-November.

It has been strange not to see their comforting beacons on the dark eastern edge of the Cape. But Highland Light has already reached its new location 600 feet back from the edge; if all goes well, in a few weeks its 1,000-watt beams will be revolving again, and a small but historic hiatus in the rhythms of our night sky will be over.

Lighthouses, like certain other human features of the Cape Cod landscape—ancient cemeteries, old houses, harbors, church steeples, cranberry bogs—have existed for so long that they seem a part of the natural landscape around them. But lighthouses also assert their presence in mysteriously compelling ways, so that we who live on this constantly assaulted land often forge strong, if unconscious, connections with these illuminated towers. The connections are probably stronger now for those of us who live on land than for those at sea, since for navigational purposes lighthouses have for many years now been supplanted by on-board electronic positioning systems. Nonetheless, standing as they do in harm's way, on the brink of destruction, they emanate a human meaning that few other manmade structures do.

Like most of us who live on Cape Cod, I have taken the presence of these lighthouses for granted—like the sunrise, or the annual return of songbirds. It has only been during the past few years, when the fate of these two particular structures seemed literally to hang in the balance, that they began to compel my active attention in ways they had not done before.

One moist evening last April, as I was driving past Pilgrim

Lake on my way home from Provincetown, I became unusually aware of the great flashes of Highland Light, moving in quick spaced arcs from east to west. Its glow was intensified, magnified, by the haze in the air. It rose and set, rose and set, over and over, like a fugitive sun, like the wink of God, like the shadow of the bright hand of God over the face of the night. It seemed to say its own name—*Highland-Light, Highland-Light*—again and again to a night sky that remained unconvinced.

I found myself strangely drawn to it, perhaps because I knew that its light would shortly be extinguished, never again to shine from the spot where it had shone for nearly 150 years. Like a moth drawn to a light bulb, I turned off Route 6 at the North Truro exit and followed the dark road eastward as the flashes expanded and began to tower over me. I drove past the Truro Historical Society's museum, past the clubhouse of the Highland Links golf course that flanks the lighthouse, past the ranks of beige golf carts lined up beside it, and finally out to the empty parking lot. I was surprised that I could actually do this. I expected someone to stop me or check me. And then there I was, standing beside, beneath this incredible radiance.

The white brick tower looked somehow larger at night, its dimensions expanded by the beams emanating from it. Two gauzy cones of light, directly opposite each other, wheeled in stately symmetry from the glassed tower, washing the hills, the trees, the fairways, the museum, the clubhouse, and other structures at its perimeter. It was clear, from this perspective, that the beams were not horizontal, but slanted downward, pointing, it seemed, directly at the horizon. The lights moved in magisterial isolation and dignity, and I was filled with a sense of its magnanimity and beneficence as it dispensed its largesse of light across land and sea alike.

I had been out to this light at night many times before, but strangely I could not remember any of them. It was as if I were seeing it for the first time—or rather, as if the presence of the light tonight had washed away all previous memories of it, as a new and glowing love for someone can wash away all memory of former meetings.

The light tower and the attached keeper's house were fenced off, but I could walk around them out onto the bluff. I made my way haltingly, the way one goes through a dark room during a thunderstorm by flashes of lightning. My way was lit by the slow-motion strobe effect of the rotating beams —image and after-image—so that I advanced and stepped to the beat of the light and its intervening shadow, in what I gauged as five-second cycles. It was a curious, formal movement, as if I were engaged in some stately gavotte—step, step, halt—step, step, halt.

As I walked west along the dark edge of the cliff, a series of small, raw ravines gave evidence of recent storm erosion. There still remained the broken arcs of an old walled road that once circled in front of the light. From the edge of the bluff the light lit up the surf below, illuminating furious over-lapping skirts of dead-white lace pounding against the dark base of the cliffs. It also lit up the clouds overhead, revealing with each sweep sudden panoramas of silvered cumulus formations far offshore.

To the west, out of the dark wetlands behind the Clay Pounds, came the anomalous singing of spring peepers against the ocean roar. Their singing had a chanting pulse to it, as if these amphibious tintinnabulations were also linked to the whorls of light sweeping over them, as if the great revolving spokes of light were, in fact, a kind of cosmic metronome, setting a beat that drew all of us—waves, frogs, and me—into a hypnotic dance of light.

Back in the parking lot a yellow flag on the seventh green whipped wildly in a south-southeast wind. I stood again, beside my car, watching the long shafts of light turning slowly, smoothly, powerfully, like a giant incandescent helicopter that had landed and might lift off at any second. It struck me as a beautiful thing, a source of wonder, something otherworldly and monstrously delicate, balanced for a moment on the edge of our world. It embodied the human spirit and the human condition in so many contrasting ways; but most of all, that night, I liked thinking that it must retreat to survive, and that, knowing this, we have chosen to have it retreat.

Long Nook

I would give up much to live near Long Nook, perhaps the loveliest of Cape Cod's ocean " hollows"—those dozen or so long, glacial valleys that are truncated perpendicularly by the Cape's Atlantic cliffs from Head of the Meadow Beach in North Truro to LeCount Hollow in South Wellfleet.

Long Nook, in Truro, is one of the highest and steepest of these Outer Beach accesses. Set between high, camel-hump dunes and ridges, it drops vertically some sixty feet down an unvegetated sand slope to the beach. There are no permanent steps or trails. Instead, diagonal foot paths are made and remade throughout the year as the cliff face itself is constantly reshaped by storms.

One April morning, following an easterly blow, Kathy and I arrived at the small parking lot about 9:30. The air was sunny, calm, and full of water vapor and negative ions. We felt exhilarated even before we saw the water, which gradually appears between the steep dunes that form the sides of the hollow, as if filling up a giant, V-shaped vase. The ocean was astonishingly glorious, as it often is the day following a storm. What struck us first, even before we could see the surf, were the colors on the sea's surface: contrasting shades of opalescent greens and pale moire blues, spread out over the ocean's vast surface like some fabulous Oriental bazaar of silks blowing in the wind. The blues were of the exact hue and texture of the vapor-softened sky, so that sky and sea blended indistinguishably at the horizon, and from there to the shore islands of blue sky floated on a jade sea.

Then the surf came into view—a magnificent milky aftermath of yesterday's blow—a quarter mile of range after range of foamy, plunging breakers, blanketing the shore with a continuous, thick roar. It was nearly low tide when we arrived, so that the beach was a good seventy-five yards wide, leaving a hard, wide, nearly flat sandy highway for walking. We headed south and at first were aware only of the surf to our left. Its impending power translated irresistibly into images of assault: enormous breakers pounding ashore like waves of amphibious panzers. The lines of swells were perfectly parallel to the shore and, crashing far out in the calm air, they exploded like watery mortar bursts, sending up unchoreographed geysers of spray into the air. By the time the fury of the breakers reached the beach, it had been rendered into viscous sheets and probing fingers of foam, like scouting parties, advancing up the shallow incline twenty, thirty, fifty feet, then retreating with whatever information they had gleaned. It was D-Day on the beach that morning, but a benign invasion, a symphonic version of destruction, heavenly warfare.

At first it seemed as if the night's high-ranging tide had swept the beach clean in a shallow arc that flattened near the water. Ours were the first footprints of the morning. But a closer look revealed signatures of the deep reach and throw of yesterday's storm. It had scattered dozens of sea clam shells along the beach, including two that were still whole and alive, which we retrieved to sweeten the previous evening's oyster stew. It had torn several brightly colored lobster buoys from their moorings and tossed them along the very uppermost part of the beach, where they lay like a string of party lights. During the night the retreating tide had left a series of light, overlapping arcs of rockweed down the face of the beach.

Close to the surf we came upon the washed-up, wave-battered form of a common murre, a penguin-like pelagic bird, the size of a small duck, that breeds on the rocky cliffs of Newfoundland and Labrador. Its black-and-white plumage was matted; its breast had been cleanly plucked by something in the ocean; but its light-blue eyes were still intact, and the serrated lining of its long, thin, black beak was as yellow as a child's raincoat.

At this point Kathy decided to turn back, but I continued on to the first break in the cliff, about a mile from the parking lot. From there I gained the crest and headed back along the cliff edge trail. The landscape of the crest still had a solidly wintry look: bare, blue-grey jungles of scrub oak branches with a few dangling dead brown leaves; wind-burned tufts of creeping pitch pine; bleached-straw waves of beach grass on the dune slopes, and grey rags of poverty grass lining the trail.

But as I rose and dipped across its contours, this drained and unresurgent terrain gradually dropped hints of a new season already in progress. Here, small, efflorescent, pale-green rosettes of dusty miller protruded from the sand; there, sharp-pointed, bright-green spears of new beach grass blades rose out of last year's dead collars, like souls half-emerged from their bodies. Mats of bearberry were beginning to undergo their mysterious transformation from dark wine to dark green hues; and from the thickets of bare oak branches came the clear, territorial song of the song sparrow.

At such moments we are filled with a profound satisfaction with life and with our body's own motion, with the health of the landscape before us and its existence independent of us—the wide expanse of sea and sun-washed beach. Whatever personal avulsions we carry with us, whatever nagging mental knowledge of the earth's worsening wounds that dogs our heels, stay gratefully at the edge of consciousness, and for the stretch of a morning we can assent to Thoreau's triumphant assertion that "Surely joy is the condition of life"—in all its amoral, physical totality. The flattened blossom of grey feathers I find on the path, sign of a violent and fatal encounter, are as beautiful and healthy as the forced narcissi on the breakfast table. The strong scent of skunk that filters through my nostrils is as sweet and bracing as the flowers' perfume, or the smell of a newborn's head. How lucky are we who live in proximity to such a landscape, that has such easy powers to lift us out of our narrow lives, to strip away our self-made blinders, and so seduce us into being who we really are!

As I descended the final hill to the parking lot where Kathy waited in the car, I could see a mile to the north the two white radar domes of the North Truro Air Force Station. Once a primary target for the defunct Soviet Union's ICBMs, they now appeared like twin full moons rising against the sun-bathed camel's hump of Long Nook's dunes—as if even these reminders of the human urge to self-destruction had been transformed by the spell of the morning into a benign version of themselves—a double blessing on the earth and of all its inhabitants.

War Story

For over half a century the slowly deteriorating hulk of the SS *James Longstreet* was a conspicuous and legendary seamark to those of us who lived in towns at the elbow of Cape Cod. Weighing 7,200 tons and measuring 423 feet at the waterline, she was one of over 2,700 so-called Liberty Ships, or cargo vessels, built during World War II to carry supplies to Allied troops. At the end of the conflict, she was towed out into Cape Cod Bay and deliberately grounded in some twenty feet of water to serve as a target ship for practice bombing runs by fighter planes based at Otis Air Force Base near the Cape Cod Canal.

For several decades the bombing, by both day and night, attracted crowds of local residents and summer visitors to the beaches of Brewster, Orleans, Eastham, and Wellfleet, providing a form of free entertainment and vicarious excitement. When the bombing runs were ended for safety reasons in the early 1970s, the ship, which had unintentionally become an artificial reef for marine life, became a popular fishing spot for both humans and seabirds. Though officially off limits, the rusting hull of the ship also became a perennial

lure for the young. During severe winters, when Cape Cod
Bay froze over, adventurous adolescents would sometimes try
to walk on the salt ice out to the ship (which appeared much
closer to land than it actually was). They usually became
marooned on the shifting ice and had to be rescued, and rep-
rimanded, by the Coast Guard. In later years, as its metal
plates fell away, the blackening hulk of the ship became more
and more skeletal and ethereal in appearance, and a strange
lush jungle of vegetation began to bloom and flow over its
remaining superstructure, decks and sides, both seeded and
nurtured by the guano of several generations of gulls and
cormorants.

Finally, last winter, the remaining vestiges of its crumbling
hull disappeared forever beneath the waves, and for thousands of local residents the blue horizon of the bay was
strangely empty the following summer. For many of us it was
a loss, not only of a piece of history, but also a visible
reminder of personal memories. Local newspapers recorded
many anecdotes regarding the ship. Other stories were told
more surreptitiously.

One day, while I was waiting for a haircut, the man in the
barber's chair told about the time he was tied up to the ship
at dusk, fishing for blues, when all of a sudden the planes
began to fly over and commenced bombing. For some reason
he had a chainsaw with him on his boat and he began to rev
it up, hoping the pilots would hear him. "I also smiled a lot,
thinking maybe they'd see my teeth in the glare. I've had people ask me, Did you ever see the bombing? Hah!"

"Hah!" said the barber. "You know that forest of plants
that was growing up there on the decks? Well, some of them
was funny plants. About twenty years ago a friend of mine in
town—he's quite a character—called me up one evening and
said I had to take him out to the target ship in my boat. This
was in October. I asked him why and he said, 'Never mind, I
just need to get out there.' So I took him out and it was some

cold out there with a stiff breeze out of the northwest. He climbs up the side of the hull using the bomb holes, just like they did in that movie—what was it?—*Waterworld*. Yeah, a regular Kevin Costner. I used to be able to do that when I was in the service, but already I'd put on too much weight.

"Well, he goes up and I'm sitting there freezing my ass off and after a while he comes down and hands me some plants. They had points on them, y'know—funny plants—and I said, 'Oh, no you don't—I'm not getting caught with these on *my* boat!' And he says, 'C'mon man, there's supposed to be a frost tonight!'

"Can you believe that? On U.S. Government property, in an officially restricted zone, no less! He's quite a character!"

Last week another local landmark vanished, though few remarked its passing. It was a rickety, derelict wooden building that had stood for decades overlooking Duck Creek at the foot of Bank Street. It had served for decades as Wellfleet's first police and fire station. When the new station was built outside of town, the highway department continued to store some materials and maintenance vehicles on its ground floor, but in recent years it had developed a noticeable list to leeward and was considered unsafe, as well as being, in the eyes of many, an eyesore in the middle of a tourist-oriented waterfront. So decrepit and wobbly had the building become that, last fall, when an article to appropriate funds for its demolition was presented at a town meeting, one voter stood up and said, "Why waste good money tearing it down when the next northeaster will do it for us at no charge, and probably float it out on the next moon tide to boot!"

But it was a mild winter, and this spring the town finally did the job itself. The whole process took only a few hours,

and it was not a particularly newsworthy event. I doubt that many of the summer people returning this year will even notice its absence. It had no architectural or historic significance and little aesthetic appeal, except perhaps to those of us who like to have old boats, buildings, and other wrecks of our past lying about, if only to remind us that we weren't always so prosperous and might not be again.

No stories about the building were circulated when it came down, and its fading from communal memory will probably be rapid. Few people, I suspect, marked its passing with any sense of personal connection, but I was one of them, for it played a role in a pivotal incident during my life here, an incident that also connected me with the much more celebrated SS *Longstreet*.

During the winter of 1963–64 I was taking a walk on the outer shore of Great Island in Wellfleet when I spotted a cylindrical metal object on the upper beach. I did not know what it was, but suspected it might be an unexploded dummy shell from last summer's bombing of the target ship. Though they were called "dummy shells," these cartridges still contained flare explosives to indicate to the pilot the accuracy of his drop, especially at night. Nonetheless, with that youthful conviction of invulnerability, I picked up the bomb and walked back into town with it to the old police station, located on the second floor of the wooden building on Duck Creek that even then had a shaky appearance to it. I carried it up the outside flight of wooden stairs and into the office, where a middle-aged woman sat at a desk.

"Is the police chief in?" I asked.

"No," she replied, "he's out to lunch."

"Well," I said, "I found this out on Great Island and

thought I shouldn't leave it there. I'll just put it here for him to look at later." And with that I set the capsule on her desk and departed, leaving her pushed back up against the wall and staring, as if I had just deposited a live snake in front of her.

A year after this incident the United States Congress passed the Gulf of Tonkin Resolution, legislation that Presidents Johnson and Nixon would both use over the next decade to justify the pursuit of the ruinous war in Southeast Asia. Like most of my generation, I was only faintly aware of the event at the time, and had no inkling of what it would signify for us and for the nation at large. It seems to me now that if I had looked a little harder at the ship then, I might have guessed.

The summer after I carried the unexploded bomb into the Wellfleet police station I received a notice from my local draft board to report to my hometown in West Virginia for an induction physical. My main concern was that I was planning to be married in September and needed to earn as much money as possible that summer. Having to take time off to travel back to West Virginia would be both inconvenient and expensive. I am not sure I was even aware that a marital deferment was in effect at that time, but even if I was, I'm quite sure I had no intent of trying to manipulate or evade the system. If anyone in those innocent, ignorant days was considering draft resistance or escape to Canada, I was certainly not one of them.

So the following week I went down to the draft board office in Hyannis to file a request for a transfer of venue for my physical to the Cape. Again, I encountered a local secretary working for a government agency. She was friendly and helpful, but when I explained that my request involved plans to be married the following month, she gave me a curious look and said, "Well, I'll be happy to file your request. Of course, you realize, that sometimes papers get misplaced around here."

"Pardon?"

She gave me another look, this time as if I were the dumbest boy in her class. "I *mean*," she replied, leaning on that second word, "there may be some delay in getting your request processed."

"Oh, I see," I said, though I didn't, not really, not at that moment, but somehow I had the sense that it would be in my best interest to pretend that I did and gracefully retreat.

As it turned out, my transfer request was delayed for five weeks, by which time I was safely in the arms of a marital deferment. I would like to think that the woman who was that secretary is still around and that she might happen to read these words. It would please me enormously to offer her my gratitude, also delayed, for her unsolicited and unauthorized act of compassion.

I am sure that there are many who are happy that the summer bombings have ceased, who would, in fact, prefer to have all traces of military presence removed from these long-peaceful shores. But just as it might be salutary to have a few old boat hulks and dilapidated buildings lying about town, it may also be useful to keep the visible artifacts and appurtenances of warfare in front of us—decommissioned ships, abandoned military bases, defunct artillery ranges, obsolete gun emplacements, and so on—for the machinery and the policies of war are still with us, and no place, as we now know, is beyond their reach.

An Eclipse

The other day I was out walking with Ollie along the abandoned railroad bed that runs in back of our property, when suddenly I was struck by a fiery patch of brilliant red lying on the pine needles in front of me. Ollie, color blind and somewhat olfactorily challenged pup that he is, trotted by it without stopping, but I was held, transfixed, even before I recognized it for what it was, as if a shard of the sun had fallen from the sky.

I picked it up and cradled it in my hand. It was a male cardinal, its body still warm in the cold morning air. I thought for a moment it was merely stunned and would revive momentarily, but its breast was still and its eyes were shrunken in death. There were no apparent wounds or other signs of injury on it; only the sides of its thick beak were abraded slightly, as if it had been rubbing them on a cuttlebone.

More than most creatures, birds allow you to appreciate the essence of their beauty in death. I thought of all those eighteenth- and nineteenth-century naturalists and artists, including Audubon himself, for whom shooting birds, in

order to examine them scientifically or depict them artisti-
cally, was an accepted practice. The usual historical justifica-
tion is that, before binoculars, telescopic lenses, and mist
nets, this was the only practical way to observe small birds in
detail.

But holding the cardinal in my palm, it seemed as if there
was more to it than that, something that we may have lost in
the name of humaneness. Even a vivid close-up view, photo,
or videotape of a cardinal is a completely different experience—and in some ways a lesser one—than that of holding
the real bird, even a dead one, in your hand.

I took the bird home, laid it out on my desk, and began to
examine it. The eyes, black and squinted, were hidden in the
recesses of the sable face mask that surrounds the large,
opalescent, red-orange beak. Other than this jet-black face
muff, red pervades all the other parts of its body in subtle and
wonderfully contrapuntal ways. Even its thin scaly legs,
crabbed padded toes, and delicate curved talons are pig-
mented a dark, purplish hue. I scratched the thickened skin
of my thumb with its long, thorn-like talons, a pleasant
sensation.

When I began to explore the plumage more closely, however, I discovered not only a remarkable variety of hues, but
also that the colors are often not what they seem to be. The
breast, for instance—which appears as the area of purest,
most saturated red—is a chromatic illusion. Plucking out a
few of the breast feathers, I found that the barbs on the lower
third of each feather are actually a pale grey, that those in the
middle third are grey at the base but red at the end, and that
only the barbs of the last third near the tip are completely
red, and of a tint much paler than the breast itself. On the
bird these feathers are overlapped like courses of shingles, so
that the grey portion is hidden from view.

These breast feathers are so light and airy that my breathing stirred them off the page of my journal as I attempted to

examine them with a magnifying glass. When I overlapped two of the breast feather tips, red over red, I got, as expected, a deeper hue; but when I lapped them red over grey, as they are on the breast, it produced an even more saturated red. As in mixing pigments, where adding black intensifies a color, it appears to be this shingled arrangement, placing an under-layment of grey beneath the red portion of each breast feather, that produces the most intense red to be found on the cardinal's body.

This is but one of a number of unexpected and ingenious structures and arrangements I discovered that are used to produce the extraordinary variety and texture of color on the body of a male cardinal, strategies it takes a visual artist years to learn: shading, tinting, pigment juxtaposition, variable saturation, mottling, washes, iridescence, multiple textures, structural color—to name only a few.

I fell into a kind of trance of alert wonder as I probed and explored the different parts of the bird's body. It was like sinking into a vast lake of feathers, descending into deeper and deeper layers of light and softness. It would take many pages to describe in detail what I learned in only an hour or so of investigating this one bird's plumage. Yet I had only begun to scratch the surface of the artifice used in creating such an intricate and stunning symmetry of form and color.

When at last I surfaced, I realized that the appearance of the bird had suffered noticeably from my probing and plucking. Despite my efforts to preen it back into shape, the body remained permanently ruffled in places. Yet it had yielded to me not only a greater aesthetic and intellectual appreciation of its complex beauty—which I might, perhaps, have obtained nearly as well from a nature video or a CD-ROM encyclopedia—but also a personal, layered, sensuous perception of its body that can only come from an encounter with the thing itself.

Moreover, an integral part of the experience, perhaps the

most important part, was its unexpectedness. It was the serendipitous coming upon the bird on the railroad bed that had sparked my curiosity, leading me to questions I did not even know I wanted to ask. Always, it seems, what I have learned most deeply I have not intended to learn, or have not learned to any purpose but the fulfillment of the moment. Such experiences have fallen at my feet or appeared unexpectedly on the horizon, and asked me to follow.

I felt grateful to the bird, and an obligation to return or restore what respect I could. Our culture has few accepted rituals for such urges. As a child I used to bury dead birds in shoe boxes in the backyard, complete with the trappings of Protestant rites (though I often dug them up a few days later to see if birds really did go to bird heaven). I am long past such innocence, but neither was I willing to put it in a plastic bag, as I have done with other dead animals I have found, and place it in the freezer for future "research."

No, best to return it where I found it, to let foxes, beetles, fungi, bacteria, or possibly my neighbor's cat perform their own ornithological investigations, transforming, like me, that which they examine into themselves. So I did, and in the evening I found my desk still littered with curved, downy breast feathers, half-red, half-black, as the Skidi Pawnee are said to have once painted the bodies of their human sacrifices, representing the sun in eclipse.

Off Hours

The other evening we drove out to White Crest Beach—well named, with its high, bare, old-ivory shoulder of a dune cresting the hill, and several foot trails creased into its flanks leading down to the shore and the surf.

It is a mystery to me why there are not more people on the beach at this hour (in fact, most seem to be leaving just as we arrive). As far as I am concerned, this is the best time of the day to be here in summer, for it is now that the human presence recedes and assumes its proper proportion. This is the time when the rounded contours of the bluff begin to throw their soft grey shadows across the baked sands like a benediction; when a few surfcasters appear and heave their heavy lures out beyond the breakers, the repeated, arching casts of the lines forming a human counterpoint to the rollers coming in endlessly upon themselves.

Compared to the display of human flesh here earlier in the day, people are not only much fewer in number now, but seem to be friendlier as well, less contained, and with a sense of sharing, rather than defending, their stretch of beach. At high noon we are like dense colonies of nesting gannets—raucous, defensive, aggressive, bristling at intrusion, irritated at the common lot. In extreme cases these birds kill each other's young and defecate on one another. We don't do that, of course, though sometimes we behave as if we would like to.

Now, amid coolness, quiet, and space, we are more like the shorebirds that flock leisurely and feed up and down the beach. The dark, ring-necked plovers with their necklaces of white stay below the high-tide line, and the lighter-colored sandpipers with their long, dark, chisel-like bills patrol both the slant of the upper beach and the rumpled terrace of sand behind.

We saunter down over the white brow of the hill. A boy of about ten, slightly chubby, is showing off for his mom, cartwheeling and somersaulting with careless, imperious abandon down the face of the bluff. We descend more soberly along one of the slanted footpaths, an improvised trail worn into the sloping sand as if by a camel train in the Sahara. We walk only a few yards south of the base of the trail, but it is enough—space is generous this time of the day. We go down almost to the high-tide line to catch a few minutes of the westering sun before the shade of the cliff engulfs us. Then we spread out our grey wool blanket, beach chairs, towels and wicker picnic basket and simply sit, unwinding, falling outwards into the rhythms of this hour of grace, this hour of day yielding to shadows and the soft sounds of evening.

The beach still seems to vibrate with the vanished energy and cacophony of the day. That, in fact, is part of its pleasure—the sense of noise and frantic activity recently dissipated, the peace of a classroom just emptied. The tide rises languorously toward its climax in soft, sand-saturated surges to smooth the foot-furrowed brow of the summer berm. Farther out, the swells are dark jade, marbled, miniature Alleghenies, ridge after ridge, sometimes breaking with a muffled crash, sometimes with a voluptuous seethe thick with the grate of gravel. Sometimes the overlapping lines of breakers along the shore fall into momentary alignment, their sine curves merge into phase, and there is a series of wonderful half-seconds of pure silence between the crashes.

It is this, probably more than anything, that defines this time of day: that the soft pulse of the surf has once again become the dominant sound and presence on the beach, the metronome to which everything, including us, sets its tempo. Terns sail like silvery origami sculptures offshore and suddenly plunge into the dark-green bulges of the sea for sand eels. Gulls rock indolently in small rafts offshore like sea ducks, or plant themselves in front of us, arrogantly demanding chicken bones, which I dutifully throw them just to watch their naked greed and aggression. Flocks of shorebirds now appear to reclaim this stretch of beach, from which they have been exiled all day by the press of human presence. A few dogs are allowed to run free, despite the regulations we all know, and no one complains. There is room for all of us now.

Every now and then a much larger wave—the "seventh wave"—hurls itself in and reaches, with a hundred foam-laced fingers, just up and over the high-tide break in the beach, then recedes. It will go slightly higher in its flood, but only slightly. All things are regular and contained this evening, steady; all things know their territories, and respect boundaries. Even the unbounded power of the sea is sheathed.

The shadows of the bluff have enveloped us for at least twenty minutes when suddenly there is a palpable drop in the temperature, as when a low pressure system moves in. Something has shifted, some turning in the evening's clock has occurred, and it spurs us to think of talking a walk.

The beach to the north, a series of undulating cusps, wears a thin mantle of mist, giving it a slightly mysterious look. In the distance, a mile or so off, we can see the foreshortened stick figures of the larger evening crowd on the beach at Cahoon Hollow, anchored there by the presence of the Beachcomber nightclub.

We put the food back into the basket, zip up our backpacks, and leave everything there, something we would never do during the day. Even trust is somehow more apparent now. As we walk north, I watch the ghost-sheen on the slanted lower beach as each wave recedes: the luminous shadow of moisture in the sand that traces in slow motion the retreat of each wave like a lingering, unsubstantial caress.

A mother and daughter, preceded by a nervous, yapping, yellow lab-mix, come toward us. They stop and chat, make us formal introductions to "Chloe," who relents some, but remains suspicious.

Two young girls, perhaps ten and twelve, romp in the surf, totally relaxed with one another and themselves as only young girls can be—playing with the waves and screaming in mock terror as a surge side-swipes them, then going right out for more.

We pass some of the day's debris—the wrecks of beach chairs and plastic trays, shards of broken jars and glasses, odd bent metal poles with concrete weights molded around their bases. There are also more benign signs of the day's occupation: a large rectangle outlined in eelgrass, probably demarcating a makeshift volleyball court.

Coming back we pass a woman sitting in a beach chair: heavy-set, with jet black hair and a bright red jacket draped over her shoulders. She is sitting alone, looking peacefully out at the sea. Beside her, near her hand, is an open pack of cigarettes. She isn't smoking.

For us and for all of these people, this time of day allows us to reconnect ourselves to what is around us, to engage our senses, our bodies, our imaginations, our propensity to story, with this elemental seascape. It is now, in these off hours, when the allure, the enduring mystery of the beach insinuates itself into our perceptions and our memory—when it makes our day, speaks to us in recollection, and when, because it is no longer so intensely and exclusively ours, it becomes more truly ours.

Blackberrying in Africa

This morning, following a hard and heavy rain during the night, I took a walk to Africa. Well, that's what my neighbor Tracy calls it, the expanse of hundreds of acres of open wet meadows, marsh islands, and thick borders of wild cherry, pitch pine, swamp maple, and vine thickets that lies less than half a mile from my house. It is, in fact, an evocative metaphor, for there is something about the place, especially in summer, that reminds me of the open veldt country and river plains of Kenya.

Walking the rutted dirt road that borders its open stretches, I almost expect to see howler monkeys or mambas hanging in the liana-like vines that festoon the maples and birches. In spring the pinkish-white sprays of blooming shad-bush look like groves of mimosas, and the tortuous shapes of wild cherries call to mind the twisted branches of the thorn trees on the Serengeti Plain. In June the dry, toneless screams of the breeding toads are like the strange nocturnal cries of the tree-climbing hyrax. The beaten trails that snake through the ten-foot-high reed grass might be those of elephants winding their way through bamboo forests of the Abadare

Highlands. The tall, long-beaked silhouette out on the marsh looks like that of a Goliath heron, the largest wading bird on earth, spreading its massive wings and turning to face the wind so as to lift its ponderous form into the air. And the slow, brown current of the Herring River is as winding and lush in vegetation as Tana River, down whose slick, muddy banks I once watched the flattened, corrugated bodies of crocodiles slither in the shadow of Mt. Kenya.

Oh, it's a pleasant fancy, to let one landscape call up another. There are of course no monkeys, poisonous snakes, or elephants. The vines are wild grape, not liana. The bird is not a Goliath but our own great blue heron, and only muskrats, not crocodiles, slip down the river's muddy banks. Frost said, "We love the things we love for what they are," but we also love them for what they call up in memory and imagination.

I love the openness and the agricultural feel of this land-scape, its wet meadows and fields, its twisted old apple and pear trees hanging over the bordering upland, the patchwork of deer trails running through the tall grass, the mallards and muskrats along the river, the large flocks of autumn starlings winging out over its expanse. It is for me the closest we get to an extensive pastoral environment on Cape Cod, though, like my African fantasy, this, too, is largely an illusory one—or at least an "unnatural" one.

A hundred years ago this entire valley was a open naviga-ble saltwater estuary bordered by extensive salt marshes. Then, in 1906, the town constructed a dike across the mouth of the Herring River. The dike was the brainchild of Captain Lorenzo Dow Baker, Wellfleet's preeminent entrepreneur, shipping magnate, and founder of the United Fruit Company. By diking off the tidal flow into the Herring River valley, Baker claimed, the wetlands would become arable farmland, the bordering uplands (much of which he happened to own) would become developable, and the town would be rid of the scourge of the dreaded saltwater mosquito.

Lorenzo Dow Baker died two years after the dike was completed, and most of his schemes did not materialize. A modest amount of pasturing and haying took place in the former floodplain, but it had disappeared by the 1950s. New development, other than a golf course, was minimal, in part, perhaps, because the saltwater mosquito was replaced by the equally obnoxious freshwater varieties. In any case, the river valley, its meadows, and much of the surrounding upland became part of the Cape Cod National Seashore in 1961.

Still, because of the dike, much of the salt estuary has been transformed over the past century into a fresh- or brackish water wetland. It is in that sense an artificial or, in ecological jargon, a "human-disturbed" landscape, but nonetheless one that has developed its own wildness, pleasures, integrity, attachments, and cycles.

Recently, as part of an effort to restore several natural habitats within its boundaries, the National Seashore has proposed gradually opening up the dike and returning the Herring River valley to its former saltwater/salt marsh state. It is a scheme that, in the abstract, any self-respecting conservationist would support, one that promises several environmental benefits, including an expansion of wetland acreage, improvement in water quality, and an increase in the number of the eponymous herring that migrate up the river each spring to spawn in the ponds above.

And yet, as a resident and walker of the area, I find I am not so sure. In my years here I have grown to value this area for what it has become. I would miss the masses of flowering shadbush welling up like perfumed fountains in early spring; the rich ferment of May birdsong that depends on the cherries, shadbush, blueberry bushes, catbrier, blackberries, and poison ivy; the creamy-white mounds of multiflora rose lining the dirt roads in summer; the rafts of edible watercress in the upper river; the wild hedgerows of shrubs and vines; the open meadows that give me foot access to the river's wooded islands; the thick fields of ripe goldenrod in early autumn, dotted with migrating monarchs that flit and graze and attach themselves, like small black-spotted orange flags, to the yellow-tasseled stalks; the blaze of red maples lining the riverbanks in September; the bright-red winterberry bushes that attract flocks of waxwings in December. Much, if not most, of this particular richness would eventually disappear if this environment were restored to its "natural" state.

Mostly, though, I would miss the blackberries. I have never found blackberries in such lush profusion anywhere else on Cape Cod. Most of them grow right at the edge of standing water, or open swampland, which probably accounts for their lushness, even in dry years. In winter the spiked, leafless, purple vines roll beside the roadside like dark coils of accordion razor wire. In June they are part of a vast display of white-against-green foliage: billows of white blackberry blossoms crashing against waves of white and pink multiflora rose and the yarrow-like, lime-ivory crowns of viburnum flowers. By July the purple-green tangles of vines already sport an impressive crop of tiny lime-green beehives that will become the dark-purple fruit of August.

The blackberry season lasts for only a couple of weeks, and as it progresses a maze of paths begins to appear among the tangle of vines, matted down by the traffic of pickers. As August wears on, one must go deeper and deeper into this sweet heart of darkness to find unpicked ripe berries. Each of us carries his or her weapon of choice: coffee-cans on neck strings, plastic bags, juice pitchers, buckets, colanders. We follow the paths with a certain single-mindedness, hardly thinking of how we will find our way out of this spiky labyrinth.

After several minutes of tracking the berries into impenetrable dead ends, or reaching through gaps in the limbs of shad trees to snare some high-growing fruit, we may suddenly come out of our trance and stand, disoriented, in the midst of a green jungle, wondering where we are. Then—a mysterious rustle beyond our sight, and a shadowy shape glides horizontally, obscured by leaves. A lion? A Masai warrior stalking his quarry? His movement is silent, mysterious. Then a straw hat and a blue blouse moves above the bush line—just another berry picker intent on her own prey.

This morning, a heavy haze hangs in the air, rendering everything—clothes, towels, sheets, computer paper—limp and sagging. At a little after six I set out for Africa. A damp mist cloaks the open wet meadows and marsh islands, hiding the herds of zebras. Sparrows, mostly savannah and swamp, are everywhere, and early flocks of grackles make auguries against a burnished late-summer sky.

The night's rain has saturated the parched earth, creating little lakes in the sandy ruts and leaving the arched vines of the blackberry thickets bejeweled with rain-diamonds and rain-pearls. Though it is barely August, the vines by the roadside are already covered with luxuriant patches of large, ripe blackberries. Many are the size of the first joint of my thumb, and darkly, watery-sweet.

Near High Toss Bridge I spot a pickup with a landscaping logo on its door. In the patch of vines nearby are two women picking berries by the basketful. "You need blackberry cobbler," one calls out by way of greeting, "just to get through the summer traffic."

Not expecting such an early harvest, I have brought no basket or pail; but using my cap, I step down into a patch of vines and begin gathering the ripe berries. There is a fine, but crucial difference between ripe and not-quite-ripe blackberries, like that between the right and the nearly right word. If any portion of the underside retains the slightest tinge of lighter reddish-purple, I leave the berry unpicked. Yet even a uniform black-purple drupe is no guarantee of complete ripeness. The real test is tactile. Each drupe should almost fall off its little newel-post—at most a very gentle tug should release it. Any palpable resistance on the part of the berry is a sign to let it be another day or two.

It is a moral question, in a way, a contest between desire and patience, similar in some ways to the testing of character one experiences when going after blue crabs with chicken legs tied onto a piece of string. The crab must catch itself, pincing onto the ripe chicken leg and holding on while you gently pull the string back within reach of your crab net. The trick is to find the precise tension of pull that will keep the crab holding on as you draw it in. Pull too fast or too hard, and the crab will let go. You must learn to let his appetite exceed yours or you will lose him.

So it is with blackberries. If you pull too hard, you may get the berry but you will lose the full sweetness of it. On the other hand, if you leave it, it may be gone the next time you come by. Each person must find this point of equilibrium for himself. The more one has to pull, the more tart the reward will be. The sweetness of the blackberry must be freely given.

So ripe are these berries, however, that they seem to give themselves to me. By the time my hat is half-full, those at the bottom are already partially crushed by the weight of those above them, staining the fabric. The immortal mosquitoes are out in abundance, feasting on my blood. My hands, too, are stained with the stigmata of this thorny fruit. I lick them off, relishing the combination of syrupy sweetness, salty blood and sweat, and bow my head again to labor in Lorenzo's gardens.

A Day of Roads

When I pulled into Newcomb Hollow in Wellfleet, the beach was curiously empty. There were only three cars in the parking lot, and two of those left almost immediately. The waves were low and quiet, silently tossing massive logs and bright flags of sea lettuce about in the surf. A muffled fog was sitting on the beach like a cool shroud, though I could feel the hot sun, like a weight, beating down upon it.

In August the beaches of Cape Cod are normally paved with human bodies. Here, on the Lower Cape, the flexed forearm of this glacial peninsula, some five million people each year visit the Cape Cod National Seashore, most of them during the summer months. A century and a half ago the Cape's most famous literary visitor, Henry David Thoreau, remarked on this very stretch of beach that "a thousand men could not have seriously interrupted it, but would have been lost in the vastness of the scenery as their footsteps in the sand." Even Thoreau's perceptive vision, however, could not have imagined the extent to which humanity would someday occupy these sands, so that those same footsteps would actually threaten to alter the scenery itself.

As a year-rounder, I usually avoid the ocean beaches in summer, saving my walks there for the off-season. But this morning, all it had taken was a little moisture and sea breeze to blow the crowds away like sea foam and restore the beach to its ancient vastness and majesty, and so I came, with no purpose in mind except to experience the beach in its unaccustomed solitude.

I began walking north, my eyes smarting from a stiff, moist north wind. Above me, on my left, loomed the sand cliffs of the outer beach, part of a nearly continuous twenty-six-mile marine scarp running from Coast Guard Beach in Eastham to High Head in North Truro, interrupted only by a series of dips, or "hollows," in the cliff wall. At Newcomb Hollow the bluffs are about fifty feet high and nearly completely barren of growth, in part from the constant foot traffic of the beach-users. Farther on, the cliffs double, then triple in height, and the vegetation begins to reassert itself, climbing up the smooth slopes out of the wrack line.

A dense fog continued to blow down the beach, shrouding visibility at both ends. In the distance I saw what appeared to be figures on the beach. But when I came closer, they proved to be improvised driftwood structures, decorated with colorful bits of washed-up fabric, netting, and lobster buoys, the kind of whimsical sculpture one often finds here. In places footprints and vehicle tracks were so numerous that the beach resembled a railroad yard done in sand, yet I neither met nor saw another soul from Newcomb Hollow to Brush Valley in Truro, nearly three miles away. This abundance of mute signs, the strange absence of people, and the desolate feeling of the fog, gave the impression of a mass exodus, a ghost beach.

As the cliffs began to rise, near the Wellfleet-Truro town line, I left the beach, climbing up one of those diagonal foot trails cut into the face of the scarp—something like a mountain path, narrow and flat, and comparatively firm after the recent rain. Reaching the top, I continued on the path that runs along the crest just back from the edge. This path, like the beach itself, is both a permanent and ephemeral road, in this case man-made, but constantly forced to relocate as the cliffs recede from year to year.

I looked out over a vast and undulating plain of stunted vegetation, across one of the most dramatic stretches of the outer beach of Cape Cod. To the north the bluffs dip and rise precipitously in long, rolling waves. They rise up out of wooded hollows to the west, cresting in shaggy, grassy overhangs at the cliff edge, so that they appear as massive frozen swells, terrestrial counterparts of the ocean breakers that nibble away at their foundations below.

Here, I thought, is one place where the Cape's extremes are vertical as well as horizontal. The highest point of land on the Outer Cape is along this stretch of cliff, a summit officially designated on the U.S. Geological Survey maps as "Pamet," which climbs a giddy 177 feet above the beach (though this figure likely changes from year to year). Yet everything is on the Cape's characteristically diminutive scale, so that one feels like a giant striding in several minutes from one summit to another along a sandy mountain range, complete with miniature peaks, cirques, bowls, and knife-edges. As the crest trail swung out to the edge, I peered over and startled a flock of gulls that were roosting on the slope, sending them out into the fog where they disappeared, reassembling farther north. Each time I caught up with them they flew, as if newly startled, and waited for me farther on— a kind of larger version of the shepherding game one plays with flocks of shorebirds along the beach.

At intervals the crest trail swung inland and joined a wider and more substantial jeep sand-road. Along its soft surface were numerous fresh tracks of deer that had apparently been coming in my direction, had scented or heard my approach, and turned off the road. I could feel their presence nearby, bedded down probably within yards of me somewhere in the low, dark-green thicket of scrub oak. But I knew I could wait there all day and never see nor hear a sign of them.

I strode, with my folded umbrella set across my shoulders like a yoke, across an open field of bright, rounded tufts of beach heather surrounded by tall, waving beach grass, among hardy stands of gnarled and weathered chokecherry, through thickets of beach plum with their hard green fruits already as large as marbles in this year of excellent berry sets. Their stiff twigs were entwined with numerous vines of wild grapes, all sprouting clusters of lime-green fruit as yet no bigger than grape-seeds, glowing beneath the broad, arched leaves. How lush and thick, how heavy with promise these eroding fragments of beach bluff can be!

Shortly beyond the Pamet summit I descended to the beach road again, staying on it until I reached a break in the cliff face at Brush Valley, a short distance south of Ballston Beach in Truro. As I walked up the hard narrow path of this ancient glacial valley, the uninterrupted hills of scrub oak rose sharp and huge into the fog. The screams of the invisible gulls loomed over me, dwarfing my presence. We need to be overwhelmed like this, from time to time, by some unpeopled expanse of the land where we live, even to fear it a little— that it goes on so long without us.

I came out of Brush Valley onto the paved surface of South Pamet Road near the head of the Pamet River valley. The Pamet is a tidal river basin that comes in from Cape Cod Bay a few miles to the west and ends just behind a thin line of ocean-fronting dunes—thus nearly cutting the Cape in two.

North and South Pamet Roads run roughly parallel on either side of the river and once formed a loop road that ran directly behind the dunes at the head of the valley.

About two decades ago a small but important environmental decision was made here. During the great winter storm of February 1978, the ocean breached this dune line, spilling over into the headwaters of the Pamet River and temporarily separating the northern half of Truro and all of Provincetown from the rest of Cape Cod. As a result, the town of Truro decided to close off the valley loop road at its head—thus turning North and South Pamet Roads into dead-ends—and to fence off the dunes to walking. The strategy appears to be working: the dune line has migrated completely over the old paved road surface, and beachgrass has weaved its network of underground runners, like a hair transplant, beneath the sand surface.

I was struck at the time by the town's original decision to close the road, not merely because it showed uncommon environmental sense (allowing, as it were, the dune to continue to march down *its* road unobstructed), but because it ran directly against the grain of road history in our time. It is unusual enough to hear of any established road being closed or abandoned, but in this case the passage being terminated was one of the oldest in existence in New England. According to several eighteenth-century maps, this section of the Pamet Road was part of the original King's Highway, the first road running the entire length of the Cape, laid out during the reign of Charles II. Yet this historic thoroughfare had been sacrificed, truncated, at no small inconvenience to some of the local residents, for the long-term good of a natural system.

I emptied the beach sand from my shoes and continued along the narrow, winding course of South Pamet Road toward Truro Center, about a mile and a half to the west. Certain areas of the Cape have always been comparatively fertile, and the narrow floodplain of the Pamet River is one of those. This lovely low valley, filled with old farmhouses, orchards, marshside gardens, and the strong smell of a few remaining cowyards, breathes a rural use and settled continuity that is rare to encounter here anymore. Many of the old houses today are occupied by summer residents, retirees, artists, and writers, but it is a benign occupation, full of deference for the past. At one spot there is even a small brook running under the road into the marsh that Thoreau took notice of in 1849. He had read somewhere that there were no fresh brooks in Truro, but noted, "I am pretty sure that I afterward saw a small fresh-water brook emptying into the south side of the Pamet River, though I was so heedless as not to taste it." A century and a half later I decided to rectify his uncharacteristic oversight, and so I knelt beside the stream and drank. It is, indeed, Henry, sweet and fresh.

Farther down the road I came upon two frizzy-haired young women standing beside their car and looking at it as though it were a sick cow. They had just come off one of the dirt side roads, they told me, where they had rammed a fender against one of Truro's rare glacial boulders. The left front wheel looked seriously out of alignment and the radiator was dripping.

"The radiator? Oh, is that what that water is?" said one. "Well, Marian, it's not a very big leak, is it? I bet if we stopped and put water into it every half-hour we could make it back to Brookline."

I persuaded them that they should have it looked at first, gave them directions to a garage south of Truro Center, and watched them as the car went roaring, weaving, and squealing off down the road, looking for all the world as if they were riding a wild pig. Ten minutes later, when I reached the town center and came out onto Route 6, I was surprised to see them again, driving by me in the breakdown lane, emergency lights blinking, the left wheel protesting loudly, as they headed, not off-Cape, but north toward Provincetown. They saw me and waved, with hopeful, trusting, desperate looks on their faces. Innocents from Boston, I thought—another venerable Cape tradition.

Perhaps, though, they felt safe from disaster having gotten back to the familiarity of Route 6, which is the main tourist highway running down the spine of Cape Cod from the Bourne Bridge at the Canal to the Cape's tip at Provincetown. Pedestrians, however, risk their lives crossing this road in summer. I had planned to wait in Truro Center for the afternoon bus to take me back to Wellfleet, but by the time I finished lunch I felt refreshed, the fog had lifted, and I decided to complete the circuit on foot.

I struck off south on one of the narrow dirt roads east of Route 6, intending to make my way back to Newcomb Hollow along a network of wood roads shown on my 1972 U.S. Geological Survey map. But the road I had chosen quickly petered out in the puckerbrush, and I soon realized that it currently existed more on my map and in my mind than in reality. Nonetheless I forged ahead, the passage growing leafier and needlier, until with each step I had to push the branches ahead of me with both arms, as if doing the breast stroke through a layered green sea of foliage. It occurred to me that I could very well be the last person ever to attempt to walk this particular road, and I was just about to give up and retrace my steps when I suddenly emerged back out onto the paved highway.

This was not Route 6 itself, but one of those old side loops of the original highway that were cut off, like oxbows on an old river, when the road was straightened and widened in the 1950s. There are a dozen or more of these little bits of old Route 6 along the Lower Cape, curving off the main highway here and there for a few hundred feet before rejoining the mainstream of traffic. (It is easy to see where they veer off, for the telephone lines, installed down the Cape before the road was straightened, still follow the old route.) Some are completely barricaded off now, the pavement bulldozed over and replanted with bayberry and other native shrubs. One is a storage area for the state highway department. Most, however, are still accessible by car, and for years I had promised myself I would someday trace their route. But always, while driving, I seemed to be too pressed by the surrounding traffic or my own momentum to pull off and do so.

So I decided to walk them now, following the old, nearly continuous route as it weaved its way back and forth across the busy new highway like the loose end of a thread in a needle looping across the taut strand. On one loop was an unpublicized parking area by a small pond; on another were a few old houses from the 1700s and 1800s, set off like roadside exhibits from a previous age; on yet another, some modest pondshore cottages built in the 1930s, 1940s, and 1950s, before John Kennedy, a summer resident of the Cape, signed the Cape Cod National Seashore into being in 1961, effectively preventing new building within its boundaries.

It occurred to me that the history of most roads seems to be the opposite of that of rivers, in that roads tend to grow younger, straighter, more rapid with age, meandering less and less, cutting their channels deeper and faster through the surrounding terrain, bypassing more and more of the old roads, villages, even—in the case of interstates—entire towns and cities, some of which themselves in time grow more sluggish, cut off from the main flow, and are left to stagnate and silt in at their own, unremarked pace.

I have, in nearly three decades of living here, covered a great deal of this peninsula on foot, retracing many of my favorite routes year after year, carving, no less than the bulldozers, my own personal history here. My first set of USGS maps, printed in the late 1950s and now retired, are heavily

annotated with exclamation points, where with rank enthusiasm I first noted discoveries of bank swallow colonies,
prime beachplum or bayberry sites, fox dens, wild cranber-
ries, hidden ponds, the remains of shipwrecks, eagle sightings. The notes on my current set of maps, themselves nearly
a quarter-century old, are less excited and tend to record the
passing of things: beach cottages claimed by the ocean, shifting sandspits, encroaching woodlands, whole sections of
towns lost to development, abandoned cranberry bogs, and
old wood roads become impassable with time. Sometimes,
after walking what I thought was some unexplored stretch of
road or section of beach, I have been surprised to find it
recorded on one of my earlier maps, unrecognized after many
years.

The highway I was on now, Route 6, is the youngest of a
series of roughly parallel roads that run down the lower arm
of the Cape from Orleans to Provincetown, and in so doing
weave deeply through the Cape's history, each strand having
a traveled and storied history of its own. Route 6 (that is, in
its original, more loopy configuration) represents the first
continuously paved road down the Outer Cape, completed
in 1923. Along its length came the first large waves of motor
tourists to Provincetown in the years after World War I.
Provincetown's art colony flourished in those days, and the
tourists were joined by hosts of painters, writers, and theatri-
cal figures—among them, Eugene O'Neill, Karl Knaths, Jack
Reed, Mary Heaton Vorse, William Daniel Steele, Edward
Hopper, Edna St. Vincent Millay, Edmund Wilson, Conrad
Aiken, and John Dos Passos—all traveling this road.

More than a mile to the west at this point, running
close to Cape Cod Bay, is the abandoned bed of the Old
Colony Railroad, which first reached Wellfleet in 1869 and
Provincetown four years later. It conveyed such distinguished
figures as President Theodore Roosevelt, who laid the cor-
nerstone of the Provincetown Monument in 1907, and such

disgraced ones as the Reverend Horatio Alger, who fled his
Unitarian pulpit in Brewster a few decades earlier. According
to the church records, Alger was dismissed by the church
elders for "molesting young boys" and was ordered to take
the next train out of town—to Boston or Provincetown. He
chose Boston, where he later made his literary fortune with
a series of rags-to-riches pulp novels about young, enterpris-
ing boys.

Lying between the railroad bed and the present Route 6,
and older than either, is Old County Road. A long, narrow,
winding stretch of this old nineteenth-century road runs from
Wellfleet Center to Truro Center, mostly within the National
Seashore. To some of the older inhabitants it is still known as
"Whiskey Road," not, as many suppose, because it was a
thoroughfare of choice for transporting bootlegged goods
during Prohibition, but because for many years after Repeal,
Wellfleet remained a dry town, and the shortest route to
liquor was along this road, to Truro.

Only a few hundred yards east of Route 6's roaring summer traffic one can still find portions of the original Old
King's Highway, laid out in 1660. It was in November 1778,
following the wreck of the British man-of-war *Somerset* on
Truro's backside, that 480 survivors of the Royal Navy, in
the custody of Captain Enoch Hallett and the home guard,
were marched down this road from North Truro to Boston
through a chain of cheering and jeering villagers.

And still farther east lies the oldest land road of all, the
beach itself, the most changing and unchangeable of our
thoroughfares, walked over the centuries by the Pamet,
Punonakanit, and Nauset Indians, by the first hapless ship-
wrecked sailors, by early beachcombers and professional
wreckers, by generations of lantern-carrying surfmen of the
Life Saving Service, and by countless vacationers and beachgoers today.

I have walked or ridden each of these north-south routes at one time or another, but now, crisscrossing the stream of roaring trucks and buzzing cars on Route 6, I was struck anew at the cumulative history they represent, and at how various have been the routes by which we have all made our way up and down this peninsula, and for what various purposes. Each way has taken precedence at different times in our collective history and at different seasons in our individual lives, and each is, to a remarkable degree, still here, intact and available for passage, if not by vehicle, then on foot.

But where did we think we were going all this time? Perhaps that is the question I had been wordlessly framing for myself as I started out on the beach earlier in the day, a day, it had turned out, of roads. Perhaps it is useful, on occasion, just to wander like this, along the thoroughfares of one's home ground, with *no* purpose in mind, just to try to get some sense of where it is they have led us after all these centuries of earnest and frivolous travel.

At the Wellfleet town line I struck off east on the first dirt road through the woods back toward Newcomb Hollow. About a third of a mile in I came upon the longest remaining continuous section of the original King's Highway. At this point the old colonial road is no more than a narrow dirt cartpath running through shady and quiet woods, indistinguishable from any of the other wood roads that labyrinth their way through this section of Wellfleet. Indeed, I wondered at first if this was in fact the Old King's Highway as designated on the map, for it ran due south over a fairly steep hill that would have been difficult for wagons and coaches to negotiate. One would think that if the early settlers had taken

the trouble to lay out a road, they would have chosen an easier route. But I soon passed a brass plaque, set in a granite
slab beside the road, that read:

> KINGS HIGHWAY
> HERE WAS BUILT
> THE FIRST
> SCHOOLHOUSE
> IN WELLFLEET
> W.R.

No dates, no hint of who the local historian or grown-up
schoolboy "W.R." might have been, and of course no sign of
the vanished schoolhouse itself. But farther along there are
eighteenth-century Cape farmhouses, the sites of old stage-
coach inns, and ancient pear and apple orchards that still
grow heavy with fruit in late summer, all giving further
evidence that this out-of-the-way cartpath in these semi-
isolated woods was once a vital artery running through active
settlements.

To the east I began to hear music. The secluded pine woods
rippled and hummed with the muted and overlapping sounds
of drums, cornets, mandolins, guitars, and stereos. They
came from a scattered, extensive community of summer cottages, most of them older ones predating the National
Seashore, which are strung out around the ponds at the head
of the Herring River and along a bewildering complex of
sand roads. The broken strands of music that filtered through
the afternoon air had an impromptu, lackadaisical quality to
them, starting and stopping in midphrase, like birdsong.

In their haphazard rhythms and snatches of melody I
sensed the strong role that these woods and the houses they
hide play for their seasonal inhabitants, a role that they can
never play for one like myself who lives here year-round. For
these summer refugees this is a place out of their accustomed
life, removed from its familiar and inexorable flow, a locale

of wide margins where, for a weekend, two weeks, a month, or a season, they can rediscover aspects of themselves, or explore new ones, lost in a maze of unregulated soft dirt roads that are identified only by some rough wooden sign tacked to a pine trunk at an unnamed intersection in the woods, relaxing and making tentative music for its own sake, music that now echoed anonymously back and forth across the waters that separated them.

So musing as I walked, I came at last to where the Old King's Highway crosses the Herring River, not far from its headwaters in Wellfleet's Herring Ponds, and only another twenty minutes to my car. Here the "river" is a shallow stream only a few feet wide, deep-sunk, slow-moving, well-shaded, and extremely clear. On the downstream side it exits from beneath the road out of a concrete culvert. There was a slight commotion in the water here, and I saw that thousands of small herring fry, each about three inches long, were swimming downstream in thick clumps, like swirling patches of long, slender blades of grass. These were the year's crop of alewives, migratory herring that each spring make their way up hundreds of New England rivers and streams to spawn in freshwater ponds, and then shortly return, leaving the young to hatch and make their own precarious way back out to sea in late summer and early fall.

The culvert out of which they swam—or, more accurately, were carried—was dark beneath the road and seemed to issue out of the earth itself, gushing up wave after wave of tiny fish that already seemed ocean-bent in their determined motions. Traveling from east to west they would cross, before they reached the bay, the entire series of roads and thoroughfares striating the width of the Cape, in a largely unrecognized and unnoticed journey. Yet here was perhaps the oldest road of all traveled by life on this peninsula, predating all highways, railroads, wagon paths, and Indian trails. It is a road originally laid out, not by men, but by tremendous ice sheets plowing down from Canada's Laurentian Shield while Europeans huddled in caves in France and Spain. Its course was dug and graded, not by bulldozers, but by the meltwaters of the glaciers' retreat, perpetually maintained and resurfaced by the flow of the ponds above it. For how many thousands of springs have alewives come in from the cold seas, making their way up this watery highway to spawn, leaving these tiny young to yield to late summer currents, to be carried out like autumn seeds to the unfathomable waters of their maturity?

Once navigable, over centuries the river has been shrunken by dikes and filled in by marsh, so that it is a way we rarely travel anymore. Nor are we likely to be aware of these herring fry as we speed over them on our various human highways. My own way home that afternoon lay in an opposite direction to that of the fish, but watching their little forms darting through the lucid waters with such fresh and undiminished energy, I could not help but feel in some measure brought back to my own beginnings.

Ghost Music on the Dunes

These are the wine days, the high autumn days on the Cape, and there is no better place to spend them than in the dunes. Thanks to the generosity of our friends, Gary and Laurie, Kathy and I are spending a few days at Peg's, one of eighteen remaining dune shacks spread thinly across the broad, sandy expanse of the Provincelands from Race Point to High Head.

The Provincelands encompass several square miles of dune ridges and valleys that sprawl between the town of Province-town and the Atlantic Ocean at the very tip of Cape Cod. The dune shacks lie along the outermost ridge of dunes, and many of them date back to the early years of the twentieth century. The first ones were said to be built by crew members of the Life Saving Service stations that used to line the outer beach here, enabling the men to bring their families along in the summer months. Others were built later by local and sum-mer people, many of them writers and artists who used the shacks as retreats. Today several are still known by the names of their former owners: Boris's, Zara's, Frenchie's, Sunny's, and Peg's.

Peg's is named after its former owner, Peg Watson, who

was a social worker in New York City. About a mile east of Peg's was the shack of Charlie Schmid, the legendary "Bird Man" of the dunes who lived there year–round for twenty-three years. Charlie and Peg were said to have been close friends, lovers actually. Over the years Peg spent as much time as she could at her shack until her arthritis became too bad and she went to Boston for knee surgery.

After the operation Peg returned to the dunes to see Charlie, though friends said she really wasn't fit to come. The story is that, on the day of her death, she drove over the sand road in her jeep to Charlie's. When she left in the evening, Charlie watched her go until she disappeared in a dip, and then he went inside. What happened next is conjecture, but apparently, the jeep either stalled or got stuck in the sand, and Peg, using her walker, tried to get to the nearest shack, Zara's, for help. There were two women staying at Zara's and one of them had a dream that night in which she seemed to hear someone crying for help. The next day they found Peg's body in one of the wild cranberry bogs, a place still marked with a cairn of stones gathered from the beach.

Charlie inherited Peg's shack. After his death in the early 1980s, it was acquired by the Cape Cod National Seashore and gradually fell into disrepair. By the time Gary and Laurie leased it from the Seashore, the porch was gone, the floor boards were rotted out and the roof was about to fall in. Today Peg's has been restored to its original soundness with loving care and attention to detail.

In the mornings we wake to unexpectedly inland sounds: the calls of towhees and bluejays poking and flitting among the thick scrub oak and beachplum shrubs that surround the shack. A song sparrow jumps up out of the brush to the top of a bayberry twig to see what is going on, chipping loudly. Hundreds of tree swallows buzz low over the shack, all heading west toward Race Point, skimming within a few feet of my head, as if they were flying bombing patterns.

Dragonflies—hero darners the size of small helicopters—chop through the soft air, thick with memory.

To the south heavy rains have flooded the cranberry bogs across the jeep trail, turning them all to small, deep-blue lakes. Beyond them, along the crest of the high dunes, the sky-blue water tower and the top of Provincetown's Pilgrim Monument loom like the Dakota Towers and the Plaza Hotel over Central Park, but in reverse scale and relationship. Here it is the park, that is, the Cape Cod National Seashore, which surrounds and dominates Provincetown's miniature metropolis.

We are lazy and grateful, basking in the clear, lucent light under arching, autumn skies. All day the old yellow sightseeing plane drones overhead along the dune ridges. A friend, visiting us, remarks that the same plane has been flying across the same route every summer since he was a boy here forty years ago, "and probably long before that. I bet it's been flying since the 1930s, maybe the 1920s. It's that vintage. Heck, it's been flying so long it's worn a groove in the air. They don't even have to steer it anymore, just give it a kick to get it going."

By late afternoon deep shadows begin to curl into the north-facing hollows of the dunes. We see deer tracks and large pairs of paw prints that might be coyotes. In one place the seed stem of a beachgrass plant has been carried along the smooth side of a dune, making a jagged lightning-bolt track in its flank.

Kathy says that the air surrounding these shacks is "old," by which, I take it, she means that it is full of memory. Peg's, like many of the shacks, has a log in which visitors are encouraged to write. In addition to the numerous expressions of gratitude for the gifts of solitude and beauty, there is a wealth of small, careful observations of weather, wildlife, and the shack itself that gradually forms a collective memory of this place. On one wall is a sketch by Bill Evaul, the Truro artist, of the view out the shack's eastern window. In it he has carefully indicated, against the silhouette of the dunes, the former and present positions of the tower of Highland Light, several miles to the southeast, that was moved back from the edge of the sea cliffs this past summer. An event that was publicly reported and celebrated is here recorded as a small but significant milestone in the history of this shack: a fixture in the landscape, already old at the shack's birth, has shifted slightly, but momentously.

Shortly before sunset, I come in off the porch into the shack and am immediately aware of faint music. Kathy has fallen asleep on the bed, and I think perhaps she has left the portable radio on, but no, it is turned off. There is, nonetheless, unmistakable music in the air, just above the auditory threshold. It sounds vaguely Middle Eastern: a low flute, or wordless voice, with soft percussion. Perhaps someone in one of the shacks to the west is playing music that is drifting down on the wind. I go outside again, but hear nothing except crickets and surf.

Doubting my ears, I wake Kathy, and she confirms what I hear: low serpentine melodies with a steady, muffled beat underneath. We begin to search the shack from one end to the other, trying to discover its source, lying down on the floor, then standing up on the bed; but it seems to grow no louder or softer no matter where we listen from. Ghost music, it seems—like the crying of babies said to be heard at the sites of certain massacres of Indian villages in the west.

Then the music stops. The indistinguishable words of a woman's voice follow. I turn on the portable radio, twist the dial, and eventually find WOMR, Provincetown's community radio station. Yes, it is their broadcast, but that only displaces the mystery: where is it coming from? We are very close to its transmitter here in the dunes, so close that the station comes in on eight different frequencies across the dial. Could it be that the whole shack—its metal screens and spoons, its iron pump and aluminum pots, its steel refrigerator and stove—are all acting like some kind of enormous antenna, the way that metal fillings in a mouth are sometimes said to do? It's a far-fetched idea, but there seems no other explanation.

Gradually we become more and more obsessed with finding the source, realizing we will not sleep unless we do. We open up drawers, haul out boxes and duffle bags from under the bed, scour the shelves, dig through piles of blankets and clothes. Eventually, we unearth an answer. At the bottom of one of the storage boxes Kathy finds an all-band portable radio. The radio is, in fact, tuned to WOMR and, apparently, was accidentally left programmed to turn on at this time by the previous occupants.

There is relief, of course, in solving the mystery, but as with all mysteries revealed, a certain disappointment as well. Even as we sink into surf-smothered sleep, I continue to hear a low, disembodied, plaintive voice, singing somewhere out among the dark dunes and memory-flooded bogs.

A Terrible Beauty

*"Think of the ghastly beauty of the mushroom cloud at
Alamogordo, rising heavenward, soon to visit
obliteration on two Japanese cities."*

CHET RAYMO

I have never seen a month for mushrooms like this September.
The last week of August set it up, following a long dry spell,
when Hurricane Bonnie brought us a couple of wet, gusty
days, followed by a stretch of cool, dry weather—perfect conditions for an eruption of 'shrooms that lasted through most
of the month.

Yesterday I took a walk through the oak forests of Merrick
Island and found that overnight a low blaze of early autumn
foliage had ignited the woodlands, a bright deadly carnival
in miniature. The forest floor resembled the lighted board
of a vast pinball machine, glowing and blinking with fantas-
tic lights. There were large round domes the hue of deep

bruises, white skeletal umbrellas with a single red spot in their centers, overlapping assemblies of irregular fornices like mounds of soft-shelled turtles, the radiant-red, white-carbuncle-dotted cap of the Destroying Angel, seductively cheerful yellow disks bright as a cheerleader's sweater, frilled columns of deadly aminitas, bronze disks with dimpled centers the color of burnt suns or soiled sandstone, chalk and alabaster spools that looked like marble statues of themselves, thick russet skulls split to reveal yellow meat, huge folded golden leaves like thick catcher's mitts, pinkish-brown parasols with furled edges, spongy convoluted green-tinted domes like the enormous exposed brains of sci-fi aliens from my youth, shapeless lumps of cream stained with dirty orange like pieces of Miss Havisham's moldy wedding cake, and on and on.

I did not know most of their names, and I was glad not to. I wanted to see them all with fresh eyes, without prejudice, though I knew some were likely poisonous, others edible, a few possibly even hallucinogenic. One cannot easily tell from their appearance, of course, and that's the rub with mushrooms. A fungus that looks perfectly benign to the casual eye may, in fact, be quite lethal; another that has a lurid, daemonic appearance may be a coveted delicacy. Moreover, many edible mushrooms and toxic toadstools resemble one another closely, may in fact belong to the same family, or even genus, so that only spore prints or expert taxonomical analysis can distinguish them.

The most striking plant I saw that day was one I first mistook for a small hedgehog. It had a large, chocolate-brown dome, nearly five inches across, covered with a geometrical pattern of studs tipped with spurs, like the scales of a pine cone. This was the only one I took with me, and later showed it to my friend Norma, to whom I resort for facts and reassurance about these seasonal fruits. She exclaimed in delight,

"Oh, it's an Old Man of the Woods!" What a wonderful name, I thought, perfectly expressing its dark, eccentric, retiring appearance. Edible, too, it turns out. This was the first time I had ever noticed this species, but over the next few weeks of this *mensis mirabilis*, I found and collected dozens.

The common names for mushrooms suggest that they have long possessed a strong hold on the human imagination. Their names are, in fact, anything but common, and a random list of them (read them aloud for full effect) suggests a collaboration among Lewis Carroll, J. R. R. Tolkien, and Stephen King. There is Artist's Fungus, Earth Tongue, Crowned Earth Star, Dead Man's Finger, Spreading Hedgehog, Rusty Hoof Fome, Death Cap, Destroying Angel, Strangulated Aminitopsis, Clouded Clitocybe, Velvet-Footed Collybia, Delicious Lactarius, Abortive Clytopilus, Gem-Studded Puffball, Striate Bird's Nest, Collared Stinkhorn, Cottony-Margined Milky Cap, Wood Blewit, Slimy Gomphidius, Smoky-Gilled Woodlover, Deceptive Craterellus, Slippery Jack, Black Witches' Butter, and (my favorite) Confusing Peziza—just to name a few.

Beyond their contemporary metaphoric connotations of nuclear destruction and their often poisonous nature, mushrooms have a much more direct link with death. They are the necrophages of the plant world. Their strange beauties stem directly from decay, from which they draw their life—or, more accurately, from which the underground network of thready mycelia (of which the visible mushroom is the fruiting body) draws its nourishment. In doing so, they perform some of the most essential work on the planet, recycling organic nutrients and thereby keeping us from being up to our necks in the corpses of plants.

One of the startling things about mushrooms is the rapidity with which they themselves decay once, as Mary Oliver puts it, "they are done with perfection." Pick a mushroom only hours after it reaches its peak and you will find its surface covered with fuzzy mildew, its stem and cap infested with crawling maggots. Perhaps they decompose so quickly because, feeding on death as they do, they have no truly healthy stage themselves, no firm prime of life, or only a very ephemeral one, before the worms bore in, molds bloom on their skin, and they melt away before one's eyes, like the Wicked Witch of the West; or, to use the botanical term, they *deliquesce*—a strikingly lovely word for a sensorially horrific process.

Despite their dazzling diversity of exotic form and surreal color, however, the closest relationships I have with local mushrooms are with a few of the most ordinary-looking ones: the common boletes. Boletes are the daily bread of the amateur mushroom-hunter on Cape Cod, and over the past few weeks my kitchen counters have overflowed with bags and bags of them. Boletes are one of the more edible groups of fungi and come in a variety of names expressive of their appearance or personality: Admirable, Lurid, Painted, Bitter, and King.

The staple species here is *Leccinum aurantiacum*, or the Brick Top Bolete, prized because of its relative abundance, good taste, and ease of identification. Most boletes have the classic shape of the animated Oriental mushrooms in Disney's *Fantasia*: rounded hat-like domes cupping a thick, pestle-shaped stalk. They tend to grow beneath stands of conifers, and the Brick Top is commonly found on the floor of open pitch pine woods.

Safe, reliable, and familiar, boletes are the color of warm buns just taken out of the oven, held out to me, a six-year-old again, in the thick, glove-padded hands of my Hungarian grandmother: "Here, *megutselah*, have some..."

Some have a warmer, brickish hue, almost a kind of blush

on top of their little rotundas, reminding me of Utah sandstone or Tuscan roof tiles. It seems incongruous that these fruits of darkness and damp, cool shade and black earth, should look like something fresh-baked in the sun. Yet though we tend to think of mushrooms as denizens of the dark, some species grow on the open beach or among the sand dunes out of some rotting piece of driftwood or buried plant. Many boletes, in fact, pop up in the open sun, among the carpet of bearberries fringing the pine woods.

I love to take hold of their firm, muscular stalks, grabbing each one with my fingers beneath the broad cap and gently working the bulbous base back and forth, pulling it out loose and whole, still dangling a shaggy nest of mycelia and dark brown soil. This hairy ball exudes an earthy aroma that the nearly scentless stalks and caps lack. The thick white mature stalks are finely creased and stippled with brown or black marks called scabers; the undersides are white and spongy, the caps like fine, thin leather.

For most of September the boletes were almost laughably easy to collect. Once I gathered twelve pounds in a forty-minute outing. At home I removed the spongy underparts, sliced up the stalks and caps, and placed them in the gas oven on racks covered with aluminum foil. The pilot light on our oven produces just enough heat to thoroughly dry several racks of cut-up boletes over a twenty-four-to-thirty-six-hour period. When they were done I weighed them: barely eight ounces of dried boletes. In other words, over 95 percent of a mushroom's mass is water.

Perhaps such a superabundance of mushrooms had occurred before, but I had never encountered one, and other gatherers I talked to confirmed that this was a bumper, if not a record, year. However reduced in weight, the plastic bags full of dried boletes retain the luscious, condensed flavors that will sweeten our stews and soups and sauces all winter. It was an unexpected harvest from an unexpected source, showing me once again that at all points of the universal cycle of life, death, and decay, nature finds something that appeals to our unbiased senses.

Special Delivery

For the past month at least, and I suspect longer, a spider has been guarding a clutch of eggs she laid near the back corner of our mailbox's plastic red insert. The egg sac is a white, fuzzy sphere about the size of a small pea. The cocoon surrounding it is white and formless, like a bit of drifted snow lodged in the crease of the insert. When I pull the insert forward to examine the sac, I see that its gauzy interior is speckled with tiny black irregular dots that may be hatched spiderlings, though they do not appear to move.

How surprised she must have been to discover that the dark, empty, out-of-the-way place she chose on a Sunday or a postal holiday or some no-mail day in which to lay her eggs was, in fact, a way station in the vast national web of communications—and a moveable platform at that. But then, she herself may have arrived on the box through a kind of arachnid air mail known as ballooning, that common method of dispersal where young spiderlings release multiple strands of webbing and are wafted on gossamer parachutes to new habitats by autumn winds.

She is a brown, hairy spider with a body about five-eighths

of an inch long; at first glance I thought she was probably some kind of common wolf spider. But when I looked through my *Golden Guide to Spiders and Their Kin*, the body patterning and her position on top of the egg sac resembled that of a wandering spider (*Zora spinimana*), a member of the spider family Ctenidae. This group, however, is tropical and subtropical, and it is unlikely one of them would still be active in an exposed metal box this late in the New England year.

Each weekday, through the warm first half of October, the colder days that followed, and the first wet dark days of November, I would open up the box, pull out the insert to retrieve the mail, and find her there, on alert, poised on her "toes"—though whether for defense or flight is uncertain. She seems not to be of the family Thermopylae, an unquestioning defender willing to give her life to protect her egg sac. Once I prodded her gently with my finger and she dashed to the very back corner, pausing by a small drainage hole there, as if she would squeeze down through it if I advanced on her. I couldn't imagine what she would defend the sac from in there: ants? snakes? a mouse? perfume samples?

She is doomed, yet she is steadfast. Why do we admire that so? The last few mornings have had the edge of winter on them, the touch of frost that kills light things. The other day, when I opened the box, I thought she was dead. She was draped over the egg sac cluster like a fallen soldier, her body contracted and still. But she held on tenaciously to the threaded bed beneath her, and, after a few minutes in the weak afternoon sun that fell upon her, she came back to life.

This morning she was again completely torpid, which allowed me to remove the liner and get a closer look at her in the sun. The cephalothorax, or front half, appeared light yellow with dark brownish stripes, but her long hairy legs were arched over her abdomen, obscuring the body markings there. I caught sight of one poppyseed eye shining in the sun, but I could not make out the eye pattern. (Spiders usually have eight simple eyes, variously arranged, whose patterns are used identify families.) Oddly, a small dwarf spider, no bigger than a sesame seed, rolled with alacrity across the back of the box liner.

The other day I asked my friend Eric Edwards about these mailbox spiders. Eric is a poet and amateur arachnologist, but what gives him special knowledge about this group of spiders is that he is also a full-time rural mail carrier in the Upper Cape town of Mashpee. In fact, with his father, Robert Edwards, a research associate at the nearby Woods Hole Oceanographic Institution, he has published two scientific papers on mailbox spiders.* The shelf in front of his sorting case in the post office is piled with plastic film cartridges in which he collects his specimens, a fact about which his postal colleagues seem to be both aware and unperturbed.

Eric has collected over 1,250 individuals, representing over 200 species of spiders, from the 350 to 400 mailboxes on his route during every month of the year. Many of these species are only seasonal, with the number of species peaking, as one might expect, during the summer months. Most are also commonly found in nearby natural habitats, such as fields, understory bushes, and on the trunks and foliage of common oaks and conifers. At least nine of the species collected, however, have been found *only* on or in the mailboxes, suggesting perhaps that some spiders may be becoming uniquely adapted to these artificial environments. It might be interesting to compare the pools of spider species in towns that have rural delivery, like Mashpee, with those in other towns that don't, like Truro. Also, one wonders, are spiders more common in mailboxes that are only seasonally active? Do people with spiders in their boxes get more or less mail

*Edwards R.L., Edwards E.H.: Spiders (Araneae) associated with rural delivery mailboxes, Mashpee, Massachusetts. *Entomological News* 1991; 102:137–149; Behavior and niche selection by mailbox spiders. *The Journal of Arachnology* 1997; 25:20–30.

than those without? Do the spiders ever get mail themselves, the way, say, Socks the Presidential Cat does? ("CONGRA-TULATIONS MS. GLADICOSA PULCHRA — YOU MAY HAVE ALREADY WON TEN MILLION FLIES!")

The mailbox spider is dead, and in death I can see more clearly who she is. Last Saturday I saw that she had left one of her legs on the egg sac (a rear one, it turned out—torn off by a piece of mail being inserted?), and was hunched, shrunken, and crabbed up with cold in a back corner. I thought she was dead then, but she arched back into protective life, running over to the sac when I prodded her with a pencil. But yesterday she was truly dead, and I brought her inside, along with the liner and the sac.

We have had a warm spell over the weekend, with temperatures rising near to sixty degrees. Three crocuses bloomed in front of the house. Having endured the first light frosts, it is almost as if she hung on, only to let go in this stretch of unseasonable warmth, perhaps thinking spring had come round again. She is, I can see clearly now, a funnel weaver, family Agelenidae, one of those who spread their dewy webs, or "fairy handkerchiefs," across the grass on summer mornings. She seems to match pretty closely the picture of the grass spider, *Agelenopsis* sp., in my guide. Eric's list of mailbox spiders, in fact, includes two species of this genus, *A. pennsylvanicus* and *A. potteri*. Both of these are listed as seasonal, and "appear briefly in late summer and early fall as adult females and deposit egg sacs in the mailbox." My guess is that she was a particularly hardy or stubborn *A. pennsylvanicus*, which Eric has found as late as October. "In fall," my guide says, "the female deposits a disc-shaped egg sac in a crevice, then dies—often while still clinging to the egg sac."

I can also see now that what I thought might be small

hatchlings in the sac webbing are just flecks of debris, or perhaps spider feces. The spherical white pea of the sac remains intact under the net of webbing. Later in the day I will replace it and the liner in the mailbox, to see what might be delivered in the spring. Since spider hatchlings are often cannibalistic, I will also put the spider body back on top of the sac, so that her progeny may feed on her when they emerge.

I find I miss the daily encounter with this opportunistic arachnid, this bit of wildness inhabiting official government property. Given that the Postal Service is now honoring comic strip characters, movie monsters, and entertainment celebrities on its stamps, perhaps it wouldn't be too much of a stretch to suggest they some day issue a series commemorating these mailbox residents. Eric could given them a wide list to choose from.

"This Living Hand..."

I spent most of the morning in a Zodiac inflatable launch in Loagy Bay in South Wellfleet trying to help shepherd a stranded pilot whale out into Wellfleet Harbor. The whale— probably an adult male, given its size of eighteen feet or so— had first been spotted near Mill Hill island about 7 A.M. on an incoming tide. By the time we arrived, shortly before nine, it had grounded itself on a ledge of high marsh near the Lieutenant Island bridge.

When Ed Lyman, rescue coordinator for Provincetown's Center for Coastal Studies, arrived with the Zodiac, it was just about high tide, and we knew we had to work fast. With Phil Fox, a shellfisherman who lives in the area, Ed and I motored out to the whale, which was lying on its side, breathing regularly, about one-huncred-fifty yards offshore. We nudged it off the marsh and into the deep channel where, on the advice of Phil, who knows these waters well, we decided to drive it north and out through Loagy Bay, rather than south through the narrow channel under the bridge.

With little difficulty we managed to herd it out into the

deep waters of Wellfleet Harbor in less than an hour, where, under its own steam, it plunged vigorously away from us, heading directly toward Great Island. "Take a left!" Ed shouted after it, and we headed back. We were pleased with our efforts, but knew, as with all such strandings, the ultimate outcome was unknowable. We were back at the dock by eleven-thirty.

I went home and worked until three, when I debated whether to use the rest of the afternoon light chopping wood or getting some oysters. I decided on oysters. Although, like most Wellfleetians, I usually go to Chipman's Cove, where the bulk of the noncommercial oysters are, I decided on a whim—perhaps because I felt some need of solitude to further digest the day's events—to go to Area 2, south of the breakwater on Indian Neck Point.

There were no other cars in the shell-littered parking lot when I pulled in about three-thirty, and no other footprints on the smooth sloping beach where the tide stood, some two hundred yards out. The sun was already settling down into a thin wispy nest of spun clouds over Great Beach Hill, and the wind was a mere breeze from the west-northwest.

Oysters are scarce here, compared to the midden-like beds of the cove, but so are oyster gatherers. The shellfish here tend to be found in scattered clumps of two, three, or four, attached to small rock holdfasts, sometimes trailing dark green mops of dead-man's-fingers seaweed, which drag them shoreward in onshore blows. At this time of the year, though, it is still relatively easy to gather one's ten-quart limit.

I walked out to the tide line where the clumps were most numerous, lifting them up with my clam rake, prying them off the holdfasts with a screwdriver, knocking off the undersized seed. They were the thick, plump, restaurant-quality oysters of early winter, not the elongated, anorexic mollusks one is reduced to harvesting later in the season. A small scat-

tering of gulls waited patiently along the tide line. Not subject to the Town of Wellfleet Shellfishing Regulations, they
picked up the seed oysters I discarded and carried them to
the parking lot where they dropped and broke them open on
the asphalt.

I had chosen the right spot for my mood. I enjoyed seeing
the commercial shellfishermen on the other side of the stone
breakwater, each of us in his own sphere. Beyond them the
town's signature outline was being transformed by the dying
sunlight, surmounted by the glowing white steeple of the
Congo Church. To the south, the first of the returning fishing
boats steamed up the channel toward the wharf. I walked
along the smooth sand, picking up nuggets of shellfish strewn
like dragon's teeth at the edge of the outgoing tide.

I had gathered about two-thirds of a bucket when I was
suddenly aware of heavy breathing over my shoulder. How
long it had been there I don't know, but it was at once manifest, unexpected, and familiar. It was whale breath. I turned
and looked out over the water. In a few seconds my gaze was
directed by another loud intake to a familiar shape, long and
black, with a single tapered fluke rising up out of the water
like a black marker.

The whale lay on its right side about a hundred yards
inshore of the green channel marker, just as it had lain on the
marsh that morning. (For some reason, all of the live stranded
pilot whales I have ever seen on open beaches were resting on
their right sides. Why should this be?) I greeted the sight as
an old inevitability, some ordained correction to our human
desires applied to the world at large. I suppose I was struck
by the irony of our being thus reunited, but not by the occurrence itself, which I had somewhere half-anticipated since
this morning.

I did not drop my bucket and run toward the car to sum-
mon help. Rather, I kept gathering oysters, sizing up and

rationalizing the situation in my mind. I looked at my watch. It was now 4 P.M., dead low. The whale's situation was at its nadir. By the time Ed could get here with the boat again, assuming I could reach him, it would be dark. The tide would have risen to the point where, if the whale had not become too exhausted, injured, or disoriented, it would be able to swim back out into the channel on its own.

The other alternative, as I saw it, was to mount a rescue effort in the dark, try to take the whale into deep water in the inner harbor and somehow contain it for the night and assess its situation in the morning.

Perhaps I have encountered too many stranded whales in my days here. It is not that I have become too inured to their plight to care anymore; rather, I have become confounded by the variables and unknowns in their equations. Who could say that the whale was not doing what was best for it without our aid or interference, or that it was not resting instead of stranding? Truthfully, what I was most drawn to do was to walk out and be with it as darkness descended; but this, too, seemed to be denied me. It lay in at least three feet of water, far above my knee boots. I was not willing to endure a soaking in freezing water for some dubious communion with this animal, or spurious offering of companionship in its isolation, or even a positive identification of it as this morning's whale, which seemed all but certain anyhow. No, I would spend a few more minutes gathering my oysters, then go ashore and call the Center and let them decide what, if anything, to do.

I went back to my work, but the breathing continued, loud and proximate over cold water in the calm air—the explosive exhale followed by a sudden intake—until finally I put my rake and pail on the upper beach, still several dozen oysters short of my limit, and walked out toward the whale, curious how far I could or would go.

The sunset had settled into a smoky intensity over Great Island, and overhead the first evening stars had pricked out of a clear, dark blue sky. Surprisingly, the water remained little more than a foot deep as I slogged out toward the gleaming wet form. I could see now it was pointed directly toward shore, flexing its great body to raise its head every ten seconds or so for another breath.

I reached it just as the waters and the whale's own skin began to swim with the oily acrylic colors of the sunset's afterglow. The whale, apparently, had wallowed out a hollow in the sand a couple of feet deep, providing it with a pool that kept it moist and largely buoyant. Deliberate or not, this at least protected it from desiccation and suffocation from its own weight. There seemed no doubt that this was our morning's animal. It was the same length, and though I could not see its right fluke with its distinguishing rips, it had the narrow triple rakes on its right flank that Ed had noticed. Moreover, it *sounded* and *felt* like the same animal. Though trapped in this depression of its own making, it did not seem in obvious distress. At regular intervals of eight-to-twelve seconds it raised its globular head until the intake valve was just above the water line and, with remarkable efficiency, exhaled a great burst of air and vapor and gulped another intake of breath before lowering the great head into the pool again, where it rested, if not comfortably, at least quietly between exertions.

I took off one glove and put my hand on its cheek, rubbery and cold to the touch, and it responded instantly, thrashing its entire length, not desperately, or as if trying to escape, but more as if shrugging off an unfamiliar and unwelcome presence, as a cow would a blue-bottle fly. I removed my hand at once, not wanting to cause it any unnecessary exertions. Its exposed left eye was squinched tightly shut, with a thick, sticky, cloudy fluid streaming out of it. I assumed it had closed it for protection against sand and/or drying out. Nor could I expect it would receive any comfort or encouragement from beholding a vision of my bearded shape looming over it.

I walked around the body, looking for any signs of injury, but saw none. When I got to the blowhole, a great *whoosh* of warm air hit me in the face. I have experienced whale breath before and was struck again by its clean, fresh, ozone-like smell. But this time I was impressed even more by its warmth in that frigid air. Our scientific knowledge has informed us that whales are fellow warm-blooded mammals, but sheathed as they are in their great protective shells of blubber and rubber-like skin, it is hard to feel it. Blood will do it, red and steaming to the touch, but even more, the sudden, unexpected feel of warm, living respiration bathing my face, like a lover's breath, jolted my sympathies and my sense of helplessness. What can we say, or sing, to a whale in its isolation to comfort it? Where is the research that will tell us how to alleviate two and a half tons of loneliness?

So I stood there, doing nothing, but loathe to leave. The returning boats were now coming in with running lights, just this side of the buoy, less than a hundred yards from us. They must have seen us in the dying light, this curious sight of a grounded whale and a sentinel figure, but they showed no sign of recognition. Perhaps they, too, had seen too many whales, or knew nothing could be done. In any case, they had fish to unload and families to return to.

The boats' passage stirred the whale, sensing the low thrumming of their motors, to new and useless exertions. I reached out and stroked its cheek again, hoping it might somehow sense at least a sympathetic presence. In the end though, it was the whale who provided me with the only tangible comfort out there on that wet, dark plain. I stood in the lee of its long body, using its bulk as a breakwater to keep the boats' wakes from washing over the tops of my boots. As the light vanished and stars peppered the sky, I took off my other wet glove and warmed my cold hands in the stream of the whale's intermittent, living breaths.

Nothing But Net

A place like Cape Cod rarely hands you what you expect. This is a truism I have learned to accept over the years, though not always to anticipate. It is especially true at the Cape's outer edges, and even more so in winter.

One day last January I decided to take my first walk along Chatham's new South Beach, at the elbow of the Cape's crooked arm. A dozen or so years ago this beach was part of a continuous, narrow, twelve-mile-long barrier beach that stretched south from the mainland to the north, enclosing and protecting Pleasant Bay and Chatham Center. The beach was dotted with dozens of cottages and, in summer, with hundreds of beach buggies.

Then, in 1987, a series of vicious winter storms severed the fragile dune line. The break gradually widened into a gaping mile-long breach that has exposed Pleasant Bay to the open Atlantic and the full force of its winter storms. Among other effects, this break turned the southern half of the barrier beach into an island, significantly altered the ecology of the bay, provided a new, if somewhat treacherous, access to the sea for Chatham's fishing fleet, and has claimed over a half-dozen houses on the mainland shore and threatened dozens more.

Then, about five years ago, South Beach, as the new barrier island was now called, did a strange thing. It began to bend landward at its northern end and eventually attached itself to the mainland shore just below the Chatham Lighthouse, creating an elephant-trunk appendage to the mainland. Few predicted this development, and even fewer expected this improbable geological formation to last. But it seems to have stabilized, at least for now, and in so doing has unexpectedly provided pedestrian access to a new municipal beach some five miles long. Formerly accessible only by boat, South Beach has now become a mecca for summer bathers, shorebirders, and winter beach strollers.

My plan was to walk to the southern end of this beach, where hundreds of harbor seals winter over and the southernmost breeding colony of gray seals in the world whelps its pups in mid-winter. That was my plan, but, as I said, the Cape rarely hands you what you expect.

For one thing, I had prepared for a typical winter's day, when the wind on the outer beach can insert itself like knives through the tiniest crevices of your clothes and foul-weather gear, where stinging, blowing sand often forces you to walk backwards on the beach, and where you remove your binoculars from their protective case at your peril. Instead, it proved to be a "January thaw" day: warm, calm, and remarkably clear with temperatures in the high fifties. So I carried only a light jacket, my binoculars, and a small backpack containing a bird guide, gloves, a change of socks in case I got my feet wet, and a thermos of tea. Given such inviting conditions I also decided to take my poodle, Ollie, along for company.

We set off from the base of the steps below the lighthouse and headed out on the curving arc of beach that forms the south boundary of the new inlet. The breach, though wide, was shallow and full of foaming rips and shoals, and beyond it the open sea shone in restless splendor. Inside the breach, however, the water was as placid as a lagoon. Low, curling waves rolled along the sands' edge, and each break of the wave was followed by a spangle of glinting light racing after it along the wet swash like a comet's tail.

The tide was low, and to my right rose the tall, slanting muscular beach of pure clean sand that wind and sea have built up in the past few years. It rose like a huge desert dune, sheltering us from the northwest breeze and blocking from sight everything that lay beyond it: the grassy dunes, the wide tidal flats, the glacial bluffs of the mainland, and the waters of Nantucket Sound far to the west.

In its young muscularity this beach could be the shoulder of Maushop, the giant of native Wampanoag myth, whose pipe-smoking was said to be the source of the prevalent Cape Cod fogs, whose tossings and turnings on his bed of the Outer Cape formed the valleys and dunes there, and who, when he emptied his moccasins of sand into Nantucket Sound, created the islands of Nantucket and Martha's Vineyard. I have always liked these local creation myths, for they seem to reflect the human scale and contours of this gentle and approachable land.

Ollie scampered up and over the crest of the beach out of sight for a minute or two, then plunged back down to the water's edge. There was little for him to chase; even the winter flocks of dunlins seemed to be elsewhere. Occasionally I also walked up to the crest, where I could see dozens of winter soft-shell clammers in the distance on the wide inner flats. Kneeling in that immemorial pose of clam-diggers, they dug into the wet black mud with their short-handled clam rakes, extracting the fragile, bluish-white shellfish. They kept their backs to the wind, working their way methodically forward with the intentness and uniformity of a flock of dowitchers feeding in August.

Spaced along the top of the beach for the first mile or so were a series of odd stacks: tepee-shaped structures constructed of driftwood poles, old lobster pots, plastic bottles, beach grass, ragged sheets of foam insulation—anything, it seemed, that came to hand. These were not the familiar, ad-libbed beach sculptures I often find on the outer beach in summer, creative assemblies of random finds erected by beachcombers. Despite the eclectic nature of their materials, these structures were of roughly uniform size and shape and were regularly placed every few hundred feet along the top of the foredunes. I guessed that they had been recently built by fishermen and their families as improvised landmarks, aids for locating the treacherous approach to the new break-through channel.

We approached one of the largest of these stacks, a skeleton-like structure perhaps ten-feet tall and bristling everywhere with beach grass. It brought to mind those hairy, man-shaped wicker structures that the ancient Celts constructed during the winter solstice, and on which, it is said, human sacrifices were sometimes burnt. So eerily humanoid did it appear that Ollie began barking furiously at it.

The poles that formed its skeleton were crossed at the middle and cinched together with green polypropylene rope and horizontal sticks. On the top was a crown of sticks that had been placed in such a way as to suggest an osprey nest—an unlikely possibility, I thought. But when I climbed onto the girdling rope and peered over the edge of the top, I found, in the center of the loose bowl of sticks, clumps of matted fur and fiber such as these fish-hawks line their nests with, suggesting that in such a setting even human structures are appropriated for ends we never intend.

As we progressed down the beach, its smooth, uniform slope was broken only by an occasional scallop shell or a buried length of an old hemp hawser. The offshore shoals were disappearing, and the surge of the open ocean began to push along the outer shore. The sand here was fine, wind-distilled, and compacted by the waves, so that it provided an unexpectedly firm base for walking. Within an hour I estimated that we were nearly two miles below the lighthouse, more than a third of the way down the length of the beach. With luck, I thought, we would reach the seals before lunch.

Just as I was beginning to congratulate myself on what good time we were making, I saw a large, dark bird sitting near the crest of the beach, facing the water. It looked about the size of a goose, and had a long, narrow, sharp beak. It was a loon.

Loons are common winter visitors here, often seen off-shore from September to May. Bereft of their striking checkered breeding plumage and haunting repertoire of breeding songs, they nonetheless bring a bit of northern summer lakes to our winter beaches. But loons rarely come ashore, especially in winter. Their legs and feet are not made for walking, and they are very awkward and vulnerable on land.

A trail of webbed foot marks, beginning about halfway up the beach and leading up to the loon, indicated that it had come ashore only a few hours ago on the last falling tide. We approached it from below and, as we got close, the loon began jabbing out at us with its long, sharp bill and serpentine neck. Ollie started barking in his ambivalent, fight-flight mode, and I called him back, more for his own protection than the bird's.

There appeared nothing obviously wrong with the loon, but I knew I could not examine it further until I leashed the dog somewhere. There was a large piece of driftwood projecting from the very top of the beach about ten yards from the bird. I shortened Ollie's leash, hooked the handle over the projecting spike of wood, and began walking back toward the loon.

As I did the bird flopped awkwardly several yards down toward the water, then stopped. Now I could see that it was hogtied in some fashion with monofilament gill netting, which it had probably gotten entangled in while diving for food in the offshore shallows. Of all the deadly legacies with which we have laced the ocean, gill netting is one of the most insidious. In many offshore areas, lost or discarded netting lines the ocean floor for thousands of square yards. Nonbiodegradable, these nets continue to catch and kill fish and other marine life long after the boats that fished with them have left, long after the men that set them have themselves died.

I took out of my knapsack a pair of thick leather gloves (without which I'm not sure I would have risked that beak). I slipped them on, circled down below the loon again, then walked up slowly toward it, speaking gently and extending my hands. When I got within a few feet it suddenly jabbed out at me again, pecking my hand and my leg, but the entangled netting restricted the force of its blows.

It began uttering the loon distress or warning cry, those short little leaping laughs that I associate so much with their northern breeding lakes. Here it seemed foreign and anomalous. I opened the small blade of my pocket knife, quickly circled behind the bird, knelt down beside it, grabbed the scissoring beak with my left hand, and held it shut. Immediately the loon began trying to row away from me with its wings. I twisted its neck around so that I could hold its head down with the same hand as I held its beak with, leaving my knife hand free.

It worked. The bird subsided, glaring at me with one round red eye. I saw that a rat's nest of thin, light-green monofilament was wrapped at least a dozen times around its left leg. I began cutting the strands as carefully as I could, grateful that I had just sharpened the blades last week, for the netting was tougher than I thought. The loon, understandably enough, started to struggle again. I had to press its head down harder and cursed softly, wondering if I was inadvertently twisting its esophagus, and thus cutting off its air supply in my efforts to free it.

From above us Ollie barked on his leash, then settled down, digging himself a hollow in the sand. I continued cutting. The binding strands seemed endless, but finally I sliced the last one and released the bird's leg. It was then I saw that that was only the beginning of its entanglement. More filaments wound around its body, looped under one wing, and circled its throat. Some lengths of crinkled line dangled from its serrated mouth like pieces of green dental floss, likely caught there when the loon had tried to bite itself free.

With its leg now loose, the loon renewed its efforts to escape. To keep it restrained, I straddled it from behind, clasping its feathered body between my knees. At least in this position I could hold its neck in a straighter position and so avoid strangling it. I pulled off my right glove with my teeth so that I could trace with my fingers the lines of filament beneath its dark feathers and cut them without injuring the creature. It occurred to me that to anyone coming upon us now it would look as if I were clumsily trying to stab the bird to death, or worse, attempting to sodomize it in some grotesque reversal of the Leda and the swan myth.

At last I managed to cut all the visible strands away and to tug the crinkled lines out of the loon's mouth. I released it and stood back, wondering, for the first time, what its actual physical state was. If it was uninjured, I expected it to head immediately for the water. To my surprise and discomfiture, it turned and, extending its wings, began to come at me with glowing eyes and darting beak. I stumbled backwards, nonplussed. I had, of course, been thinking of myself as its savior; but obviously, and not unjustly, the loon regarded me as a clear representative of the species that had inflicted this outrage and threat upon its person.

But its clumsiness on land protected me. After several feints that fell short of their mark, it turned again and made a series of awkward wind-and-leg hops down to the water's edge, where it stopped. Was something wrong? Had I missed some entangling strands? Would I, please God no, have to try to catch it again to see? But it seemed that it was just disoriented, lightly shocked, perhaps, by its ordeal. After a half-minute or so, it made a few more clumsy hops seaward, like some large, avian rabbit, then stopped once more.

But now I had no doubts. I knew that the loon would shortly move again down to the water, that it would go in and be all right. I knew it with the surging confidence of my successful effort. I knew it with the calm assurance of a basketball player who knows, even before the nubbled surface of the ball leaves his fingertips, that the arc has already been drawn and that he has shot nothing but net. I was, I realized, *pumped.*

And sure enough, this time the loon hopped down to the edge of the low, curling waves, looked out for a few seconds, waddled into the gentle swash, and then, as soon as it felt its native medium gently lift it, shot underwater, its powerful pinkish feet pulsing it along. It remained submerged for over a minute, then, nearly a hundred yards out, the loon broke water, cried out, and immediately dove again. I echoed its triumph, and Ollie, still tied to the driftwood, mindlessly echoed mine.

I walked up and freed him, and the two of us set off again down the beach, into the face of the low winter sun, flushed with importance, not looking back.

Sometimes I Live in Town

Sometimes I like to pretend I live in town. I almost did once, or like to think I did. It was several years ago, when Kathy and I were looking for a year-round place to rent or buy. Shortly after Christmas, a friend mentioned an old house in the center of town that might be for sale. Though the asking price was somewhat beyond our financial limits, we went to look at it. It was on a narrow side street just off Main Street, and we fell in love with it at once. It was a vintage three-quarter Cape, a sweet old house on a quiet cross street of sweet old houses, with a central chimney, a large yard, and a spreading Norway maple tree shading the house. It sat at the top of a low arch that the street makes, facing toward town. To its immediate left was another large antique Cape that I was told used to be the summer home of one of my old college professors. It seemed propitious.

The current owner had once lived in the house but had moved to the West Coast a few years ago. He had been renting it out, though at the moment it was empty. When we contacted him, he was initially noncommittal, but arranged for us to get the key to the house. It was even better inside than out. The interior architecture was largely unaltered, retaining much of its original paneling and trim, and it had a large bright front room, an open keeping room, a kitchen-bedroom ell with wonderful wooden counters painted by Cape Cod folk-artist Peter Hunt, two downstairs fireplaces, and a pair of capacious rooms upstairs that had never been finished.

Still, we wondered if we could afford it. For one thing, it had never been properly insulated and the only source of heat was a coal stove. In all likelihood it would require a new septic system. The exterior had been sadly neglected and would need a new shingle roof, clapboard siding, some new windows, and possibly some sill work. The front steps were completely missing, and several piles of bricks, which looked as if they had been there for years, sat in front of the door in anticipation of a restoration project that had never gotten under way. A friend who had bought another old house just a few doors down from this one some fifteen years ago warned me, "You want to continue being a writer? Then don't buy an old house. You can't serve two masters."

But all these potential problems and drawbacks, not to mention the owner's diffidence, were minor details in the face of a sudden overwhelming conviction that this was the house I wanted to live in. I had never really desired to live in an old house, but, for some reason, I was consumed with the idea. This was the house I was meant to live in, that I *would* live in. The small front room could be Kathy's study. I would turn one of the upstairs rooms into a temporary shop while I finished off the other gable room to be my study. I would make the deep kneewalls into closets, plant the garden at the back of the yard, set up a hammock under the maple tree...all this before I had even left the house during that first January visit.

We waited for the next several weeks to hear again from the owner. In the meantime I began trying to figure out how we could afford it, realizing, with some trepidation, that I was prepared to put myself in debt up to my ears for this house, if necessary. I also began to haunt the house at every opportunity, peering through its windows, daring the neighbors to call a policeman, who would show up and ask me what I was doing there. I would simply reply, "Why, I'm going to *live* here!"

At night I would stroll up the side street to the house, passing beneath the single street lamp across from it. It was a motion-activated lamp that switched on as I came within its charmed circle, as if it were lighting up just for me. I began to observe my future neighbors, smiling at them as I passed and thinking how I would get to know them intimately, their quirks and habits, over the years. I will grow old here, I mused, and a bit odd, just like them.

I drove into town early in the morning, parking in the side yard of the house, and walked down to Main Street, just to know what it would feel like to go into town every day for the paper and a cup of coffee. As with the house itself, I had not realized before that I wanted to live in town. I had spent my first quarter-century on Cape Cod living as far from other people and other houses as I could; yet now I found myself increasingly drawn to the idea of village life, of settled streets and settled neighbors, of its daily comings and goings and the patterns of its human life.

Moreover, it was not just any town I wanted to live in, but this one. If this was the right house, then Wellfleet was the right town. Its narrow, tree-shaded streets had always appealed to me. Lined with old Capes, substantial Greek Revivals, sea captain's mansions, and a few apricot-colored summer cottages with gingerbread trim, blue shutters, and spare white interiors, the streets possessed a quintessential New England loveliness.

Still, many other town centers on the Cape had preserved their visual charm. Wellfleet's was uncommon, though, for it had remained a real center, fully functioning, not just an historical facade. During the summer its Main Street, like others

here, fluffed out with a variety of art galleries, trendy clothing stores, pricey restaurants, ice cream shops, and other seasonal enterprises. But between Labor Day and Columbus
Day these estival accretions gradually withered and blew
away, leaving a classic village Main Street of civic buildings,
year-round residences, and modest, locally-owned businesses.
These included the public library, a florist shop, two book
stores, a small auto garage, a funeral home, a local bank,
three churches, a restaurant, a liquor store, a pharmacy, a
grocery store, a real estate office, the Wellfleet Historical
Society, and the Town Hall. On one corner lived a pair of
musicians, with a cello-shaped sign outside their house that
offered, in intriguing sequence, "WEDDINGS—RECEPTIONS
—INSTRUCTION."

But these homey, small-town components hardly accounted for the almost-visceral passion I had acquired to live
here and nowhere else. One of the things that appealed to me
about the town was its imperfections. Although most of the
establishments along Main and Commercial Streets kept up
a well-maintained and freshly painted face for the tourists,
Wellfleet had not yet become so self-conscious a resort community that it could not tolerate a certain run-down and
unkempt element. Especially on its side streets, many of the
houses sported peeling paint, deteriorating porches, rotting
trellises, and worse. There was at least one true derelict off
West Main Street, and I was gratified to see a genuine trailer
home bordering one of the church parking lots—a rarity
under most current Cape Cod zoning laws. My house (as I
had already begun thinking of it) would fit right in—at least
until I got around to fixing it up.

I even took a perverse pleasure in the town's reputation
for eccentricity. During the nineteenth century, Wellfleetians
were referred to by other Cape Codders as "Bible-faces" for
their excessive devotion to reading Scripture, particularly
among the Methodists. Early in this century, the populace

was somewhat notorious for its inbreeding, though it probably had no more than most other rural towns. When I told
an old friend of mine, a Cape native from a neighboring
town, that I was moving to Wellfleet, she said, "Oh, that's
where all the idiots come from. It's improved some lately, I
guess, with all those artists moving there. But it was always a
backwards town."

Yes—backwards. Different. Peculiar. I wanted my town to
be a bit crazy, crooked in its nature, like its old lanes and
wildly curving streets. I was delighted one day to encounter,
in the front yard of an old house on one of the side streets, a
live peacock feeding on the lawn.

Even the church bells were offbeat. The ones in the steeple
of the Congregational Church (or the "Congo Church" as it
was locally referred to) rang the hours and half hours in a
code that baffled newcomers. When it was one o'clock, they
rang two. When it was seven o'clock, they rang four. When it
was noon, they rang eight. More than once I observed visitors, nonplussed at hearing the bells, looking at their own
watches, first in puzzlement, then with a condescending
shake of the head as if concluding that Wellfleet was yet
another small town that couldn't keep its clocks running
properly—unaware that they were listening to the only public clock in the world that rings ship's time.*

As the winter wore on, we received no definite reply from
the house's owner. Still, my faith that we would eventually
possess the house on Cross Street was unshaken. I had
already taken up residence there in my mind, and physical
occupation would follow shortly. I had the faith of a true
lover who knows that it is only a matter of time before he
wears away the obstacles and objections of his beloved and
the world.

---

*Ship's time is a repeating four-hour cycle using eight bells; e.g., one
o'clock equals two bells, two o'clock equals four bells, three o'clock
equals six bells, and four o'clock equals eight bells, with an extra bell
added on the half hour.

I continued imagining, and even practicing, what it would be like to be an actual resident. I took out a library card and an auto insurance policy at the local agency. I stopped in regularly for lunch at the Lighthouse Restaurant, bought occasional flowers at Kelley's, and beer at the Wellfleet Spirits Shoppe. I opened a charge account at Lema's Grocery where Charlie, the singing butcher, held court behind the delicatessen counter. Charlie had moved to Cape Cod from Glasgow in 1972, and in his rich Scotch burr he sang along with Sinatra and Tony Bennett on the radio that was always playing at the back of the meat department. He flirted openly with the woman customers, who all seemed to love it. I think some of them came in for it.

I began filling my prescriptions at the Wellfleet Pharmacy, a small independent drugstore whose owners decorated the plate-glass windows with changing, seasonal scenes. One day I bought a memo pad there, and a tall, gangly, curly-headed boy behind the cash register took my money. "Is that all, sir?" he asked. "That'll be seventy-two cents, sir—which means you get *three shiny new pennies* back! Have a good day, sir!" I smiled at his extravagant courtesy and put one of those three shiny pennies into the old weight machine that stands by the door.

I spent time watching the local teenagers hanging out in the parking lot next to the Town Hall, or on the small green before it, shaded by a large maple to which, I was told, a local woman had chained herself a few years ago when the selectmen proposed cutting down the tree to create a pullover space for the twice-daily bus that stops there on its way to Provincetown. Younger kids sat on the benches or played hackysack on the grass, while a somewhat older group, mostly boys dressed in black with reversed caps, and a few girls, gathered in the parking lot around a battered black sedan whose speakers pumped out rap and hip-hop. I liked their townie energy, all flailing arms and mock fighting, their noise and display an expression of that mildly rebellious, small-town camaraderie of limited options and baffled desire, as if they were taking their inarticulate grievances to the municipal authorities.

One day, on the other side of the street, in front of the Lighthouse Restaurant, I passed by a gaggle of four men (one of whom I recognized as a local selectmen) as they stood looking across at the kids. "Well," one remarked with practiced sarcasm, "how do you like the new Town Recreation Area?" and received equally practiced comments in reply.

I loitered on the periphery of their group, mentally rehearsing for the time when I, too, would become An Official Main Street Observer, espousing different attitudes or politics, perhaps, but standing with my own group of cronies, one of the old farts of the town, expounding on what was right and wrong with this microcosm of the universe.

Sometimes, when in town, I walked down Bank Street, a short steep street that leads from Main Street down to Duck Creek Harbor, once the commercial center of the town when commerce was primarily by boat. Here a narrow wooden footbridge, known as Uncle Tim's Bridge, crosses the creek to Cannon Hill. Cannon Hill is a small mound of glacial deposits, dotted with pitch pines and surrounded by salt marsh, used by local residents as an informal park. The vegetation of this marsh island is sparse and fragile, and the hill has a worn and overused look, with several severely eroded gullies scarring its sides. But it offers a commanding prospect of the town, a place from which to stand and gather it all in in one sweep of the eye.

One afternoon in November I drove into town to get something at the lumberyard, which borders Duck Creek. It was an unusually warm day and the town was enveloped in

fog, the tide out, and the sere marshes and dark grey mud-
flats of Duck Creek exposed and redolent. I walked across
Uncle Tim's Bridge up the scarred and tattered flanks of
Cannon Hill. From the top the outline of the town was obscured in the middle distance. This time of year the pleasure-
boat moorings and wharf fingers at the marina were hauled
out, and with its small fleet of weathered draggers, trawlers
and oyster boats, the harbor had a pleasing working look to
it. A fast tide was beginning to course through the old railroad dike, filling the marsh, and the mist-hidden steeple of
the Congo Church chimed seven bells: 3:30.

To the north I could make out a flock of some ducks pad-
dling and feeding at a bend in the upper creek. A large bird
flew from the east over the trees and marsh toward the
church. I recognized it as a harrier, not from any visible markings or even its shape, which was obscured, but from its
wavering, feathery flight, so seemingly unstable, so unlike the
steady, imperturbable flight of gulls, who always seem in perfect agreement with the winds they fly through. The harrier's
flight by contrast appears nervous, uncertain, as if the hawk
were about to be overturned by each slight shift in wind or
position, though in fact it is superbly fashioned for shifting,
low flight and gliding among the dunes and marsh grass, and
must therefore fly that way, no matter where it is, never having learned or needed to soar.

So, too, I knew the ducks in the creek as black ducks, even
before I caught the intermittent wink of silver wing-linings as
they flapped over the water. I knew their manner of congre-
gating like sheep, all beaks tending to point to a common center.

I knew these birds, I realized, not by appearance or field
marks so much as by gestalt, by long acquaintance and frequent meetings over many years, so that the recognition was
a fitting together of memory and image. This, I thought, is
the advantage of growing old in a place we know, with famil-

iar surroundings and familiar inhabitants. As our senses falter and dim, we continue to recognize the things by their more general form and motion, their distilled essence combined with our memory, just as we recognize instantly the rhythm and inflection of an old friend's voice, or her posture and walking gait, even when we can no longer make out her words or features at a distance.

This was the kind of belonging I had sought in the natural world for most of my time here on this narrow peninsula in the sea. Perhaps this longing I now felt to live *in town* was a reaction against all the years of trying to escape the human landscape, of forging my own personal vision of where I lived. Perhaps I was simply tired of making clearings and tracks for myself in life's "pathless woods" and yearned for settled streets and known neighbors at this point in my life.

I wondered, too, if my urban background might be reasserting itself with a long-buried need for communal life. Of course there were few apparent similarities between the working-class, polyglot suburb of Newark, New Jersey, where I was born, and this small and increasingly upscale seaside resort town. And yet I recognized, along Wellfleet's narrow New England streets, the same old trees, the same old houses, the same old garages and cluttered yards, the same density of settled community and daily platter of human interaction that I had known in childhood and that, perhaps without realizing it, I had come to long for again.

But I also began to suspect that the longing was deeper, more subjective, and more complex. I knew it must have something to do with the break-up of a thirty-year marriage and the subsequent uprooting from a house I had built and lived in for two decades, the profound physical and psychological dislocation of the next several years. I had a deep need to be *settled* again, rooted, unnomadic, yes—but I was looking for that stability now within structures made by others, for I had come to distrust deeply those of my own devising.

Once I spent a month in a small medieval town on the coast of Tuscany. Each morning I walked into the piazza and had espresso under the awnings of a cafe where Michelangelo had stayed for several weeks, purchasing marble from the nearby quarries of Carrara. Since the fourteenth century the lives of the people in that town had been marked and regulated by the tolling of the ancient bell tower. Every hour, the ringing of the bells scattered hundreds of pigeons out of the tower crevices and over the square, casting a momentary shadow of fluttering wings over the people and the buildings, until the bells stopped and the birds flew back into the tower and perched there until the next hour, when they would scatter again as they had for six hundred years.

Like the long-settled residents of that town, I yearned to participate and submerge my individual personality in the established rituals of this community, to place myself within ordained patterns that had predated and would outlast me, to be part of the daily and generational passing of its human life. What I wanted, it seemed, was nothing less than to live the rest of my life beneath the shadow of the Congo Church, walking the stations of the village streets like some Yankee monk, offering responses to the rhythm of those inscrutable ship's bells as they tolled out the canonical hours.

In the end we did not get the house. When I eventually pushed the owner for a decision, he proved terminally ambivalent about selling. Just as I had developed an irresistible need to establish ties in the town, so he, too, it seems, had an immovable reluctance to sever his own. In both cases it was a matter of subjective and irrational need, but his was rooted in an existing reality, and in the end I had to give it up.

The following year Kathy and I found a small house in

good repair, about a mile outside of town, that we could comfortably afford. It is a good house, with a pleasingly eccentric character, built by two artists about ten years ago, and we have grown to love it.

I have even come to acknowledge that buying the house in town would probably have been a practical and financial disaster. Aside from its obvious needs, I would no doubt have had to contend with a myriad of other concealed ills that old and unmaintained houses are heir to. Just the other day I spoke to a woman who is now renting the house year round. Her boy friend, she says, spends nearly all his spare time cutting and chopping wood to avoid the expense of the coal it takes to keep the house heated. "And even then," she said, "it's almost always cold in winter."

Still, for the first year or two, I occasionally experienced deep pangs of regret—for the house, yes, but even more, I think, for the missed chance of living in town. I was most vulnerable to these feelings in the fall, which was when we had first seen the house, but also perhaps because autumn has always been for me the season of loss and regret as well as new beginnings. Perhaps it was also because the town—the center, that is—is always at its best at this time of the year, especially in October, after Columbus Day, when the last real weekend of the season has come and gone, the crowds have left, the frivolous shops are all closed, and the clear light gives everything a more vivid edge, a deeper dimension of reality.

It was on such a day, about a year after we moved into our present house, that I went into town for a walk. It was a warm late-autumn afternoon, and yellow maple leaves were pasted to the wet sidewalks. The light slanted on the old houses. A man sat on a front step rubbing his dog like a scene from an Edward Hopper painting. Two young women passed me, talking about—what were they talking about? If I lived here and walked by this spot every day, I would know.

I passed the short cross street and looked up the lane. There was the house, crouched beneath its tall Norway maple, its beige gable peering out from behind the dark red clapboards of the house in front of it. I was suddenly struck by such unexpected regret, such longing, such a sense of missed rightness, that it was like being gut-punched without warning. It pushed through all the barriers of knowledge of why we could and should not have had it: its indecisive owner, all the necessary expenses, the constant upkeep, and so on. All this burned like dry leaves before the rekindled intensity of desire for this, the right house on the right part of the right road in the right town at the right time of my life. There had been no other like it. It was, simply, the right place, and I had lost it.

Of course I did not think those words then. What I actually thought was that I could spend years just learning to paint that view from Main Street up the gentle arching rise of the road toward the house peeking out from behind its neighbor. But that is always the keenest form of regret, when it takes the shape of sharp, specific, even trivial, unlived possibilities: watching snow softly limning the trees that line the street, or raindrops dancing on the asphalt just outside our front bedroom window, or the yard maple beginning to leaf out once again, seen through the small upstairs gable window partially blocked by the ell roof...

Over the past five years, the sharpness of regret has become blunted, or taken new forms; but like all profound desires, it abides and, whatever path our actual life takes, it remains part of who we are. And so, every fall, it seems, there comes a day when I find myself in town. The sky is a deep, deep blue, the maples along Main Street are catching red and yellow fire, the white clapboards of the old houses all seem freshly painted, the first brown fugitive flocks of cottonwood and locust leaves begin to scuttle along the pavement, and small clumps of old men stand on the sidewalk outside the Lighthouse Restaurant talking about how the town is going to hell in a handbasket. Then the life I think I might have had suddenly becomes more real than the one I do, and, for a time, I walk about the town, pretending I belong there.

Acknowledgments

Many of the essays in this book first appeared in an earlier form in the following publications and collections: *The Cape Codder, Country Journal, New Age, Harrowsmith, Orion, The Georgia Review, The Nature of Nature* (ed. William H. Shore), *and The Place Within: Portraits of the American Landscape* (ed. Jodi Daynard). I am particularly indebted to *The Cape Codder* newspaper, which first gave me public exposure as a writer a quarter century ago and which, I am pleased to say, still accepts my occasional pieces.

This book owes its existence to many people. Among them are my agent, Ike Williams, who knew where to send it; Jack Shoemaker, who had the faith to accept it; my editor, Trish Hoard, who helped guide it into its final form; my copyeditor, Julie Kuzneski, who improved it greatly; and especially my chum, Kathy Shorr, who believed in all of it. My thanks again go to Eric Edwards for sharing his knowledge about Cape Cod mailbox spiders, to Gary Isaacson and Laurie Schecter for generously sharing their dune shack, and to

Norma Simon for her mushroom expertise. For information on the *SS Longstreet* I am indebted to that indefatigable historian of Cape Cod trivia, Noel Beyle, and his book *The SS Longstreet*.